THE GRAN]

Confessions of an Old Scuuui noteller in the Digital Age

A TRILOGY
PART I : THE GRAND JOURNEY BEGINS
1946–1967

by

PATRICK L GRIFFIN OAM

with

JULIANA PAYNE

NATIONAL LIBRARY OF AUSTRALIA

A catalogue record for this book is available from the National Library of Australia

Publisher:
ASPG (Australian Self Publishing Group)
P.O. Box 159, Calwell, ACT Australia 2905
Email: publishaspg@gmail.com
http://www.inspiringpublishers.com

National Library of Australia Cataloguing-in-Publication entry

Author: Patrick L Griffin OAM with Juliana Payne

Series: **THE GRAND LIFE: Confessions of an Old School Hotelier in the Digital Age**

Title: **A TRILOGY – Part I : The Grand Journey Begins 1946–1967/**
	Patrick L Griffin OAM with Juliana Payne

ISBN: 978-1-922327-42-0 (Print)
ISBN: 978-1-922327-43-7 (eBook)

Dedication

There have been three men in my life whom I feel played a significant part in my development, my life and my career. I would like to dedicate Part I to my father, Frederick John Griffin (1908-1989). He was six when World War I broke out, twenty one at the start of the Great Depression and thirty one at the start of World War II and after these tumultuous years, at the age of thirty eight he faced a greater challenge: I was born. As was his nature it was he who gently guided me through childhood and the traumas of adolescence, which I feel may have been greater for him than for me. I am grateful for his perseverance and that he encouraged me to maintain the path I had chosen in hotels. A kind and loving father who sacrificed much to give me an opportunity to enjoy a grand life.

FREDERICK JOHN GRIFFIN
1908–1989

Introduction

1954 - 'Patrick is terribly slow and difficult. Very forgetful and lazy. Does not seem to realize that he is growing up. Conduct: Must be more reliable.' *Miss R.C.Bean, Headmistress*

1992 - 'Patrick you are booked to New Orleans in first class and on the Concorde from New York to London, a suite booked at the Ritz and will board The Orient-Express to Venice the following day'. *Malcolm, The Travel Agent.*

Miss Bean would have been shocked out of her sensible woollen stockings. Mr Bryant, my next headmaster, would have snorted in disbelief, whilst J.M. Merriman, my Housemaster at public school might have mulled over his final sardonic comment of "A smooth and plausible boy this, I am sure he will do well in his chosen trade."

Whilst being treated for a third bout of persistent (and thankfully non-fatal) cancer, I indulged in some inevitable soul-searching. My wonderful haematologist, Dr Julie Crawford, exhorted me - 'don't stress, enjoy life to the full and pray'. I was used to doing the first two, and the third didn't appeal at all, so I concluded that now was the time to write the bucket list.

With the nurse's selection of 1960s music playing in the hospital ward, I realised that my life had already been spectacularly full and privileged. I had family and friends; I had indulged in a luxurious lifestyle in fabulous places, and had met the rich, famous and notorious along the way.

There was very little left to include on the bucket list, but I had a full complement of wonderful memories.

In a hotel career spanning fifty years, I encountered many people of note and notoriety. Some appeared kind and charming but were absolute bastards; others who presented as absolute bastards were, in fact, kind and charming.

In Australia, I opened two hotels that hosted hundreds of public figures, stars of film, theatre, music and society. Most fell into the category of kind and charming, but some were less so. Those of us 'below stairs' were privy to it all, especially their indiscretions. I've recounted a few of these tales, but due to the high cost of defending defamation claims as an impoverished pensioner, I have chosen to err on the side of caution, and many will remain unspoken!

The greatest lessons I had learned had been on the working floors of hotels. I came to appreciate the opportunities that were presented to me every day, and by helping others fulfil their dreams, I was able to fulfil my own.

Recounting my memories (or confessions in some cases) has given me so much fun, pleasure and reward. This is the first book of the trilogy, and I hope that you also read Parts II and III, and enjoy the story to the end.

I am still uncertain as to how I actually achieved what I did, and credit is due to those around me, but one thing I do know is how lucky and fortunate I have been to be able to say, without reservation, that it's been The Grand Life.

Acknowledgements

I have to thank so many who have helped me with this project, my late father, who for reasons only known to himself, kept all my school reports, letters and other documents. My good friend Jonathan Webley, and his PA, June Pockett from The Grand for the copy of their book 'The Grand Hotel' by Peter Pugh, and for photocopying lots of information. Also the many friends from The Observatory Hotel, together with others who reminded me of names and events that I had long forgotten. These memories I have recorded with as much accuracy as I am able. I have mentioned some people by name, hopefully spelt correctly, I have also changed some names, for discretion or simply due to the fact that I really can't put a name to the face. My special thanks and gratitude are extended to all, and my apologies to those that I have inadvertently forgotten to mention. For much of the general information used to elaborate on some issues I must give thanks to the contemporary fountain of knowledge, Wikipedia. Any mistakes in regards to names, places and dates are entirely of my own making and I would be happy to correct any in future editions. The photos are either from my own personal collection or taken from the hotel's publicity. I am also grateful for the generosity of the celebrities who so willingly provided many signed photos'. Likewise, while I have endeavoured to locate the copyright holders of the few photos I have downloaded for this book, which has not been straightforward or easy, again I would be happy to correct any omissions or errors in future editions.

Most of all my appreciation must go to my dear friend Juliana Payne, who gave me considerable help in reviewing, editing and publishing the books, as without this help, encouragement, and knowhow, I would never have completed this endeavour.

Last but not least, my three sons, Steve, himself an accomplished author*, Tim, a uniquely gifted IT specialist, and Charlie, a hotelier after my own heart. Finally, but far from least, my wonderful wife Gan, for her patience, encouragement and support in times of 'sickness and health' ... and for supplying the bottomless pot of coffee that has kept me going.

* www.steve-griffin.com

Events That Shaped The Era 1946 - 1967

1946 - Churchill delivers 'Iron Curtain' speech - the UN is formed - First bikini on sale - I am born.

1947 - Start of the Cold War - India-Pakistan Independence.

1948 - Gandhi assassinated - The Berlin Airlift - 500 Caribbean immigrants arrive in Britain aboard HMT Empire Windrush.

1949 - Apartheid begins in South Africa - George Orwell's 1984 published - Soviet Union detonates its first atomic bomb.

1950 - NATO is formed - Korean War begins - Petrol Rationing ends in UK.

1951 - Festival of Britain celebrations in UK - First Oral Contraceptive (the Pill) invented - I'm hospitalised with double pneumonia and I develop my aversion to big needles.

1952 - King George VI dies - Food Rationing ends in UK - London Smog kills 4,000 people.

1953 - Queen Mary dies - Queen Elizabeth II Crowned - Mount Everest conquered - but for me more importantly: We get our first TV, a Baird 14" screen & Sweet Rationing ends.

1954 - Fourteen years of rationing comes to an end when meat officially comes off ration – "Rock Around the Clock" by Bill Haley and the Comets - Elvis Presley begins his music career - Tolkien's 'Lord of the Rings' published - Back to hospital, had my tonsils removed - Roger Bannister runs 4 min. mile.

1955 - Commercial ITV starts in UK - starts in UK Salk Polio vaccinations, more big needles - I develop a new aversion : against large bosoms - Start my interest in music, buy my first 78rpm record, The Dam Busters March by Sir Malcolm Sargent & London Philharmonic Orchestra.

1956 - The Suez Crisis - UK opens first nuclear power station - First CND Marches in UK - Music interest continues with a favourite, Poor People of Paris by Winifred Atwell.

1957 - Russians first launch Sputnik - Asian Flu Pandemic, 1.1 million deaths worldwide - I join 80% of UK males and inhale my first cigarette, a Peter Stuyvesant, making me very dizzy - Smoking goes on to cause over 480,000 deaths per year in the USA alone - Favourite music, That'll Be The Day by Buddy Holly.

1958 - Stereo LP's first sold - The Microchip Invented - Peace Symbol created in UK - I'm sent off to boarding school - I take my first airplane flight, Le Touquet to Lydd in a Bristol Freighter - I see the stage musical West Side Story. Thank you Margie Booker for my first kiss ! Favourite music, All I Have To Do Is Dream by Everly Brothers - Big Man by The Four Preps'

1959 - Direct Dial Pay-Phones launched in the UK - Barbie Doll launched - I drink my first beer with cousin Nick in the Garrick Pub in Stratford on Avon - Grandpa Langley dies. Favourite music, It Doesn't Matter Anymore by Buddy Holly, it didn't he was killed.

1960 - Coronation Street first aired - Soviets shoot down Gary Powers, the US U2 Spy Plane - Lady Chatterley's Lover goes on sale in UK - Chubby Checker starts The Twist craze which I demonstrate to the family to their amusement - Favourite music, It's Now or Never by Elvis Presley - Handy Man by Jimmy Jones - I'm Sorry by Brenda Lee.

1961 - The Berlin Wall goes up - Vietnam War begins - Russia puts first man in space - Diners Club Issues first plastic Credit Cards - IBM Golf Ball Typewriter introduced - Favourite music, Wooden Heart by Elvis Presley - Crying by Roy Orbison.

1962 - Cuban Missile Crisis - See Dr. No, the first James Bond film - Marilyn Monroe dies - Favourite music, First Beatles single Love Me Do - So did I, meet my first real love.

1963 - President Kennedy assassinated - Martin Luther King's 'I have a dream' speech - France vetoed UK's entry to the Common Market - First Doctor Who aired on BBC - I leave school - My first job - Brother Chris takes me to the Windmill Theatre, Soho. Favourite music, From Me To You by The Beatles - Be My Baby by The Ronettes.

1964 I buy my first pair of flares (Tulip Line) in Carnaby Street - First offshore 'pirate radio station' Radio Caroline - I passed my driving test - Favourite music, I Feel Fine by The Beatles - House of the Rising Sun by The Animals - Love Me Do by The Beatles.

1965 - Death Penalty abolished in UK along with Flogging - 70mph speed limit in UK - Have my first accident and crash my friend's Austin Healey Sprite - Favourite music, Satisfaction by The Rolling Stones - My Girl by The Temptations.

1966 - England wins the World Cup - Aberfan disaster in Wales - I notice that mini skirts are getting very short - Necessity is the mother of invention, tights replace stockings - Motown arrives, favourite music, Reach Out I'll Be There by The Four Tops.

1967 - I turn 21 - Torrey Canyon oil spill, an ecological disaster - End of Pirate Radio - Arab-Israeli 6 day War - Favourite music, Ain't No Mountain High Enough by Tammi Terrell and Marvin Gaye - San Francisco by Scott McKenzie - Move to Amsterdam during 'The Summer of Love'- Join Hilton Hotels International - Too many late nights, lagers and cheap cigarettes hospitalise me with a collapsed lung - I return to England.

PART I:
THE GRAND
JOURNEY BEGINS

1946 – 1967

Numbers in superscript throughout the text refer to the photos on pages 370 to 396

Chapter 1

#Eastbournein64 #punctualityavirtue #friedeggsonflannelette

It was February 1964. I had just turned eighteen and I thought my career was over before it had begun. He lay there motionless with a fried egg on his chest, looking rather absurd. I stood there rooted to the spot, staring at the egg. God. Was he dead? Had I killed him? Oh bloody hell.

The morning had started out like any other since my training had begun a few months earlier. Through that early morning haze between sleep and waking, bells were ringing deafeningly. An image of a fire truck flashed through my mind, and then one of an old black Wolseley Police Car with the bright silver bell at the front of the radiator. Or was it the school bell? Shit, was I late for my bell monitor duties? I started to wonder what I was doing still in school, when the warmth of the fog that surrounded me lifted. I gradually opened one eye to see the large round white face of my alarm clock angrily staring back at me, its pale green luminous hands and numbers a beacon in the dark announcing that it was six o'clock. Bugger. Morning already and I was a long way from those bell monitor days.

I watched the little hammer move back and forth, striking one bell then the other. I tried to make it stop by force of concentration, but still it kept going. Where had I found the strength to wind it so tightly? The mechanical spring surely has got to reach the end of its spiral soon. The hammer started to slow and just as I was about to declare the victory of human willpower over the machine, the thin wooden partition that divides the staff accommodations shook as if it were about to collapse; Davidson my next door neighbour had thumped the wall.

"Turn that bloody alarm off!"

I was beaten. In a second effort of gargantuan concentration I managed to focus my strength to lift my arm from under the warmth of my blankets, to reach out and press the little knob on the clock that brought instant silence to the room.

I lay there as if paralysed, wondering if the pain that made itself felt between my temples was sufficient to give me a day off. The taste of the sixth pint of beer from the night before invaded my mouth and suddenly I caught the smell through the darkness of the last cigarette I had stubbed out in the ashtray beside the bed. Oh God it really is morning, and I am on the early shift for room service. Why can't I be dead?

I tested the outside temperature by sticking my right foot out from under the blankets. It was freezing. I took another look at the evil luminous face of the alarm clock which reminded me that it was five minutes since I was dragged awake from the warm sleeping embrace of the blankets. The decision was made for me; I threw back the covers, and leapt out of bed aiming for the switch at the door six feet away that would bring light into my dark English day. More pain, as my moving toe came into contact with an immovable object on the floor. I let loose a cry of pain that quite ironically harmonized with the ringing pitch of the object with which my toe had come in contact. Still in mid flight, my hand hit the switch and there was light. As I steadied myself I tried to focus on what shared the floor with my discarded clothes from the night before. A large opaque white globe with the Shell Company emblem emblazoned upon either side, normally seen on top of a petrol pump in a public garage, had found its way to my room, where did it come from and how did it get here, what did we do last night ?

The clock's increasingly malicious big hand was now moving to its midpoint. I had fifteen minutes before I was due to be serving breakfasts to some of the world's most eccentric old wrinklies who were still warmly ensconced in their comfortable beds in their home: The Grand Hotel.

I had no time to review the results of what had obviously been a first-rate night out with the lads the night before. Instead I focused on getting my brain into gear. I headed for the bathroom down the corridor. Washed, cleaned teeth, back in four minutes. Donned my whitish shirt (must wash that today), on with my black trousers and waiter's jacket. Where is my bow tie? *Panic.* Where is it? In the corner of my eye I catch a glimpse of it only to be disappointed to find a sock. Speaking of which, where is the other one? How does one lose things in a room that would usefully serve as a broom cupboard? Ah there it is and - thank God - there is my bow tie.

Seven minutes to go; I was down the stairs and out of the staff house that I called home. Into the early morning darkness; and the icy blast of an Eastbourne February north easterly nearly stopped me in my tracks. Suddenly, now fully awake, I realised it had to be a sprint to the hotel. The light from the street lamps gave the frosty pavements a phosphorescent glow as I approached the large imposing doors of the rear entrance to the Grand. The vision of that clock's demonic hand approaching six-thirty spurred me on. There was no option, I would have to risk the short cut - up the richly carpeted marble staircase two at a time, in through the lounge service entrance, past the kitchen hot plate.

"You eez-a fucking late Griffin."

The shout from Chero the Italian breakfast chef rang in my ears. I grabbed a tray of freshly baked bread rolls as I skidded to a halt in front of the antiquated service lift that plied its way up and down the four floors of the hotel. Pulled back the gates, jumped in, only two floors to go and I'd be home and dry. Through the metal grid of the gates I watched the old brickwork pass by, so symmetrically laid nearly a hundred years before. I bet you they weren't working at six thirty in the morning. At last I clunked to a stop and threw the gate open.

"Where the bloody hell have you been?"

Cartwright, the other floor waiter on the early shift, pulls a tray from its rack to lay it up in preparation for breakfast service, removing the cigarette from his lips and carefully placing it on the shelf alongside the numerous other scorch marks that pay tribute to long forgotten cigarettes of the past.

"You're bloody late."
"I wouldn't have been had the kitchen got the rolls out sooner. Bloody chefs."

On that note of mutual contempt for the kitchen staff, he went back to his cigarette and trays.

The first standing breakfast order I had was LadyPrince in suite 234 at quarter to seven, so I now had plenty of time. An elderly woman, Lady Prince had been a resident at the hotel for the fourteen years since she was widowed. Inheriting the fortune her husband had spent his life accumulating, all she ever consumed was two slices of lightly buttered wheat crispbread and a pot of Lady Grey. I joined Cartwright in setting up the trays awaiting the ring of the telephone.

Just about anywhere I can think of is more exciting than winter in Eastbourne on the south coast of England. It is better known as being populated by genteel old ladies and gentlemen in the autumn of their lives. Its unique charm was summed up by a famous English wit, who would now be older than any of them: "Brighton and Hove are full of very old people and Eastbourne is where their parents live."

As a result, the halls of one of Britain's finest and oldest five star institutions, and Eastbourne's most revered luxury hotel, were cloaked that winter morning in a silence that only fourteen residents and a few guests can create when they are the only occupants of a 200 room hotel.

Morris, the head room service waiter, appeared in the pantry. A short man who did not carry the black tails and starched wing collar of his uniform well, but woe betide anyone who mistook his Chaplinesque appearance for weakness. He had been butler to one of England's noble lords, but there was nothing servile about him. If anything, he had an air of superiority, nourished by his unshakeable belief in his role. His *raison d'etre* was to ensure the guests in his care were to be gently directed and duly protected from any embarrassing errors that may reflect poorly on themselves.

Morris' genteel existence was interrupted in 1939 with the call to do his duty for King and Country. He spent the next six years in a tank regiment in North Africa and Italy. At war's end he came back to civvy street to find his beloved social structure had been turned on its head with the newly elected Socialist Government. One of the first actions of the new order was taxing the rich, and the introduction of the cheerfully named 'Death Duty' had a devastating effect on the British ruling classes.

Many of the grand old homes of England had been taken over by the military during the war, as had been The Grand Hotel. Old oak floors polished by generations of devoted servants over centuries did not fare well under the hob-nailed army boots. With little money for restoration, these houses had been boarded up as the landed gentry sought humbler abodes. With no jobs to return to once they finished their military service, the previously devoted servants headed for the grand five star hotels around the country where their expertise in private service might be appreciated and applied to earning a living, however distasteful it was considered to be serving the *nouveau riche* of post-war Britain, itself on the verge of bankruptcy.

This bloodless revolution had a curious impact on the gentry, whose attempt at a humbler lifestyle was not to their liking. Seeing their erstwhile staff, who had cared for them faithfully over several generations, ensconced in new comfortable surroundings, the masters migrated to join their servants in these grand monuments to a past era. Taking up residence in the hotels, they hoped to resume their previous lives, lives that had been so unpleasantly rocked by the rather nasty Mr. Atlee and his cloth cap Labour Party colleagues, who were hell-bent on destroying the whole fabric of British society.

Mr. Joe Morris - or simply Morris as he preferred to be called, in the manner in which no doubt he had been accustomed to being summoned by his previous employer - ruled over room service like a benevolent dictator, assisted by his two lieutenants, Messrs Atfield and Pritchard. His one focus in life was to care for every need and whim of the guests in his care, however demanding or eccentric it might be, and this morning would be no different.

It's 6.40am. Time for Lady Prince. Laid out on the large tray, bedecked in crisp Irish linen, were two pieces of crispbread, a small silver dish of butter and Lady Prince's own Antique George III English Sterling Silver Teapot, containing her own Fortnum and Mason Lady Grey Tea. Morris casts an expert eye over the tray and I was off down the long corridor that led to Suite 234. A tap on the door. Count to five. Tap again. Key in the door. Enter.

Lady Prince is up, hair perfectly in place, face perfectly powdered and the light scent of lavender wafted perfectly across the room.

"Good morning Griffin".
"Good morning m'Lady, How are you this morning?" I asked every morning.
"Very well thank you," she replied every morning.

She reminded me of the aunts in *Arsenic and Old Lace*; cheerful, jolly and polite, very possibly masking a murderous instinct. I placed the tray on her small table beside the window that overlooked the lawns of Eastbourne's seafront, only years before dug up to cultivate onions for the war effort but now returned to their former glory. It was still dark as I drew back the curtains. One could see little but the distant white crests of breaking waves, whipped up by the cold winter winds, reflected in the waning moonlight.

"May I pour your tea?"

I quietly departed, leaving Lady Prince with her thoughts and the sound of the knife scraping a very thin sliver of butter on the crispbread, probably still thinking of the austerity required with the 2oz ration of butter to which her generation had become accustomed during the war.

One down. Back to the pantry to set about the preparations for the dreaded Major's breakfast. He could make or break the routine of the day.

Sitting in a corner of the room service pantry was a large wireless set. For those who are born digital, it was a beautifully presented cabinet with delicate fretwork at the front and a large glowing dial at a window, with a rising and descending line that pointed out the array of radio stations into which you could tune. This radio was permanently locked onto the BBC's Home Service.

It would have been more than anybody's life was worth to attempt to change stations. Even if we had tried, there was not much hope of picking up the pirate radio station that had just started to broadcast 'pop music' from a ship off the coast. Apparently this new music posed a greater threat to British sovereignty than had Hitler twenty years before. At best, for the daring few, there might, with a little nudging, be a chance of getting 'The Light Programme' and *Music While You Work*. This offered a refined selection of what was known as 'popular music', but, sadly, lacked anything that even remotely appealed to the musical tastes of the rebellious young generation of the new decade – the 1960s.

The innocent onlooker might have thought that the management of the time were highly enlightened, offering staff some entertainment to listen to whilst toiling away at their daily chores, rather like Spotify does today. Perish the thought. This wireless set had special dispensation and was purely functional with one purpose and one purpose only in our daily routine

One minute to seven and Morris glided into position, fingers deftly on the knob of this grand old piece of technical wizardry. Click. The dial lights up. A soft hum as the valves behind the fretwork come to life. There's a respectful hush as the wonderfully modulated tones and rounded vowels of the BBC announcer roll forth.

"…and that is the end of this announcement; now for the BBC time signal. At the third stroke, it will be seven o'clock precisely. Dong, dong dong."

As one, we all look at our watches. Morris carefully checks his ornate hunter pocket watch, of which he is very proud. He was bequeathed it by a very grateful employer, to whom Morris had devoted half of his adult life. Such generous gifts of gratitude for a job well done, he would remind us, were something for which we would have to work very hard. In the meantime I adjusted the hands of my uncannily misnamed *Timex Ever-Right* watch, which hardly ever was, to read seven o'clock precisely.

The BBC's dulcet tones continued. "This is the BBC Home Service and this is the seven o'clock news with Alvar Lidell. Today at The Old Bailey the trial commences of the conspirators in Britain's greatest train robbery..."

I tuned out of this singularly unimportant piece of news, and focused on what was a matter of life or death to me at that moment: a final polish of the cutlery on the tray of my decisive breakfast of the morning: The Major's. Suddenly my ears pricked up.

"What was that?"

"What was what?" from over Morris's shoulder.

"What did they say about cricket?"

"Oh something about R.T. Stanyforth dying."

"Who the hell is R.T. Stanyforth?"

"God. Griffin, don't you know anything? Apart from captaining England he was also a Lieutenant-Colonel with a Military Cross. I thought you went to a posh school?"

"So bloody what? Can't stand cricket, but being military The Major will know."

For reasons that continue to elude me I am continually frustrated by the instantaneous assumption that my English public schooling has transformed me into an encyclopedia of cricket.

Whoever said 'The battle of Waterloo was won on the playing fields of Eton' had obviously no idea either of Eton or of my school, which was far removed from any such historically eloquent connection, and in any event this was deemed a misquote as apparently when the Iron Duke attended Eton they had no playing fields.

"Look, Morris, if it is to do with cricket I have to know or The Major will give me hell."
"He was English, played wicket keeper back in the late twenties, I think,"
"That'll do."

The Major was not a man to be bothered with light conversation, least of all with the serving staff, but he expected enough 'intelligence' so that he could plan his day.

If England was playing cricket anywhere in the civilised world, he expected a full report. Then again, in The Major's world, if a nation did not play cricket, it could not be regarded as civilised. This had caused some measure of consternation the previous week when I had taken my allocated day off. The only available waiter was a young Italian chap on loan from the restaurant. Quite naturally he had no idea of the game of cricket, let alone the significance of the off break that had taken the wicket of Cowdrey. The Major, furthermore, was naturally averse to the fact that the war was over and the Italians were now our allies. On delivering the breakfast the hapless Mediterranean waiter was castigated as to his lack of moral aptitude for war, frogmarched to the door and ordered never to return. Morris was never to repeat such a grave misjudgment in his allocation of manpower.

"And now for the weather forecast..."

With cricket, this was the other essential piece of intelligence required prior to entering The Major's suite. Failure to supply such information could see you court-martialed, followed by firing squad.

A final check of the tray: Cutlery spotless. Two inches away from the breakfast plate, containing two rashers of streaky bacon, two fried eggs, two half tomatoes and half a slice of fried bread, cut on the diagonal. On with the cloche. Tea pot warmed, two and half teaspoons of English Breakfast tea, pot placed top right at a 45 degree angle to the plate. Three inches to the left the milk, no sugar bowl and below a large, personally supplied, porcelain Wedgwood breakfast cup and saucer and tea strainer. Left of the breakfast plate, a side plate and knife. Above, a rack of three pieces of white toast, whole, he likes to 'tear' his toast in the correct manner. To the right, a piece of Anchor butter, in recognition of New Zealand's efforts at Gallipoli, measuring no more than one and a quarter inches square and a quarter of an inch thick. A final check on the time: seven thirteen.

Armed with the same breakfast that The Major had had since he first took up residence after the war, and the intelligence he required to start his day, I now had a very sudden and very real flash of the fear he must have instilled in his men, as they waited all those years ago in those World War I trenches for his order to go over the top, more terrified of him than the Germans.

Here we go. *Good luck.*

Stand at The Major's door. Pause, check watch, a few seconds to seven fifteen: five - four - three - two - one. Knock twice. Count to five. Repeat knock. Enter.

The room even smelled like the army; tobacco and shoe polish. The bedside light was on, as always, and The Major was sitting up against a pile of pillows in bed, dozing, or simply ignoring the intrusion as he often did.

"Morning Major!" I announced in as crisp a military fashion as I could muster.

I placed the tray carefully, so as not to disturb the precise setting, on a small trolley that he had had specially constructed that would allow the wheels to slide under the bed whilst the tray ended up in front of him. I always thought it was a brilliant idea and that someone should make them commercially. Of course someone did, and made a fortune.

I moved the tray into position and removed the cloche. A warm waft of steam rose, carrying the aroma of eggs, bacon and tomatoes, and the vital confirmation that it was still hot. Thank God.

I turned and drew the curtains.

"It's going to be a chilly day again today, sir, temperature isn't likely to get much above freezing, a little rain this morning but possibly clearing this afternoon".

The standard all-purpose weather prediction for an English morning, in Eastbourne, in winter. Now for the clincher.

"Sad news about Stanyforth's passing away… great wicket keeper in his time…"

As if I had followed his achievements with enthusiasm and truly felt some pain in his passing. Still no comment from The Major. Miserable old bugger. As if I gave a monkey's. I withdrew, only too happy and relieved that I had not had to listen to a diatribe on the State of the Nation. I headed back to the safety of the room service pantry to report back on the successful mission to my CO, Morris.

I busied myself around the pantry, taking the occasional call from some of the few guests in house, who for some utterly inexplicable reason deemed it would be a pleasant break to have a few days in Eastbourne in the middle of winter. Mr. and Mrs. Hartley ordered two full English breakfasts and Earl Grey tea, which I called down on the intercom to Chero, the temperamental Italian breakfast chef.

"Whata de fuck you want?"

Obviously, Señora Chero had not been kind to her *marito* last night.

"Just two English breakfasts, I'm sending down the check in the lift".

The lift was a strange contraption from the Victorian era. It functioned as a 'dumb waiter' that worked on a rope pulley system. It served as the main form of contact with the kitchen and the occasional method of a quick get away for room service waiters. Two minutes later the 'English breakfasts' were ascending rapidly to the second floor. On to the trolley and we're off to serve Mr and Mrs Hartley.

Room 220. Knock on the door. "Come in". I am greeted by a young man with a big smile, and a young woman with a very timid smile. I set out the breakfast and offered to pour the tea, which was accepted by the ever so shy Mrs Hartley.

"Do you take milk?"
She looks up. "Yes please."
"And for Mr. Hartley?"
"Do you want milk dear?" as she looks in the direction of Mr. Hartley, immediately realising her mistake and flushing a bright charming pink.

I smiled, poured the milk and wished them a pleasant stay at The Grand Hotel. I left the young couple knowing now why they have found it so attractive to spend a few days in Eastbourne in mid-winter, and knowing that they are now recovering from the fact that they may have just blown their cover as a 'married couple'.

Back in the pantry I announce my discovery which is greeted with the usual hilarity and ribald remarks in keeping with the moral confusion of the sixties.

It was now nearly eight o'clock: time to face The Major and collect his breakfast tray.

As I approached the door to his suite, fear started to gnaw the pit of my stomach. Had the eggs been all right? Not too runny? The bacon, had it been too crispy? It was the primeval fear of the unknown. Had he heard something disturbing on his wireless set? There was no escape; the hands on my watch were about to align with eight am. Knock twice, key in the door and I'm in. There was something strangely unsettling about the atmosphere in the room, and I realised it was… silence.

Why wasn't his wireless on? As I moved into the bed-room, I was stopped in my tracks by the sight of The Major still asleep, sitting up, propped up by his pillows, blissfully unaware of the congealed bacon and eggs sitting on the tray before him. Panic rose in my chest; what should I do? Oh God. I am stuffed.

I was *sure* he had mumbled something when I drew the curtains. Maybe I could dash back and get a new breakfast, turn back his clocks, tell him I had to take a call from my dying grandmother. Oh God, the miserable old bugger will get me sacked. Control yourself, Griffin. You're on the battle-field now. Deep breath. There was nothing for it but to accept and if possible try and deflect the wrath that was about to follow. Isn't honesty the best policy? I would be my most dig-nified, apologetic and honourable self; I would grovel to save my skin.

Now for the awakening. Having been indoctrinated by Morris, I knew that you never, ever touched a guest in trying to awaken them and to speak up was useless as half our guests were so deaf that a clap of thunder wouldn't even have woken them. So as instructed I positioned myself at the foot of the bed, hands in view, knees against the end, and nudged.

The bed shuddered. No movement from The Major, however. Once more with feeling. Nudge.

The Major stirred and, as if in slow motion, started to lean to the side. He suddenly gained momentum, and like a falling redwood fell over the side of the bed. He took the breakfast tray with him as he went, and both landed with a thud on the floor beside the bed.

I stood frozen to the spot. Shit, what have I done? Had I just achieved what two world wars had failed to do? Had we poisoned him? Surely it wasn't the shock of the news of R.T. Stanyforth's passing?

The next few moments were a daze. I found myself running down the corridor in search of the one person who would know what to do. I threw back the pantry door.

"The Major!"

The staff looked up with bored sympathy, awaiting yet another tale of woe

"Dead!"
They clamoured, "He's dead?"… "Dead?"
"Yes, I…I…"
"You killed him?"

At this, Morris moved swiftly and smoothly into action. "Come on, lad, let's go see what we can do."

As we approached the door I had carelessly left open, I bravely held back, letting Morris take the lead. As I boldly followed behind him, I found myself developing a morbid curiosity. Morris knelt beside The Major. "He's gone."

Morris picked up the phone and asked for Mr Beattie, the hotel's managing director. After a short pause, I heard the rumble of his voice. "Morris here, sir. Sorry to disturb you, but, regrettably, I fear The Major appears to have died. Yes sir... No, Griffin found him... Right sir, I will deal with it".

The phone is hung up. "Get a towel, Griffin".

I merely stood there looking down at The Major, the man who had terrorized us all for so long, now looking rather pale and sad. So this is what a dead body looked like. Having never really seen one up close before I wasn't sure what to expect or feel. It seemed rather remote to me.

"Griffin, the towel."

I handed over a towel from the bathroom. Slowly Morris cleaned the demolished bacon and the annihilated egg from his chest, and moved the debris that surrounded The Majors's once vigorous body. The breakfast had left an oil stain on the striped flannelette pajamas. "Take his feet."

I looked down at the grey mottled ankles and steeled myself. The ankles felt amazingly cold as we lifted The Major back onto the bed. Morris flicked the pillows to one side to enable us to lay him flat. In a very tried and tested technique, Morris crossed the arms across the chest. In one smooth movement he plucked the napkin from the floor, flicked it out of its carefully folded shape, whipped it under the chin of The Major and tied a neat knot on top of the head. I was fascinated to see The Major laid out in such a ritualistic, almost pagan way. "Why on earth have you done that?"

The reply I received from Morris was the defining moment in my hotel career. "Well, lad, if you don't do this then the jaw can drop open and *rigor mortis* will set in. The Major is an officer and gentleman and has been a guest at the hotel for many years; we wouldn't want him leaving The Grand looking stupid, would we?"

The Major was dead, and yet Morris' objective was to consider the needs of his guest, not merely serving a meal or clearing a room, but the maintenance of dignity and reputation. So this is what real five star service is all about.

Chapter 2

#VEdaycelebrations #Thefamily #gunrunning

Two hundred and seventy one days after VE Day that celebrated the end of World War II, it was a cold, wet and windy Sunday morning on the third day of February, in the year nineteen hundred and forty-six, the coldest winter ever recorded in Britain. Not being quite born as yet, I did not know that much about it. I gleaned from my father's diary entry the variety of events occupying his thoughts that day: *"Patrick Langley Griffin born 11.00am (6lbs10 1⁄2 oz); I should have left for demob today; took daffodils (1s/6d)"*, and, I might add, modestly and yet prophetically: *"not the most handsome baby but the nurse tells me he has bags of personality."* [8]

And so it was, on that day at the Northfield Nursing Home in Rugby, I was welcomed into the world with a sharp smack to my bottom. The first of many, it was then called 'a good upbringing' and is now more commonly known as 'child abuse'. I was not alone in this experience; it was shared by the other 955,266 children born in 1946, whose parents had celebrated the austerity and abstinence of the war years in a manner that resulted in the baby boom.

My parents emerged out of professional and trade stock. On my father's side, a banking family, his father, John, had worked for Lloyds Bank, as had his father before him as tradition dictated;

the bank had been founded in Birmingham in 1765. My father's mother, Sarah, was a fearsome Victorian matriarch who learned her discipline in nursing, and founded the local Red Cross Association. She served as a nurse to the 18th Baron Willoughby de Broke on his 'Grand European Tour' until his demise and burial at sea in 1902. For a family with such structured Victorian values my father was very creative in his youth being fascinated in the new world of 'wireless telegraphy', as radios were known, whilst his sister Madge was a keen artist, later studying at London's prestigious Slade School of Fine Art.[1, 2, 3, 4]

My mother's mother, Annie, was the daughter of a cotton mill owner in Rochdale. They were also well travelled, having been to Russia in the days of the Tsar to develop the cotton industry. Along with a good source of cheap labour, the climate there was ideal for weaving fabrics. The family likes to claim that great grandpa Walmsley developed the Turkish towel we all use today, but the proof is somewhat scant. My mother's father James Langley was one of a very large family, being the son of his father's second wife who at the age of seventeen became the stepmother to seven children and bore fourteen herself ! I believe James was 'in agricultural supplies', but whatever his business, he was full of fun and beloved by us all, especially me. My mother was one of five children. Constance the eldest married an archaeologist, some years her senior, whose home was filled with all sorts of Egyptian artifacts. Joyce married a doctor; she was my favourite aunt and the source of a never-ending supply of cigarettes in my teens. Kenneth was the only boy, a farmer and entrepreneur, and a real character like his father. A lovable rogue, he scandalously got divorced to marry a young beauty in the local hunting fraternity. And there was respectable Dorphie, the youngest, who married a very successful local solicitor. [5, 6, 7]

Being part of this archetypal English professional middle class family, I knew the saying based on our class system: *Third or idiot sons go into the church or the army.* And I was the third son. Fortunately, by the time I reached the age at which this momentous decision was made, the life sentences of church or army had been replaced with 'hospitality'. In 1946, I still had my myriad childhood adventures before me: my escapades would shape, mold and influence my future career in ways I could never have imagined.

Under family pressure and social demands my father had joined his father in the banking profession. My mother, with even less choice in the matter, filled the noble, and, I might add, *only* role open to her at the time, as dictated by her social position in 1930s Britain. She was, in politically correct lingo, a *homemaker.*

My father interrupted his banking career and volunteered for service with the Royal Air Force, prior to call up, to fight for King and Country. This caused some small yet pointed note of discontent with my mother, as banking was a 'reserved occupation', and, as such, my father would have been excused at that time from military service. She took his eagerness to volunteer as a veiled critique of her homemaking abilities, but it was nothing of the sort. Throughout his life, my father's desire was to do what is Right, Honourable and Responsible, three of his five cornerstones of belief. My brothers and I were shaped by these stones, as my father used them to chisel the rough edges from us as we grew. Sometimes these stones came up against the opposing rocks of our natural desire, the rocks of *Fun* and *A Good Time* that solidified in the fifties and sixties. I might add here that my father often invoked his other two cornerstones to shape our characters, those of Discipline and The Stiff Upper Lip.

During the Second World War, the Midlands was heavily bombed. As the home of England's heavy industry, Hitler had decided it would become the centre of the Luftwaffe's attempts to break England's spirit. My father, therefore, moved my mother and two elder brothers, once the threat of invasion had passed, to the relative safety of the small South Coast town of Swanage in Dorset. My mother, having returned to Warwickshire for my arrival, had now decided to move back to Swanage which would be the best place to bring up the family in those bleak, spartan post-war years. [8, 9]

I have a very early recollection that my father's cornerstones of Discipline and The Stiff Upper Lip may not have been as successful as he would have liked. I was at kindergarten, or nursery school as it was called, the word 'kindergarten' being a little too *German* to use so soon after the war. Having been deposited in a room full of strange children, I naturally steered myself to the safe haven beneath the table. I found it useful to sit and scream there, until Miss Shepard telephoned my mother, who was forced to dispatch my nanny, Elaine, to come and collect me. The greatest fear was that I would set off a chain reaction of infant screaming that would disrupt the Disciplined Environment of Miss Shepard's Nursery for the Gentry.

Elaine Davis, the nanny my mother had employed to assist with the duties of rearing us three boys, was not one of those nannies who spanked her charges, thereby condemning them in later life, especially if a Member of Parliament, to seek corporal punishment for their pleasure. She was the girl of my young dreams, and the girl I had decided I was going to marry when I grew up. My infant pronunciation could only manage to call her 'Yaiyai'; perhaps with so many ex-colonials about following the war, we had picked up on *ayah* - what the British in India called their nannies. Yaiyai was always there to comfort me and make me happy. [10]

In England's cold and damp climate, just about everyone was a 'sickly child', and I had more than my fair share of maladies in those post-war years. My first memory was of lying in bed, with the big concerned faces of my mother and our family doctor, Dr Kennett looking down on me. It must have been the early hours - in those days doctors would turn out at any hour of the day or night. I had pneumonia, and I was wrapped in a blanket and bundled off in Dr Kennett's car to the local cottage hospital. A nurse put me in a white cot with iron bars that was a prison to my infant eyes. There I submitted to treatment with the new miracle drug penicillin, administered by injection, which left me with a fear of needles that bordered on terror for many years.

I was held in my prison cot for nearly a month. Hospital discipline was so strict that nothing was allowed to disrupt the routine, especially not visits from parents. Wednesday and Saturday afternoons from 2.00pm - 4.00pm were the only hours when my mother or father could visit me, no children allowed. I was held near a window that looked over Swanage bay and the seafront, along which ran the road that my parents would use when those longed for visiting hours came round. At 1.30pm I would stand in my cot, scanning the road anxiously for any sign of the family car. I would wave madly with excitement when I spotted it, signalling to my heroes to rescue me. In those days, hospitals did not encourage family visits: it was seen as disruptive to the routine and upsetting - to the staff - when concerned mothers came and fussed over their sick children. Rather different to our contemporary hospital culture, thankfully.

Pneumonia was followed by chicken pox, then glandular fever. I often had glandular problems, and it was the custom at the time to coat the neck in a thick iodine gunge, much like axle grease, and a bandage, so I would parade around like a Victorian vicar in his dog collar. Then followed a very severe case of food poisoning that had the Ministry of Health involved. Cousin Tim and I discovered in the cellars of Tachbrook, a stash of forgotten American cans of sardines from the war years, which we secretly consumed to our great regret. This was followed by the incident of the boiling water. Early one morning I appeared at the kitchen door at the same time as my father was heading through it with his red enamel shaving mug filled with boiling water that ended up all over me. Another brief hospitalisation ensued and I was made a great fuss of by my father. I wore the resulting sling proudly, which attracted much sympathy and many comments as to what a brave boy I was from all and sundry.

Naturally, I also had the standard childhood operation of tonsil removal in 1954. I was bribed with the idea that if I was a good boy, then I would be allowed to eat as much ice cream as I wished following the operation. Seemed like a pretty fair trade-off to me. Maybe it was the excess of ice cream I consumed, but I have retained a vivid memory of a strange dream or half-dream from that day. In my mind's eye, Dr Kennett is leaning over me in my hospital bed with a kitchen sieve with gauze in it, pouring something into it from a chemistry jar. I hear a roar and see a man in a Biggles-type leather pilot's flying helmets and goggles riding off on a motorbike. A disembodied voice says 'that's Pontius Pilate'. Either I was closer to God at that moment than ever before or since, or I was washing my hands of my future sins.

The family grew, and at last I was no longer the baby. My mother, understandably, had found three boys quite a handful. So my parents decided to adopt a little sister for their three boys. I recall the vetting process implemented by a woman in tweeds and sensible shoes. She was interested to know why I would like a little sister? My reply took the form of a nose-bleed while sitting on her knee. Obviously this was the correct answer as a short while later we waited in the driveway for the taxi which would deliver my new little sister, Angela Moira Griffin, known to us ever after as Ginny. I had thought that in the time honoured way of the sibling pecking order, I would now have someone that I could boss about. How wrong I was.[11]

The first birthday I recall was my sixth. It was a normal February day: freezing, wet and blowy, and my mother had laid on a birthday party with my friends, one of whom was our dentist's daughter. This was strange as I regarded my dentist as the most terrifying of people, so why would the child of this fearsome man be a friend of mine? Her name was Biddy Flemming and the gift she gave me was a book by AA Milne, *Now We Are Six*. It was a wonderful book full of rhymes and I loved *King John's Christmas*.

King John was not a good man, he had his little ways
And sometimes no one spoke to him for days and days and days.

I would often shed a tear as his sad situation unfolded, as my mother was very good at emphasising the drama, but then the happy ending gave me joy. As I look up at my bookshelves now I see the rather battered and faded yellow spine of that same book, inscribed *To Paddy, Love from Biddy, Ann & Peter, 3rd February 1952*. My birthday celebrations did not last very long as three days later King George VI died and I found that we all now gave up our party hats for a black cloth armband that my mother had sewed onto our school blazers. There seemed to be a cloud of sadness that fell over our household for some time after this, albeit for me this cloud was to last much longer.

It had been the previous year that I had commenced my somewhat less than exhilarating relationship with the world of academia that lasted for the next twelve years. The elusive idea of Discipline was, sadly, to remain elusive in those years. It started to elude me within weeks of entering my first halls of learning early in the 1950s: Eastbrook Preparatory School, run by Miss Rosina C. Bean. I soon discovered the hugely witty effect of placing the emphasis on her initials of 'R.C.', and revelled in the positive reinforcement I received from the laughter of other children.[12]

This was the beginning of my undoing. When basking in the glow of attention from my peers' hilarity, having provided them with my impersonation of R.C. Bean's unique walk that was no doubt enhanced by her rather large rear end. It all came to an abrupt halt when, to my unending horror, I discovered Miss Bean had taken her place among my audience. With a clap of the hands, she ordered "Children, back in the classroom." And then, far more ominously, "Patrick, come to the front of the class, and recite the Catechism that you learned for your homework last night".

Religion was about to deal me a blow, through the vengeful Old Testament hands of Miss Bean. Inevitably, I stumbled on the first line. I watched Miss Bean's expressionless face, glaring in my direction, whilst her right hand tapped a twelve-inch ruler of solid wood ominously in the palm of her left. Equally inevitably, I froze with fear and could not continue my psalmic recitation.

Thus, at the tender age of five, I first experienced the wonderful ritual of the administration of corporal punishment. A slow, deep drum should have been beating as I was summoned to stand beside the shrine, or desk, that encapsulated Miss Bean's God-given authority. No pathetic prisoner before the Old Bailey was ever as terrified as I, as she intoned, "Patrick you have failed to learn your Catechism. As a result, you must learn the error of your ways or you will never reach your full potential. I do not take pleasure in punishing you. Put your left hand out at full length in front of you".

Before I knew it, I experienced stinging pain, as the ruler came down faster than the speed of light on my palm. 1- 2- 3 times. As many an innocent offender before me had found, the beating did not in the slightest assist with my Discipline. However I feel some measure of pride as my father's son that I did keep a Stiff Upper Lip.

Eventually, I did learn the Catechism. I also learned to play that mysterious instrument, the triangle, in the school percussion band. I had, rather unfairly I have always maintained, been banned from the bass drum. With the enthusiasm and exuberance of youth, with the drum strapped to my chest, I turned to encourage my classmates and unfortunately pierced the drum skin by impaling it on a protruding coat peg. I feel that it was this unfortunate and completely unplanned event that brought about an extended cry for help from Miss Bean, in the guise of a never-ending series of unfavourable school reports. One month after my fifth birthday the first arrived on my father's desk.[13]

Patrick finds it difficult to concentrate, but he will improve. He is a very versatile character and fond of fun. Conduct: Must concentrate and attend to his own work. R.C.Bean, March 30th 1951

Sadly it got no better by my eighth birthday.

Patrick is terribly slow and difficult. Very forgetful and lazy. Does not seem to realize that he is growing up. Conduct: Must be more reliable. R.C.Bean, July 23rd 1954

Miss Bean unaccountably had softened by December, on the eve of my departure from Eastbrook. My exit report for my new and unsuspecting teachers read:

Patrick has really made a lot of progress this term and I hope he will continue well in his new school. Conduct: Quite good, but not very neat. R.C.Bean, December 17th 1954

I can only assume that she was an incurable optimist.

I certainly had not inherited my father's disciplined and orderly character. I have never known a more honest man. He was born in 1908 and grew up during the Great War, as they used to call the First World War. He began work at the time of the Great Depression, joining the Royal Air Force at 31, and then brought up a family in the tough post-war days of the 1940s and 50s. I am not at all surprised by his respect for money, which was paramount. It showed itself in many ways.

My earliest recollection was of a small red exercise book, and it was to dictate my social existence every bit as much as another 'red book' was to influence 900 million Chinese years later. Into this small red book lined in columns, I was instructed to enter how I spent the sixpence pocket money that I received with great ceremony each week. I duly did so, little thinking that it would be to my detriment. In one week in the summer of 1952, I had entered the fact that I had consumed *two* ice-creams. This fact was met with my father's unbounded astonishment. He regarded this as a heinous act of unbridled extravagance.

Throughout my childhood I experienced cash flow issues. I found it difficult to make ends meet, even with the donations that came from aunts and uncles, in the form of Half Crown Postal Orders. My most generous benefactor was Grandpa James Langley, who always sent me five shillings at Christmas, for my birthday in February and for Easter, usually in March. Unfortunately all fell in or around the first quarter, leaving me nine months with no reliable source of additional income.

Grandfather James Langley, was my mother's father, a notable character within the family and a man I was very fond of. Apart from his generosity, he was also lots of fun. He would sit me on his knee and sing a ditty, which we called the 'chooky song'. He would sing *chook, chook, chook, chook, chooky, lay a little egg for me. I haven't had one since breakfast and now it's half past three*. After a reprise or two, came the moment of great excitement as he laid the egg, and as the chicken strained, *choook, chooooooook* and at a moment of least expectation, his knees would part and I would fall through, just being caught before I hit the floor. Even when cousin Tim and I did diabolical things, such as breaking the glass in the cucumber frames along the wall of the vegetable garden, his anger was tinged with a touch of dramatic humour, "My God, I'll throw my hat in!" he would shout, with which he would take his battered gardening hat off and throw it to the ground and stamp on it.

The stories we heard of him, as his daughters would retell, made me realise where some of my mischievous nature came from. As a young man he fell for a local village beauty called Clara, however his elder and better looking brother decided she was also the girl for him. One day after the Sunday church service his brother made his move, and asked permission to take the young woman for a picnic in the family's 'pony and trap' the following Sunday. Seeking his revenge, my grandfather, offered, in the guise of brotherly reconciliation, to get the pony and trap ready and the horse fed and watered for brother's day out with Clara. In place of the horse's normal feed he gave him a large bag of apples, oats and something else. This had a rather dramatic effect on the horse's digestion and resulted in a very angry brother returning from a less than successful picnic, somewhat earlier than planned.

"Back so early?" my grandfather asked innocently.
"That bloody horse! How could I court Clara when every few minutes as we drove to the river for our picnic, the horse would raise its tail and fart, for three miles he never stopped farting and the smell was unbearable. I had to keep stopping for fear that Clara would be ill, a bloody disaster. I don't think Clara will accept an invitation from me to go riding out ever again."

And neither, to my grandfather's great satisfaction, did she.[6]

His daughters adored him, and my mother often made the comment *"Remember you're James Langley's grandson"* as if it was something of a privileged position, so much so it became a mantra in the family for anyone we wished to impress, be it a police officer or parents of a prospective bride. "I am, of course, James Langley's grandson" we'd chant. We were so convincing that people would reach for a copy of *Debrett's Peerage* to check him out.

He was a lovely man, gentle and kind to all his grandchildren, and when he died of lung cancer, having been a heavy smoker all his life, he became the first person whom I loved who died, and had the greatest impact on my young emotions. [14]

Ursel Langer was a young German girl who joined the family as an au pair, and she rated quite high on my young fondness scale. My father felt her presence was appropriate as part of the healing process following the war. My parents had an open house when it came to hosting youngsters from overseas, believing it was *educational* for us. We meanwhile were intrigued to see what the 'enemy' would be like. Much of what was on TV at that time was about the war and how Britain had stood alone against the evil Nazis. Long before Basil Fawlty uttered the immortal statement *Don't mention the war*, my father gave us strict orders to turn off the TV if there was anything on that related to the war when Ursel was around. This curtailment of television did not endear her to me, but after a few days she had won me over. She was just lovely, and would play her guitar while we sang *she'll be coming round the mountain when she comes*. We were not the von Trapps, but she was such fun. I found myself being quite profound at an early age, questioning how one day we can be fighting and hating one another, and the next day such good friends. Over the years I lost contact with Ursel, until I managed to meet up with her again nearly fifty years later when on a trip to Berlin, which is recounted in Part 3.[31]

Never mind my contemplation of the futility of war, there was a far more concerning issue on my horizon. Even as a boy of six, I knew I needed to develop my own income streams, rather than be reliant upon my father's conditional generosity. Naturally this decision led rapidly to an early life of crime that I hasten to add I grew out of, eventually. Such choices are *not* what I would recommend to today's youth, where a totally different and, I suspect, much more punitive attitude would be applied to such youthful follies.

My first heist opportunity arose when I was playing hide and seek with a boy next door. In the course of the game I discovered a small door that allowed access to the area under the house. I opened the door and crawled in, thinking it the ideal place in which to hide. As my eyes became accustomed to the darkness, through thick cobwebs, I espied a treasure trove: shining, glistening in a narrow shaft of light that came through the cracks in the small door. They were stacked four high as far as I could see. JAM JARS. These may not seem worth the effort today, but back then they had a marketable value at the local grocer's shop of at least a penny a jar, a small fortune in those frugal times. Obviously forgotten and probably stored before the war, once cleaned and polished the jars would provide my income once I offered them on the open market.

Sadly, my new-found jar-based wealth only partly solved my problems. In the early 1950s we were still suffering the shortages brought about by World War II. Bread was still rationed, but this was nothing to me compared to the stringency of the rationing of sweets. I had a small brown dog-eared ration book in my name that permitted me the miserly amount of two and a half ounces of sweets per week, a little over half a bar of chocolate today. I recall when friends of my father came to stay once, along with their son, after supper he would be allowed a small piece of a Mars Bar that had been carefully cut into ten equal pieces. I felt it so unjust that he should have such a luxury, so one morning I pinched a piece. Unfortunately this didn't satisfy my sweet tooth so I took another. I had futilely hoped they wouldn't notice, but I found myself having to confess and take my punishment of no sweets for a week. This taught me a lesson, and the lesson was that I had to become more resourceful.

A little way down the road was a small shop, unusual in that it was housed in a Nissen hut, a curved corrugated steel structure that were set up as temporary housing for those who had been bombed out of their homes, named after the engineer and inventor Major Peter Norman Nissen, not the Japanese motorcar. This shop was run by Miss Molly Malpus, a woman not known for her warmth and charm. Neither, for that matter, was she renowned for her good looks. Sporting a large mole on her chin from which protruded a number of hairs, she bore a suspicious resemblance to the witch from the Disney cartoon of *Snow White* that I had recently seen. She lived behind a large curtain that divided her home from the shop in the front.

One morning I entered the shop and waited for her to appear magically from behind the curtain. As I waited, my eyes scanned the large jars and tins of boiled sweets of all colours and flavours, the jars of bulls-eyes and gobstoppers, liquorice sticks and barley sugars. The shop was a boundless heaven for a sugar-deprived boy of my tender years. I waited and waited; where could she be? As the seconds ticked by with no Miss Malpus, and I stood there holding my little ration book tightly, I spied the scissors. This was the very implement that denied me my indulgence in sweets beyond the measly two and a half ounces, because the scissors were the demons that cut out the precious coupons.

My childish logic then struck me. Without the scissors, Miss Malpus wouldn't be able to take my coupons. And vistas of unrationed sweets lay before me... as if I was looking down from afar, I saw my hand reach out and grab the scissors. My hand in one quick movement pulled them towards me to hide under my school raincoat. I was already committed to the act when I noticed to my horror that the scissors were attached to a long piece of string that was secured to the counter somewhere behind the jars of sweets. From then on, I watched as the disaster played out in slow motion: my tug on the string set in motion a domino-like demolition of the carefully stacked jars and tins. One followed by another and then yet another, came crashing to the floor.

The noise brought an instant response from behind the curtain. In a replay from *Snow White*, the curtain was flung dramatically back, to reveal the wicked witch glaring down at me, the mole and hairs now looking twice their normal size and twice as fearsome. I stood there, frozen to the spot, petrified at the havoc I had wrought, holding the scissors as clear evidence of my guilt. The final indignity manifested in the sudden feeling of warm dampness emanating from my shorts. My fear galvanised me, and I turned and ran. I spent the rest of the day in abject fear of my father's arrival home, as he would face the news of his son's misdemeanours. How would I face the wrath that would inevitably follow?

Inexplicably, the news never broke; but just to make sure, I spent a number of weeks making highly creative excuses as to why I was unable to run an errand for my mother to Miss Malpus's local store.

Three major events occurred the following year that changed my life as I knew it. Queen Elizabeth II was crowned, Edmund Hillary and Tenzing Norgay conquered Everest, but most importantly of all, sweet rationing ceased on my seventh birthday. I had conquered Miss Malpus's scissors.

The downside was that from that day on my visits to the dreaded dentist increased dramatically.

My narrow brushes with either the law of the land - or indeed the far more onerous laws of my father - were legion. Once I sold some gold King George III sovereigns that I found when searching my father's bureau for paper. This was discovered within days of my purchase of a new air rifle. PC Bull, the local officer of the law, came calling, having come across my childish scrawl on one of his recent trips around the antique shops. This naturally raised his suspicions, and unfortunately not only lost me my air rifle but had me weeding the lawn for three weeks.

My discovery also brought about a more serious impact on my revenue-earning opportunities. Nearby was a secondhand dealer, Mr Curtis, with whom I had regular dealings in the selling of old train sets and other old toys. My father visited upon him an agreement that henceforth under no circumstances could the dealer purchase anything from me unless I presented a written note from my father or mother, giving me express permission to sell the item.

I soon adapted and ensured that this injunction only caused me a minor inconvenience. I convinced my mother to write me a letter stating that I might sell 'this item'. I explained to my mother that I wasn't certain which toy I might wish to part with and that it was subject to what Mr Curtis might be able to offer. This tactic worked magnificently well and was used on many occasions not only to lighten my storage chest of toys, but also to relieve my father's library shelves of a few beautiful leatherbound illuminated volumes of Shakespeare.

Of course he found out. On this occasion the retribution was not merely three weeks of weeding, but one of the very rare times he tendered my behind with a leather belt. Such actions were not in his character, brought about as much by my mother's surprising encouragement, and I honestly feel that it actually *did* hurt him more than it hurt me.

These misdemeanours were merely a prelude to the ultimate, and probably the most risky action of my misspent youth, which unfolded with my cousin Tim on a trip to France with his parents, my uncle Douglas and aunty Joyce. [16]

Our trips abroad were holidays we anticipated eagerly, and we were rather fortunate to have such adventures. Trips overseas to the continent at that time were a rarity; the normal summer vacation would be to rather less exotic locations like Devon or Cornwall. We often stayed at a small hotel in Pierrefonds, near Compiegne in north eastern France, made famous for the signing of the Armistice after WWI, and subsequently the French surrender to Germany in WWII. The owners of the hotel, Madame et Fille Chatia, or aunt 'Tatti', short for Tante, and Jacquelyn, were friends of the family and also my heroes as both had been active in the French Resistance during the War and helped many Allied prisoners escape from Nazi occupied France. [15]

We often explored the rambling lofts in which British fliers and escaped POWs had been hidden. On one of these explorations we came across a small room in which we found a number of dust-laden boxes. In anticipation of finding a treasure of lost Nazi gold, we carefully opened the boxes to find, not gold, but something far more exciting to boys with a passion for war and all the heroics that went with it. Guns! There must have been a dozen or more: US army carbines, pistols, revolvers, shotguns, ammunition. These were relics, abandoned and forgotten after the war. So with an absolute lack of awareness and conscience that what we were doing might be regarded as a little illegal, we carefully smuggled an American M1 Carbine and a couple of pistols, together with ammunition, into the car and stashed them between the springs of the back seat of the MG Magnette in which we were traveling.

On returning to England at holiday's end, via the ferry to Dover, our cavalier attitude to our appropriation of these highly illegal arms and ammunition was starting to change into sweaty palms and prayers to the Almighty that if we got through, we would never do anything wrong again. We arrived at the customs shed in Dover as usual and were waved into a parking bay along with other cars arriving off the ferry. An officious customs officer came over with a clipboard in hand. "Please read this declaration."

My uncle proceeded to do so and after a few moments, the officer said, "Have you anything to declare?"

"No," firmly, from my Uncle.

"No cigarettes?"

"No, apart from the permitted 200." Not wanting to look too innocent.

"Perfume? Alcohol?"

"No, only what we are allowed."

We were certain that the next question would be "Rifles, guns, ammunition?" and by this time we were ready to confess.

The officer then asked to see the boot of the car, and then under the bonnet, our car was getting a real once-over. Had the removal of the guns been discovered and the customs tipped off? How many years did you get in prison for gun-running? *PLEASE GOD ...we will do anything if you save us ...*

At that moment the officer entered the car and started looking through the glove box. He leant over to the back seat and started to tug at it to lift it up. We were done for. My head was swimming - I thought I would pass out - actually I thought I should, just to distract him.

At that moment our frantic prayers were answered. In what could only have been an act of divine intervention, the officer from the corner of his eye spotted my aunt's handbag. He reached for it and as he did so, as if by magic, it popped open for no apparent reason and there lay exposed two bottles of Chanel No 5. At that moment and forever more, I would bless my aunt's expensive taste in perfume. With this contraband now the centre of the officer's attention, we let out a cautious sigh of relief. Although it cost my aunt the duty payable and a £3 fine for not declaring her little luxuries, she will never know how her sacrifice saved us from a possible custodial sentence, as well as having the positive effect of setting us, to some degree, on the straight and narrow. We were regular church goers for sometime afterwards. About two weeks.

And the guns? They gave us great fun out in the woods around the brook, shooting at pigeons and other small wildlife, but eventually after one burst of automatic fire it did catch the attention of a local policeman as he cycled by. Again fortune smiled on us, as at this time there had been a gun amnesty declared in an attempt to recover all the old guns and pistols that had been brought back as souvenirs from the war by returning soldiers and left to gather dust in drawers, lofts and cupboards until found by their wayward children.

So we dutifully handed in our stash of arms. As we did we couldn't help but notice to our amazement the incredible array of armaments that were being brought out and handed in, including a 2-pound anti-tank artillery piece. My God what fun we could have had with that.

My teens were dotted with the odd bits of mischief, but the stress we'd suffered at the customs shed finally made me understand just how much trouble we could get into, and how I wasn't always going to be so lucky. I turned over a new leaf from that very day.

Both my aunt and uncle and my parents believed that travel was an ideal way to broaden the mind. What luck! So did Tim and I. The doors were opened for us to new cultures and ripping adventures. In particular, apparently mountains were of special and intense interest. We literally had to 'climb every mountain' and to make it especially fun we didn't have any special gear or shoes. In France, Tim and I conquered Mont Blanc, the highest mountain in Europe, in truth by way of the funicular railway rather than by crampons and an ice axe. We had great fun climbing over the glacier, or the *Mer de Glace* (Sea of Ice) as it was known, hopping over crevasses in our ordinary leather-soled shoes that had a marvellous tendency to slip. With no gear, no ropes and no safety rails of any type, it is truly a miracle that I am still here to tell you the tale. I'm also glad I had the chance to nearly kill myself on the glacier before global warming melts it away.

We also conquered the Pyrenees via Andorra and Spain. The narrow gauge rack and pinion mountain railway up Mount Snowdon was child's play. Then in Switzerland we took the steepest cogwheel railway in the world up Mount Pilatus and rode the cable car back down. Descending via the gondola that passed through a type of halfway shed, where a little man lived who would push the gondola onto a second track to reach the bottom. My poor mother thought the shed *was* the bottom, and prepared for us to stop and get off. Much to her terror, she nearly squawked out loud as the little man ran beside the gondola and shoved us onto the next track. He let go and we sailed out over the edge of the world on the second leg of our journey down the mountain. Never have I seen a grown woman so white and so terrified. We spent the rest of the trip trying to calm her down.

Neither have I seen a grown woman move so fast when it was time to exit the gondola.

Our trips to the Continent - as it was called - had a very different feel then. In France in those post-war days the English were still seen as liberators. In mountain villages children, on seeing the 'GB' (Great Britain) sticker on the car would run alongside, giving a Churchill 'V' for victory sign. I suspect a very different hand sign would be directed at British people today. Happy memories; happy days.

These were the days when surplus military equipment filled surplus stores and if Tim got an ex-army walkie-talkie, I would also want one, along with parachute smocks, RAF rubber dinghies or anything military.

Of all our high-jinks, the best was a motorbike, a BSA 350, which Tim all but rebuilt. When we could, we would go 'scrambling' in the fields of a local farmer, Mr Gilks. We would race around doing whatever tricks we could. When we found an old tin bath that had been dumped in the bushes we decided it would make a great sledge to tow behind the bike. I was *volunteered* by Tim as the first to try it out. [17]

Hitched up to the bike, me sitting in the tub, hanging on to the sides, Tim set off. Gaining speed rapidly, we had not taken into account any scientific aspects of what we were doing, especially not that of friction. As I sped across the recently cut wheat field, I suddenly felt, apart from the bumps, my bottom starting to burn, by this time we were going at some speed. It soon became too much and I started to scream out to Tim to stop. He, hearing what he thought were screams of exhilaration and unable to make out my cries of distress above the roar of the bike engine, revved up and went even faster. By this time the heat had cut through my trousers and was becoming very painful indeed. I had to make a decision, to try and raise my bottom from the tin floor of the tub, or to bail out and at this speed risk a broken bone. The latter was the only option. As I tilted the tub, I shot out like a human cannonball. The tub went spinning into the air on its forward trajectory, pleasingly in a different one to my own. After spinning and tumbling over and over I was stopped by a pile of hay bales. Apart from a few bruises and a battered ego I was none the worse for wear. In those days, anything with a motor was exciting and we were indestructible. [18]

I looked at Tim as he returned, "That was great - now you have a go." Hiding my pain, this would give me a chance for revenge.

"No bloody fear, I'm not going to burn my arse!"

I noticed the smile on his face, the bugger. He knew all along what would happen. The tub was then returned to the hedgerow whence it came.

Throughout my childhood and my teens Tim and I were inseparable as cousins, we got up to all sorts of antics and I followed his every move. [19]

Chapter 3

#schoolreports #sparetherod #memoriesofmammaries

At my new preparatory school, the headmaster was very different from Miss Bean - Mr Walter Telham Bryant OBE M.A. (Oxon.) late of India was very much a man of fortitude and discipline. Hill Crest, was described in its prospectus as *specially constructed for the purpose of a school, is electrically lit and centrally heated... Particular attention is paid to character training and the development of a sense of discipline and of good manners and address.* These strictures poured cold water on my propensity for fun. It was here that I learned more than the mysterious musical qualities of the triangle. The arcane labyrinths of Latin, Mathematics and Physics were now part of my curriculum, along with rugby, cricket, shinty, a form of aggressive hockey that naturally came from the Scottish Highlands. Most misleading of all, the purportedly 'character building' sport of boxing was included. I use the term 'sport' in its most loose application here, for what it built was certainly not character. [20]

The quotes you see here are genuine extracts from my school reports, carefully preserved by my father, that I found in a box after his death.

1955 - Headmasters Report – Patrick (aged 9) will have to work very hard to make up for his very moderate ability. W.T. Bryant

1955 - Latin - What with absences, and the sort of mental fog which descends on him as soon as he is faced with a simple abstract idea, such as "the subject of a sentence", progress has been non-existent; in fact I have had to go back almost to the beginning. W.T. Bryant

I was not keen on boxing. The instructor was a sadist named Mr Bennet, the part time boxing coach, a retired army man, short in stature, who had not only distinguished himself in his fight against the Germans, but also in Regimental boxing tournaments against others on his own side. Mr Bennet was the man who supervised the program and delighted in the fact that I was rather a tall boy for my age with long arms, and accordingly these traits gave me some sort of advantage in his twisted moral universe. Quite naturally not at all keen on the pain that accompanied an encounter with one's opponent, in the sheer desperation of self-defence, I kept winning my bouts through simple tactics of avoidance. My unpalatable reward, however, was to be faced with ever more fearsome opponents. It was not long before my wholly unintended success in the ring led me to a place not unlike what I imagine purgatory to be: a South of England junior school boxing competition.[21]

This was not what I had in mind. Reluctantly, carrying the reputation of the school on my youthful shoulders, and yet inevitably drawn to the heady heights of popularity with my school mates that only such a suicidal venture could achieve, I headed for the first round in the competition. Soon I would learn, as have many a vain celebrity, before and since, of the sadly ephemeral nature of such popularity.

I felt like I'd gone back to the beginning of time. As I stepped into the ring I found myself faced with a sweating Neanderthal from a competing school, who sported the wholly unsuitable and aristocratic name of Harrington-Jones. As the first bell rang, we touched gloves. Surely, I thought, this sportsmanlike and symbolic act was not meant to inflict the pain that I suddenly felt, in, of all places, my foot. Stupidly I had assumed that I might suffer from a well-placed but gentlemanly blow above the belt. Instead, to my unending surprise, it appears that my opponent's foot was being utilised in exerting undue pressure squarely on the toe of the nearest of my over-large feet, thus limiting my ability to retreat which was uppermost in my mind at that moment. Whilst still marvelling at the pain being inflicted on this prominent and inherited Griffin legacy, I confusedly attempted to remove my huge foot from the vicinity of the gorilla with the hyphenated name. This minor act of self preservation distracted me from seeing – ironically, that which I had been expecting – a legitimate left hook coming at lightning speed straight to my other larger than average inherited feature, the Griffin nose.

I understand why people think they see their lives flash by in moments of inordinate stress. In a split second, I managed to feel a blinding pain, to hear a crunch, to see flashes of light, and then fall back on the canvas with a thud. I lay there gazing at the ring lights above, tasting salty blood gushing from my broken nose, aghast at the referee waving his hands manically from side to side. Was that it? Surely this is not what His Grace, the Marquis of Queensberry had in mind? I'm almost certain that he did not intend for a foot to be used in such a manner. Adding to my mortification and disbelief was the uncanny fact that this injustice was not noticed by the referee. Hideously, though, every detail was noted by my school chums. And, in the way of boys since time immemorial, far from being supportive, they simply took the opportunity to rib me about my inherited features of feet like flippers and a nose the size of a beak. Because of the role these characteristics played in my humiliation, I immediately and permanently became known as *The Beak* or simply *Penguin*.

As everything inevitably does, this was to haunt me in my later life. As decrepitude has caught up, with its concomitant sleeping problems and complications like sleep apnoea, I have sought the surgeon's advice. On viewing scans of my private inner sinuses, his first observation was, "I have never seen a nose quite like yours before."

I groaned inwardly – surely he was not going to regale me with the old school jokes.

"You know it's been broken?"

The memory of childhood pugilism flooded back. "Yes, I did boxing at school." My response was, rightly I thought, rather proud, as I now sported my pugilistic scars with a sense of honour and achievement.

"Obviously weren't very good at it…" he muttered.

Who'd have thought this throwaway line could hit me such a knockout blow? As I struggled to regain my erstwhile pride and honour, he lit up the x-ray. "So far I have counted your nose has been broken five times, no, wait a minute, six times."

At this I fell into silence, wondering with fond affection where the hell my parents had been whilst I was receiving such traumatic and life-threatening injuries. Oh, now I remember. When I did tentatively mention my concerns at being thrashed around the boxing ring, my father's solicitous response was to doggedly search out his old World War II RAF kit bag, pack it not with all his troubles, but with sand, and hang it up in the cellar as a frugal home-made postwar punching bag. He then instructed me to practice. Another of my encounters with Discipline and The Stiff Upper Lip, which was also known in those days as Character Building.

A small silver medal commemorated this brief moment of fame and pain, which sat with pride on my bedroom sideboard.

It was joined a year later by an equally diminutive cup for winning the Hundred Yards Sprint at the Schools Annual Sports Day. By that time I had learned that there were people out there who could hurt you, and as a consequence had learnt to run quite fast. This simple and yet highly pertinent philosophy I have believed in firmly during my life, and it has served me well. Unfortunately even my modest sporting successes on the track or rugby field through the years put my academic efforts to shame.[23]

1956 - History - This appeals to his sense of the dramatic, but his answers are usually rather garbled.

Maths - He has gone right back to his old ways of being half asleep, and not really trying.

In the 1950s, the need to encourage and develop confidence in a child had yet to be recognised; in fact the idea was more remote than the thought that man would walk on the moon. I have absolutely no idea what my parents thought as they read my school reports, but with humane and surprising vision, my father attempted to offer a sophisticated form of staged financial reward to encourage my academic improvement. Mystifyingly, considering my financial challenges, even this could not motivate me to do schoolwork. [22]

My tutors continued to sarcastically observe my complete lack of interest in academic pursuits. I dream of a time machine that could pluck Mr Bryant out of his arcane headmaster's den and deposit him into my office today. I could modestly parade my achievements before him, and politely ask him what he thought of his ever so 'constructive' comments sixty years ago? What would today's psychology-trained teachers think of my performance? No doubt I'd be booked into special counselling before I could say 'Stiff Upper Lip'.

The idea in my day was that our youthful self esteem was built up by learning of our shortcomings as human beings via the rapier pens of the teachers at the end of each term. We also had rather more instantaneous encouragement of the system of corporal punishment, the last resort for instilling a zest for learning in recalcitrant boys. I found myself numbered amongst this motley crew. One day, for some reason, I hadn't completed my homework for the third time and was invited to join the boys in detention. This event was cordially accompanied by an invitation to join the Headmaster in his study.

A caning was very much a ceremonial occasion, as much for the entire school as for the individual. At the end of lunch, before being dismissed to retire to our classrooms where we could either rest our heads on our desk or pretend to read our books in silence, the Headmaster would read out a list of names, all of whom were invited to report to his study. I knew what lay ahead, but with my unending youthful optimism, I was certain that I would be saved by an earthquake, or an announcement declaring the outbreak of another war. Sadly neither catastrophe eventuated, and the voice intoned, "Griffin. Harris."

The other boys filed out, and Harris and I peeled away to quiver outside the large, highly polished door, emblazoned in gilt with the single word in uppercase Times: *HEADMASTER*. I paused, still waiting for earthquakes, war, tsunami…. nothing yet. I stepped forward and knocked on the door. The firm tenor voice spake, "Enter."

The door opened with a creak of unoiled hinges. "Come in boy. Don't dawdle."

I entered the large oak panelled study which had the air of a museum. A large desk in the window bay, a filing cabinet, a bentwood coat stand, and a Victorian elephant's foot walking stick stand. Ominously this one contained no walking sticks, but instead a sadist's dream collection of canes, riding crops and lengths of bamboo sticks, all chosen for their ability to show a boy the errors of his ways. I expected to see the Headmaster sitting there in a red judge's cape, whilst donning the black square of cloth that so many prisoners knew to be the scrap that heralded their impending death. I felt like an aristocrat before the French revolutionary court in *A Tale of Two Cities*, but where was my Sidney Carton to unselfishly stand in for me at the guillotine? *It is a far, far better thing that I do…*

Judge-like, the Headmaster went through all the reasons as to why I found myself standing before him. I don't know why he thought that I didn't know and needed to hear it all again. Eventually he arrived at, "Do you have anything to say?"

Under advice, I had practised my earnest response. "Sorry sir, I will not let it happen again". A hollow promise if there ever was one.

"Well I am also sorry boy, as this will hurt me more than it will hurt you." Another hollow promise. Was the world always so perfidious? "Go and stand over there".

The Spanish Inquisition had had no more terrible Torquemada than he; and I was being burnt at my own personal *auto-da-fé*.

I moved to the corner. The Headmaster set about the ritual that was in itself a cleverly designed form of medieval torture, intended to heighten the victim's fear of the moment. Standing up, he carefully removed his cape and hung it on the bentwood coat stand. Next removed was the Harris Tweed country sports jacket, and then carefully the enamelled Oxford University-crested cuff link from his right cuff was extracted. He placed it in a cut down two-pounder anti tank shell that served rather morbidly as his desk ornament. As I watched, still praying futilely for the earthquake, he slowly rolled his right sleeve up above his elbow.

The Headmaster moved to the elephant's foot stand. Why was everything in this office reminiscent of death? He removed a bamboo cane that the boys had already christened Mr Knobbly. He inflicted a practice swing at the air, which made a sound like 'whoosh'. But Mr Knobbly is consigned back to the stand, as the Headmaster opted for another. He sorted through his bizarre collection as if looking for a 9-iron, found what he sought, and swung it once through the air. Oh dear God it's Mr Whippy, one of the most feared instruments, recognised for its downward speed that the boys are convinced will beat Chuck Yeager in breaking the sound barrier.

"Over there." He pointed to the centre of the wall. "Bend over, closer to the wall."

A cunning and cruel tactic, as the prisoner now had insufficient room to follow the natural reaction in standing up quickly once struck. In addition, in the event he tried, he will receive a bonus punishment of a sharp crack to the head as it comes in contact with the wall, to remind him not to stand up to escape further pain.

The cane was next gently prodded at the prisoner's gluteus maximus. This procedure has been found to be necessary, following the shocking discovery that boys were using school blotting paper tucked into their underpants, in the belief that its magical qualities would absorb the sting of the cane. I was now prepared to throw pride to the wind and myself to the floor, and beg for mercy. I don't know whether it was a good or a bad thing, but the *stiff upper lip* kicked in and I held my ground.

1957 - Headmasters Report – Patrick is by nature very pleasant and easy going, and this does, I fear, extend to his work; but not to the degree of willful laziness. I doubt if slave-driving would benefit him – in fact I think the reverse. W.T.Bryant

The ritual fast approached its climax. I watched, upside down, from between my legs as, carefully, with very measured strides, he walked back towards his desk. He turned, as if he was about to bowl a very fast leg break to an Australian batsman. He raised his arm and started his run up. At this stage I closed my eyes and awaited the stinging pain as Mr Whippy impacted with the ferocity of willow striking leather; in this instance the willow struck my very tender nine year old backside. My fears were not disappointed, and it hurt like hell. The Headmaster started measuring his stride back to his crease. Good God, I have to face an over of these insane deliveries.

At last the *auto-da-fé* came to an end. I shuffle, stand up, turn, and shake the Headmaster by the hand in the time-honoured manner. "Thank you sir."

I leave him thus to his dressing, so as to enable him to start the ritual over again from the beginning with the new prisoner. As I totter from the Headmaster's study, I catch the strange mix of sympathy and apprehension that runs across Harris's visage. He is next to face the onslaught of the County's ex-bowler.

1957 – Headmaster's Report – Patrick's relapse is very disappointing indeed. I am afraid it is partially due to his own want of self-confidence in his ability. W.T.Bryant

Staggering to the classroom, I fought back the tears bravely. The strength of emotion was evoked as much by the tortuous elongation of the ritual itself as from any actual pain in my nether regions. As I entered the room, all eyes swivelled in my direction.

"Up or Down?" mouths Hurrell silently.

The query in all the boys' minds, this was concerned with whether Mr Whippy had been administered with trousers up or down. Down was usually reserved for more serious offenses.

"Up," I silently enunciated to satisfy their lurid interest.

I sat down, and bounced back up like a jack-in-a-box. The sensitivity of my recent experience was felt most acutely. This immediately set off huge chuckle from the class, and received visual daggers from the teacher. Years of self discipline and close study have made him totally impervious to my, or indeed any boy's, suffering.

"Griffin, stop clowning around or I will send you back to the Headmaster".

No sooner had I carefully adjusted myself onto the hard wooden seat, than the school bell rang for the end of the increasingly misnamed 'rest period'. With this we exited the classroom, and, surrounded by my classmates, I was almost swept off my feet in the rush to get to the locker rooms. We met up with Harris who was immediately dragged into and submerged in the throng. "Come on, drop them, let's see the stripes," came the chorus.

Proudly, Harris and I turned, unclipped our school belts and carefully lowered our grey shorts and white underpants. A sudden collective gasp: "Hey Griffin, you've scored blood!"

Now I had earned a REAL medal of honour, which brought great admiration in a way that my little silver cup and medal never did. The pain faded in inverse proportion to the swelling pride I felt at being so highly respected for handling pain with such fortitude. I carefully felt my bottom, feeling six distinct ridges. In the mirror, I could see they were already turning shades of black and blue, with a few streaks of red seeping through. Just as I was savouring the oohs and ahhs that accompanied my new-found fame, the bell rang again. At that moment I learned what many more popular celebrities have not learned: with the sound of the bell and a new focus for the boys, my fame and renown disappeared at the same speed with which it arrived. Before I had finished revelling in it, it disappeared, and I fell back to earth and the disciplined routine of school with a thump.

The 1950s saw an outbreak of a dreadful disease that had a devastating effect on the young, poliomyelitis. In an attempt to control the outbreak, all children were to be inoculated at school. Having suffered pneumonia at the age of five and recalling vividly how I was used as a pincushion for penicillin injections, I naturally formed an inherent and overwhelming fear of needles.

I awaited with terror the announcement as to the day of the polio vaccinations and it arrived all too soon. My mother packed me off to school one morning as if everything was completely normal, with a cheery "By the way, today is the vaccination at school. I'm told they have new special needles that you won't even feel and it really won't hurt at all." Never in a million years could my mother have imagined my delight when this proved to be true, and it had nothing at all to do with the 'new needle' that she tried to fool me with.

At school, we had our lunch as usual in the refectory. It was announced that, before rest, Doctor Kennett was to administer the polio vaccinations. We lined up alphabetically, with our left sleeves rolled up. I stood in line, my appointment with the terrible syringe fast approaching, and I longed to change my parents and be adopted by Ben's parents, Mr and Mrs Zelda, but it was too late to arrange this as there was now only John Grant ahead of me. As he stepped forward, I desperately and futilely planned an escape.

"Patrick."

There was Doctor Kennett, busily charging up his syringe with its thirtieth dose. Naturally they saw no reason to change the needle in those days. The syringes were the size of drain pipes and probably sharpened on a grindstone. I couldn't see any sign of the special new needle promised by my mother. How could she be so false to her own son?

"Patrick."

There stood Matron, a warm and kind woman, and, in the way of matrons since the dawn of time, she had an enormous bosom like the prow of a ship.

"Patrick. Come on, your mother mentioned that you were worried about having this injection, but it really won't hurt".

Surely this kindly woman wouldn't lie, but I was paralysed with apprehension, sighing loudly as if that would help me to avert my fate. At the moment of my exhalation, Matron's arms shot out, grabbed the back of my head and with extraordinary strength pulled my head forward. Before I knew what was happening, my head was enveloped in her ample bosom and darkness descended. Amongst the scents of lavender and talcum powder, I gasped for air.

It was an eternity. I was suffocating in a purgatory of soap-scented agony. At last I was released, and I surfaced to the light of day and the unutterable joy of filling my lungs with sweet fresh air. Oh, and apparently whilst I was embosomed, I had been vaccinated. The thought of impending death meant that I hadn't felt a thing. [24]

I was not an ungrateful boy. I was forever thankful to Matron for this salvation. But her unique method of distracting me from my terror of the syringe left me scarred for life. Arm yourselves, Freudians. Since that day, the front of a young woman's anatomy has held no charms for me. The physical characteristics that have been the centre of man's admiration and fascination over the centuries, hold no interest for me whatsoever. Rather than these features being regarded with boyish adventure, expectation and excitement, to me they are simply a threat, to be feared and avoided at all costs. A young woman with fine legs, on the other hand, has always held irresistible charms for me, shapely legs being of far greater appeal. After her fine mind, of course.

1955 - Geography - He seems to have a good general knowledge of the subject, no doubt from watching Television.

Swanage, being a coastal town, had seen many beach defences, Pill Boxes as some were known, built to repel a possible German invasion during World War II, with tank stops and scaffolding off-shore to harass landing craft. As children, we found these great fun to play on. These remnants of the war, along with bomb sites, were our playgrounds; collecting old ordinance, such as spent shell casings from Spitfire battles that had raged in the skies a little over a decade before, and bomb fragments dropped by the Luftwaffe, was our hobby. [27]

Having been let off sports with a summer cold, I was returning home early from school, walking along the beach, when in the distance I espied a group of schoolboys from Forres School. Forres was the other choice of private school in Swanage, and our regular competitors at sports. Some distance away the boys were gathered around something that was causing great excitement. I recognised one of my friends and called out as to what all the excitement was about. It appeared they had found what some thought was a chest or something, and they were trying to prise the lid off with a shoe horn. He was asking me for a penknife, when we found ourselves lifted off our feet and thrown to the grown, ears singing and sand and pebble fragments showering down all around us. The chest had turned out to be a WWII landmine, and five boys died that day. It was a small town and we all knew someone lost in this tragedy. I recall the vicar chatting with us to offer some comfort over the following days, and life went on.

1958 - Headmaster's Report – His good character and charm of manners will help him out one day.

Those days of childhood adventure in Swanage offered us a million happy ways to fill our days. In spring, we picked armloads of bluebells and the wildflowers that carpeted the woods; as spring turned to summer we had the excitement of long walks in search of birds' nests, from which we would collect an egg, long before such hobbies were outlawed. Even then we had our own instinctive ecological rules; we would only take one egg, and only then if there were three or more in the nest. Amongst my school friends, there was a thriving business of 'swaps' as we competed to have the grandest egg collection.

We were also excited when we found owl pellets. These strange and unlikely items of ornithological interest were quite a find. Owls eat small rodents, birds, and bugs as part of their nightly diet, but its stomach cannot digest the fur, bones, teeth, feathers, and insect shells from its prey. These unwanted parts form into a tight pellet inside the owl and are then disgorged. Dissecting these gruesome prizes produced all manner of things of interest to a boy's enquiring mind. There was however one danger to be aware of. The pellets had an uncommon resemblance to dog-poo, and we might have a horrid surprise on occasions in mother's kitchen dissecting something of much less interest than owl pellets. Once we found three kits, or baby squirrels for you city dwellers, who had fallen from their drey, their nest, their mother having been shot by a farmer as vermin. [32]

Most Sundays were spent with family walking on Nine Barrow Down or through Rempstone Woods, a magical place that was a microcosm of nature; Dad as a keen photographer would record much of it on his latest Kodak Reflex Camera that never left his side. [25]

We would all pile into the car; there was no problem with six of us as there were no safety belts to restrict us. Dad always made the journey into an adventure, as the woods were a few miles out of Swanage on the road to Corfe Castle, another magical place in our minds. The road ran beside the single railway track that connected Swanage to Corfe Castle. Dad would drive to beat the train to the bridge that crossed the track, and then park and wait for the steam train to pass below us. To our unending delight, we would then be enveloped in the billowing smoke as it curled over the parapet around us and on occasions we would get out, leaning over attempt to drop a pebble down the engine's funnel. [26]

On our return, we'd pass an old farm shed that contained a rather tired looking green John Deere tractor left over from WWII. It marked the start of the downhill run home. Dad would put the car in neutral, turn off the engine and off we'd roll in silence, gaining speed downhill and then slowing on the flat. Each time four of us on the back seat would be willing the car on to go that extra yard, until Dad would engage the gear. We thought this was great fun, but for Dad it was a throwback to the years of petrol rationing and trying to eke out the last few yards from every drop of precious fuel.

Every December, our chests were tight with excitement, we'd board the cream and green Hants & Dorset bus, referred to with much hilarity by my father as 'Pants & Corset', from Swanage to Bournemouth, to Bobby's department store and Santa's Grotto. Clutched in our hot hands were our wish lists that had been months in the preparation.

Being a child of simple tastes, I loved the colourful bus tickets: green for adults, blue for children and - much prized by child collectors – pink for dogs. We'd battle to grab the old tickets from the receptacle, to see who could fold them together to make the longest concertina. As I said, we had simple tastes! This annual trip was quite an adventure, trundling us across a windswept heath to the chain ferry at Sandbanks, where in winter the narrow entrance of Poole Harbour made for a choppy five-minute crossing.

As summer came around our holidays were spent on the beach where my parents had the luxury of a beach hut. It boasted a little kitchen with a spirit stove to boil the kettle for afternoon tea, and we stored our deck chairs, towels, buckets and spades there. Even with this unaccustomed luxury, it didn't save Nanny Elaine (my Yaiyai) from the demands of her ward to carry all the little extras down for him to play with on the beach. I fear I caused her great angst as we awaited the arrival of the local bus to take us on our short journey to the beach. In addition to the packed lunches of jam sandwiches, fruit from the garden and a bottle of orange cordial, she struggled with a large garden shovel, as I was never content with a small beach bucket and spade. Then of course there were the fishing lines and hooks that invariably got caught up on the clothes of other bus passengers. Yaiyai's burdens ensured those days held my fondest memories.[28, 29, 30, 31]

These were often preserved on a roll of 35mm Ilford film, my father being an avid photographer and president of the local Camera Club, a hobby which rubbed off on me for a short while.[33]

As summer faded, we still headed for the beach, rather better clad for the cold, and with my father's gardening equipment of course. It was extraordinary what holiday makers lost at the beach in summer, and what endless pleasure it gave those of us left to face the stormy seas of winter, sifting through the sand with a garden sieve. Coins and jewellery were commonplace, but the most exciting piece of flotsam and jetsam I found was a sailor's hat with the simple letters, 'HMS' on the band. This was definitely from the war, as no ship name was displayed so as not to help the enemy. My imagination ran wild - it must have been bobbing around the ocean for years! And what of the heroic efforts of the sailor to whom this belonged? What of his tragic end?

The holy grail was a bottle with a message inside from a stranded seafarer. To encourage any castaways we'd put a message in an old Tizer bottle and fling it off the beach, forever hoping for a reply from a far away shore. You cannot imagine our excitement when an envelope arrived bearing a pink German postage stamp. It was marked *Helgoland Wieder Freiam 1 Marz 1952*. We nearly passed out when we found it contained a letter from a boy who had found one of our actual bottles! He lived on Helgoland, a remote island in the North Sea off the German coast. We had difficulty even finding it in our school atlas. An exchange of letters commenced, but for the boys we were, the novelty soon wore off and the pressures of letter-writing became tedious. I learned later of the island's significance as a submarine base in WWII, and the bombing they'd borne. Historically a Danish possession, it fell to Britain from 1807 to 1890, briefly managed as a war prize from 1945 to 1952, and then returned to Germany.

In autumn we entered the 'conker' season. We each had our favourite chestnut tree, from which we sought the largest conkers. Each weapon was then treated by baking or soaking in vinegar, the aim of which was to toughen the skin. Once reinforced, the conker could be threaded on the string that hopefully would make it become a 'tenner', or the champion conker in the serious competition that ensued in the Autumn School Term.

This was a blood sport. The string would be wrapped around the right hand whilst the conker was held between the fingers of the left. Your opponent would hold his string, letting the conker hang down. Taking careful aim you swung your conker with all the force you could muster and hope to strike your opponent's conker, splitting it or knocking it off its string. There needed to be much skill deployed in this, as failure to strike often resulted in bruised knuckles and other hideous injuries from flying chestnut kernels. I'm not sure if this ruthless sport is still played in the modern schoolyard; somehow I suspect that the teachers monitoring the play yards today would be using their risk management skills to consign this schoolboy tradition to the waste bin. Too much chance of injury and parental litigation in the current 'cotton wool' generation.

My preparation for the transition to secondary education was fraught with academic challenges. I had grown up with the smell of sea air in my nostrils and reminders of the great British naval history everywhere around me. I romanticised the Navy even further having found that sailor's hat bearing the HMS ribbon washed up on the beach. What could be more exciting than a life at sea? My parents never shied away from anything that they hoped and prayed would instil discipline in their somewhat erratic youngest son. I was therefore enrolled for a place at the naval academy of TS Mercury, that apparently took wild young boys and turned them, miraculously, into future officers for the Royal Navy.

I sat the exam. To everyone's great surprise, the level of which was rather unwarranted I thought, I passed. Very pleased with ourselves, we headed off to Southampton for my Ministry of Transport eyesight test. I was directed into a large room with nothing in it but a desk, a large mirror and a very large old-fashioned 'magic lantern' from which I assumed I would view some interesting slideshow of naval achievements. A gentleman entered the room, confirmed my name, and then to my surprise without a word cast the room into pitch darkness. I could not see my hand in front of my face.

A few minutes passed and I stood in the dark. With a click the 'magic lantern' burst into life. He spoke automatically, in a monotone. "This is a test for your colour sight; it represents a ship's lights at three miles at night, red for port, a white mast light and the green starboard light. You will see two spots of light reflected in the mirror, which you will read from left to right – do you understand?"

Seemed easy enough. "Yes sir." Off we sailed into the dark. Green... Red... Red... White... Green... Green... White... Green... and so we cruised on for five minutes.

As I left the room and joined my father, I was full of confidence that our next stop would be at the military tailors, to get measured up for the smart naval uniform in which I had so long pictured myself. From there I would go on to make my mark on naval history at the helm of one of Her Majesty's fighting ships, no doubt to completely outshine Lord Nelson and his paltry achievements. [34]

We were called into the office of the examining officer, who proceeded to callously and with malicious aforethought shatter my dreams. He advised me that I was slightly colour blind and therefore would not be able to enter the Navy as a future deck officer. I was mortified and could not understand the reasoning; why the hell did it matter whether I could detect colours? Apparently the Royal Navy felt I might mistake the green starboard for a red port and run one of their nice frigates or cruisers into a lighthouse. Years of mental images of myself in that gorgeous naval uniform dissipated into the salty sea air. My belief was that 'All the girls love a sailor' and I thought forlornly of a life of celibacy.

I contemplated my future on the long quiet drive home with my parents. My mother tried as ever to cheer me up, looking at the bright side. "Don't worry dear, you probably wouldn't have enjoyed it. You might get seasick, and the uniform looks very itchy".

I hardly heard as I was lost in the depths of my own disappointment. I would have gladly borne any amount of nausea in an uncomfortable itchy uniform. Now I had to face very much more unpleasant and tangible hardships: I had to study at school for the Common Entrance Exam that I had sought to escape by going to sea.

1958 - Final Headmaster's Report - We shall miss his cheerful and genial personality, but he must come to terms with the fact he cannot get through life with a smile and these attributes alone. W.T. Bryant

I was now closing in on my teens and about to say goodbye to childhood. Altogether to date it had been a very happy one and although definitely warmed by the love of my parents, physically my abiding memories of that time were of cold, always being cold. The post-war years were still plagued with shortages and blackouts were common. Our home, Magnolia House - although impressively large - was cold. There was no central heating, there were no wall to wall carpets, just large Persian rugs that covered some areas of the polished floorboards that had gaps through which the winter draughts whistled. I would often complain to my father when in bed about being cold and in need of the electric fire, or a hot water bottle, only to be told to curl up in a ball under the blankets and breathe deeply, as he had done in his spartan youth. I would often wake up and have to scrape the ice off the inside of the window to see the grey winter's morning. And - oh - the chilblains I suffered. I would sit with my feet first in a bowl of hot water then cold to help the circulation in my feet; they itched terribly. One day in an attempt to stop it I decided to apply a mustard poultice that I had heard talked about, only to find that my swollen toes were now even worse and painfully raw. [35]

My impending move away from home I felt must surely have some positives - a school dormitory with all those other boys must offer some warmth?

I was wrong.

Chapter 4

#tombrown's-a-wimp #clothesmakethman #characterbuilding

In the autumn of 1958, I failed my Common Entrance exam.

So the hunt for a school was on. The local Grammar School was excellent but still required students to pass an academic examination, referred to as the '11 plus', and I failed this as well. I fear this was only one of my many problems that caused sleepless nights for my long-suffering parents.

It was not long before I found myself in their company again heading out of Dorset, east into the county of Hampshire then north towards Basingstoke. As we sped through the New Forest, out of nowhere a deer leapt across the road in front of the car. My father's reaction was immediate. The brakes were applied with such force, that from my comfortable position sitting on the edge of the seat with my elbows leaning on either side of the seats in front viewing the road ahead, I was propelled with rocket like speed between my parents, striking the windscreen with a resounding thump, and landing upside down on top of the dashboard. My father remained calm, surveying the damage as much to the car as myself, while mother fussed around checking for blood and bumps and bruises. Apart from a large swelling on my forehead there seemed to be little damage done and none to the car, so we were soon on our way, a little shaken but none the worse for wear. A disappointment as far as I was concerned, as I felt at the very least, they might have felt it appropriate to return home and allow me to rest and recover from this traumatic event.

Leaving civilisation behind, down little country lanes, through a small village called Long Sutton, we eventually came to the imposing wrought-iron gates of Lord Wandsworth College and through the large arch bearing a crest depicting a rampant lion. The long driveway led to my future incarceration and the beginning and end of my life for the next five years. Next door was a rather less imposing establishment, called Chequers Public House, and this would play a far more interesting role in my future development

At Lord Wandsworth College, I sat for and passed my entrance exam with flying colours, much to everyone's surprise again. I will always recall the audible sigh of relief that emanated from my parents as they received the good news in a rather bulky envelope from the school that was delivered to our door. Could it have been the bump to my head that had somehow miraculously knocked some sense into me? [36]

Their unrestrained joy was short lived, as my father started to read the list of accoutrements he would need to purchase for my enrolment.

The first major blow was the clothing list: 1 School Blazer, 2 grey shirts, 2 white shirts (collars attached), 4 pairs of school uniform socks, 1 School Sports Jacket (special weave by Harris Tweed), 2 pairs of khaki shorts (for Summer), one school trunk, one 'Tuck Box', 2 red rugby shirts, 2 blue rugby shirts. The list went on. All should be labelled with the boy's name and school number sewn on and easily visible. This was a particularly onerous task that was designated to my mother, an often repeated task as I grew fast.

"This is ridiculous," my father exclaimed. "They even specify from where it is to be purchased!"

It did not relieve his ire to discover the purchase was stipulated to occur at one of the more expensive London school retailers. Having two older brothers, I had always managed with their hand me downs, quite the thing in those post-war years

It wasn't that my father was a mean man. He had sprung from the loins of two generations of bankers and had survived the ravages of the Great War, the Depression, the Second World War and England's post-war austerity. *Make do and mend* had been his mantra, and waste was his mortal enemy. The school list was seen as a pointless waste, as he no doubt had in mind that I was entering those years when puberty and hormones cause growth spurts. My father envisioned an expensive jacket in which I would be sent off at the term's beginning, with cuffs around my knuckles, only to return home at term's end with the cuffs closer to my elbows.

So it was that I found myself shopping for the actual necessities, not in London, but in the local men's store and for that matter anywhere my father felt we would find a suitable (read *cheaper*) alternative. This started to ring warning bells for me, and gave me no small concern. As with every boy growing up, I just wanted to fit in and not stand out from my peers. Thankfully, the sports jacket from our local men's store seemed to me an acceptable substitute, and the sales assistant assured me it was an identical pattern to the one on my school list. I was far less confident about my substitute khaki shorts. They were indeed khaki-coloured, but the style did not seem as tailored as I fear would be acceptable at school. My father was quick to remind me that these were military cut, and if they were good enough for the boys who fought at Tobruk, then they were most certainly good enough for my school. With the heroic feats of those fearless soldiers ringing in my ears, we departed the Army Surplus Store in Bournemouth, and my fears were distracted as I clutched my reward - an old military drill bayonet that I had promised would remain at home and not find its way into my school trunk.

I was allocated to School House, one of the three boarding houses of the school. There were three hundred and fifty boys at the school, divided between the houses that became our homes for the next five or six years. I ascended the stairs to my dormitory, better known as South Dorm. I was welcomed by the austere sight of two rows of cast iron beds, eleven down each side, topped with horsehair mattresses, sheets and a bright red blanket. A locker stood beside each bed. Three 40 watt bulbs dimly lit the dorm, each hanging from a cable with no lamp shade to soften its utilitarian aspect.[37]

My trunk was at the foot of a bed. A prefect stood at the door and ordered us to return downstairs and say our farewells to parents, and to return here in thirty minutes, no later. We dutifully followed orders. As one of the eleven new boys, I stood in the quad outside the house, shook hands with my father and rather embarrassed, I fought off the hugs and kisses of my mother, who was stifling a tear or two. As they returned to the car, waving as they drove off, I remained on the spot until I could see them no more. I suddenly felt very alone for the first time. I turned and fearfully returned to the dorm, stomach churning with foreboding.

This feeling grew, as the school prefect read out the list of rules and regulations that were to govern our days. He pointed out the ablutions area through the door at the end of the dorm. We were to pay particular attention to the bathing list on which we would find our names and the bathing timetable. We were each allocated a fifteen-minute spot for our weekly bath, which was compulsory, whether we felt we needed it or not. To the left was the clothing locker room in which we would find a shelf labelled with our name, on which we were to neatly store our clothes and an open locker alongside in which to hang our blazers. Bedside lockers were for a few personal items and wash bags. Our Tuck Boxes would be checked for contraband, and then stored in the common room. We had thirty minutes until roll-call, after which we all walked to the main refectory hall for supper. Bedtime and lights out was 9.00pm, with no more talking after 9.30pm. And so my school life's routine was established.

The first night passed quietly enough, apart from a few sniffles around the dorm as the realisation sank in that mums were now very far away. I suspect I joined in with the odd sniffle, and eventually fell into an uneasy sleep. It seemed like only a few seconds later that the door burst open and the prefect strode down the middle of the dorm ringing a very loud brass hand bell. "Come on Squirts! 7.00am! Wakey wakey! Roll call in 30 minutes."

He departed. There was a stunned silence for a moment as we remembered where we were. All hell then broke loose, as we headed for the bathroom en masse. There were 12 hand basins, 4 lavatories and a long urinal at which 22 boys were all scrambling for space. We then dashed to the hand basins, a quick splash to the face and a scrub of the teeth and a sprint back to our lockers to don our school uniforms. In time we became proficient at dressing, the secret being to keep vest, shirt, school jersey and knotted school tie as one unit. There were legendary boys who were said to have retained the same knot in their tie for the full 6 years of their scholastic studies at the school. Underpants were meant to be changed twice a week, however, frequently this was not the case. They were changed, but simply from 'inside to outside'. Contemporary Hygiene 101 was not on the curriculum in those days.

Fully dressed we rushed through the door, down the travertine staircase. Some agile types used the bannister to speed their descent. Then followed the corridor dash to the common room where we lined up for roll call, a daily routine that we were convinced was a rerun of the masters' experience in German stalags. Woe betide anyone who was late or attempted to escape. Once we'd answered and all were present and correct, we were dismissed and sent on our way to breakfast. We'd stop on the way at the small pantry where we had deposited a few of the basics we were permitted to cheer up the bland school breakfast that lay ahead. These little treats were our own marmalade or jam, often home-made by a loving mother, and of course butter, an item unheard of in the school kitchens. Rather than toast bread, they tossed it in a deep fryer to produce 'fried bread'. We made it slightly more palatable with a thick layer of butter and marmalade. Although the English climate was cool, with no fridge the butter went rancid in no time. This minor problem didn't stop us from using it, and in fact it actually enhanced the flavour of whatever it was liberally spread upon.

The next dash to the refectory was more orderly than the initial scramble to roll call, as now the camp guards - or I should say prefects - were on patrol. Anyone caught running would immediately be called out and given a *racking*: the punishment of writing out 200 lines of Latin on thin stationery that bore an uncanny resemblance to Izal toilet paper. Such was our morning hunger, it was worth the risk.

After the settling-in basics of the first week, the essential hierarchy began to manifest within the dorm. Naturally, new boys were at the bottom. Being tall, and what I thought was confident in my survival abilities, I was still not prepared for the mob mentality I witnessed. Having read *Lord of the Flies,* I started to feel a little less confident. The routine of prefects and masters was to retire to their own pastimes after lights out, and leave the boys to their slumbers. On a memorable night, the Jack Merridew of our dorm-island whose character represented the dark side of human nature, announced "Now I think it is time to initiate the new boys".

Too afraid to resist, following our survival instincts, we steeled ourselves for whatever was to come. I was to be the first. "Strip off."

Hesitantly I did, trying to maintain what modesty I could whilst being prodded to get under the first bed. Once there I was ordered to crawl under the eleven beds on this side, cross over and crawl back along the other side: *running the gauntlet*, or - more accurately - *crawling the gauntlet*. I took a deep breath and clambered along as fast as I could beneath each bed. Sudden pain as a slipper came down on my bare buttocks, then as I passed under each bed I was struck by an array of slippers, ties, belts, and, oddly enough, a pillow.

I made it in under two minutes: tired, welts on my back, raw knees and hands. Once through, I was greeted with handshakes and slaps from the other boys, and welcomed into an elite club having passed the rites of passage. Most boys made it. A few of the 'gentler' boys didn't, and found their lives were to grow considerably worse. Barbaric? Yes, but accepted by all, including schoolmasters, and especially the prefects, as the *sine qua non* of educational experience.

There were those who had the bravery to resist such school intimidations. One young man with a name that led to many a barbed jibe, Roger Bootle-Wilbraham, was a rather strange boy, given to aloofness. As it turned out, it was not surprising as he had obviously inherited his father's genes, being the son of Brigadier Lionel Bootle-Wilbraham DSO, MC, Lord Skelmersdale, who served with the Coldstream Guards, and was awarded his DSO for playing an important part in holding the Dunkirk perimeter. Roger would take his place in the House of Lords, and be appointed by Margaret Thatcher as whip, a title not unknown to a public schoolboy. He was also to serve as Minister for Work and Pensions in David Cameron's Shadow Cabinet and then as Deputy Speaker in the Lords in 2010.

The wrath of the mob was not limited to a single initiation, and it was not logical or rational in its choice of target. Bullying was a creative sport that could manifest in the physical as well as the psychological. You could be sent to 'Coventry', where the entire dorm would not speak to, nor acknowledge you. You could be inflicted with an 'apple-pie bed' wherein your sheets were folded in half, causing your feet to painfully tear through the well-worn sheet when you leapt into bed. This had the added benefit of bringing the ire of the powers that be upon you as well.

There were of course far more painful physical tactics, such as 'tossing the blanket'. A boy was thrust into the centre of a blanket laid on the floor. Half a dozen or more larger boys grabbed the edges and tossed the hapless victim into the air, the aim being to slam him against the ceiling. This could actually be less painful than the landing, if the boys in charge let go of the blanket. I was fortunate as I was rarely given the blanked treatment due to my size. The smaller boys were of course far more attractive sport being so much lighter. The severe bruising that resulted was naturally noted down as a 'sporting injury.

During one particularly unpleasant period of bullying, I would long for sleep, for the safety of my dreams. Sadly one night even my dreams could not protect me. I awoke to the sight of the bullies wrenching back my blankets, pouring a large jug of cold water over me. As I leapt out of bed, a bottle of Vosene Shampoo was poured over both me and the bed. The evil effect of the shampoo was to leave a very suspicious yellow ring at the edge of the wet sheets. I spent an acutely uncomfortable night, trying to dry my sheets out before morning. Of course there was no chance of this and when it was discovered the following morning I was hustled off to the matron, to face a 'please explain'. With no way of explaining without giving away the bullies' secret and inviting ever more cruel pranks, I had no option but to stay silent, and thereby endure a long and humiliating lecture along the lines of why boys of my age should not still be wetting their beds.

Another of my purgatorial experiences occurred one winter's afternoon. I returned to my dorm to find I was totally ignored by all. Feeling invisible, I noticed that my bed, my locker, my clothes were all gone. It was as if I had died and no longer existed. I wandered about like a lonely ghost, trying to fathom what had happened, starting to believe that I had lost my mind and didn't really belong in this dorm.

A good friend, Peter Tipping, who was never too far away, and who could not openly support me, but didn't join the ranks of my tormentors either, nodded out the window. At first I saw nothing, but then, in the light mist that enveloped the rugby pitch a few hundred yards away, I noticed a familiar shape. I headed out, and as I got closer I beheld my perfectly made bed, my locker, all my clothes neatly stacked, toothbrush, mug and all, sitting in the middle of the 1st XV's perfectly marked out rugby pitch. Peter - at what might have been personal risk to his own safety from the mob - did come to my aid but it was well after dark by the time we were able to dismantle, transport, and rebuild my bed and belongings back in the warmth and comfort of the dorm.

There are, I'm pleased to say, those who have the courage to stand by you when all others fade away. I will always be thankful to Peter for that little act of support and kindness. I have often wondered what happened to him: he was a chronic asthma sufferer and there were nights when I could only sit by as he gasped for air. I found myself faced with it again when my own son Tim suffered from it, with many midnight trips to Emergency, where at least they could treat him, and he grew out of it in his teens, I am pleased to say.

Good ol' golden rule days. It might be controversial but I will talk about the dark side of my school memories so often just pushed to the back of one's mind. It was never spoken of then, but thankfully we now live in a more enlightened age. I am talking about the 'attention' of some of the schoolmasters. These attentions could range from the simply inappropriate to downright criminal. I was never regarded as a 'foppish' boy and I didn't fall into the category of being a 'handsome' boy, so my experiences in this realm were relatively mild. One could only guess at what some of the other gentler fair-haired, more timid boys experienced. These days the teachers involved would be hauled off to court, and rightly so.

One of the masters was famous for groping boys as he marked their work. We soon caught on to this, so when summoned to sit beside him for marking, our first strategy was immediately to cross one's left leg over the right leg and lean forward abruptly, thus blocking any access to his wandering hands. Most boys managed this with amazing agility. Those who forgot, or were not fast enough, were watched with high amusement by the boys in the front row, who engaged in various lewd gestures or mouthed 'Gotcha!' at the unwitting victims.

Following an outbreak of ringworm, suspected to have come from animals on the school's farm, one of these notorious schoolmasters felt it to be an opportune time to hold a tinea and ringworm inspection, such was his great concern for the students in his care. To this end, we were summoned from our dorm and called into his study. He sat calmly with a gin & tonic and cigarette in one hand, and a torch in the other. As we approached, we lifted up each foot for inspection for tinea, and then dropped our pajama trousers whilst he inspected our groins. Some boys carefully moved their own tackle, first left, then right, whilst others seemed to need his personal help in this task. Others, disturbingly, appeared to need an even longer inspection.

People often ask me in horror, why didn't you tell your parents? I answer with another question, how could I? In those days, sex didn't exist in conversation. On television couples were never seen in the same bed together, and if they were to kiss it would be a gentle peck and, if in bed, one foot always remained on the floor. Watch the movie *Brief Encounter* and you'll understand the strict morality to which our parents were accustomed. These men were teachers, they were staunch pillars of society who were never questioned, much in the same way as the clergy were protected.

In the innocence and resilience of childhood, we just learned to deal with these events. Our schoolmates supported us, all being in the same boat as it were, and we just tried to laugh it off and somehow got through it. People say how terrible it must have been, and how we must have felt as though we had done something to encourage it. Rubbish. None of us ever felt such a thing; we knew it was always at the instigation of the dirty old man, or DOM as became the normal reference. Perhaps people start to manifest this theory once the idea is planted, but I cannot believe that this is what a child thinks. I have great empathy and sympathy with any child who has been abused or interfered with. Fortunately, in my experience, we brushed it off, put it behind us and managed to get on with life, although a couple of incidences a little later in my life rather put this thinking to the test.

If anything, I think more damage was caused by the extremes of creative bullying that occurred in the name of *character building*.

Not all of the perpetrators escaped justice and one that didn't get away was my maths teacher and scoutmaster. It has taken many years for the world to come round to exposing the abuse that many boys suffered at the hands of men whom our parents had trusted to care for us. I came across a press report many years later from which I was pleased to see that, at long last, some justice has come to some of the men.[38]

The Telegraph - *26 May 2001*
Ex-teacher jailed over sex assaults
By Stewart Payne

A FORMER teacher who abused 13 boys at a public boarding school more than 30 years ago was jailed for three years for indecent assault yesterday.

Patrick Nott, 64, assaulted the boys, mostly aged 11 or 12, during the 1960s when he was a deputy housemaster at Lord Wandsworth College in Long Sutton, Hampshire. The abuse only came to light in 1999 when one of Nott's victims reported his experiences to the police. When arrested, Nott told officers that he had thought of it as "horseplay".

Winchester Crown Court was told that boys had reported the abuse to staff in 1966 but it had been "covered up" and the school had given Nott, of Ryde, Isle of Wight, glowing references when he left to work at a sixth-form college. Judge Timothy King said: "It's difficult to conceive of a grosser abuse of your position of trust."

It appears that such things were far more prevalent than we could ever have imagined in those days as I became aware on reading an article in The Times, January 20th 2014 by Andrew Norfolk entitled *'Closed worlds where abusers groomed boys with impunity'*

Now before I am rushed off for counselling, allow me to say that I am perfectly comfortable with myself and have put all this behind me. Over time I have learned the best lesson of all is to believe in the three Rs - but not 'Reading, wRiting & aRithmetic' but in a Buddhist belief of having 'Respect for oneself, Respect for others and to take Responsibility for one's actions'.

I don't know how I ever learned respect, as I certainly did not encounter any at school. Nicknames were the most effective way to put someone in their place, and boys knew exactly what to pick on to really weaponise this tactic. I was BEAK Griffin due to my nose, FATSO Jones and ZITS Gordon were unimaginative but obvious, and ZULU Mills had curly hair. If you reacted in any way, attacks would increase. We were rather mercilessly teasing a scholarship boy's north country accent - "ee by gum, lad"- when to our mortification an English teacher told us off in no uncertain terms, saying that the regional dialect was more true English than our homogenised, plummy BBC English accents. My first real lesson in *respect*.

February 3rd 1959 was quite a significant date as it heralded my entry to my teenage years when so many new things started to become more important. For me it was notable as I was now thirteen, but for many others it was memorable as it was the day when the rock idol of the time Buddy Holly died in a plane crash along with Ritchie Valens and 'The Big Bopper'. Buddy Holly's posthumous hit record was prophetically, *I Guess It Doesn't Matter Anymore*; some years later Don McLean wrote an iconic song to memorialise his death *American Pie* or as most know it 'The day the music died'. Not many boys can claim to have a song written that commemorates the day of their birth, although for me as a new teenager the music didn't die - it became more important, as did the opposite sex and indeed fashion. I had some early challenges in this area.

The first outing of my army-surplus Tobruk khaki shorts on a summer's day is an abiding memory, as vivid as yesterday. The instruction went out that Summer Kit was to be the order of the day with the warmer weather. As we made the usual Olympic dash from bed to bathroom and back again, rapidly donning our clothes in time for roll-call, I watched with growing horror as all the other boys rushed past in their neat, tailored khaki shorts. I looked down at my father's selection of shorts that adorned my youthful legs.

The difference was stark and devastating. The unfashionably wide waistband, not one but THREE buckles at the side, and, most crushing of all, the unique flare of the shorts, made the leg holes stand out like bell tents. My long legs protruded like two long white tent poles. To add insult to my injuries, my delay had made me the only boy left in the dorm, almost certainly to be conspicuously late for roll-call. Steeling my determination, my *stiff upper lip* was ready to cop whatever was to be thrown at me. I strode across the open space of the common room, boys all standing around the walls answering to their names at roll call, my head held high, I was walking with pride as if I was one of the Rats of Tobruk going to receive his Victoria Cross. My entrance was met with a stunned silence as the figure I cut was absorbed by all. Once reaching my place I turned and gave a smart salute to the prefect taking roll-call, and my best Montgomery wave to the boys around the room. The entire school house then broke down as one in hysterical laughter, but at least it was I who had made them laugh on purpose. I did however receive a punishment of 200 lines, not for my bad impersonation, but for my disruption of the sacred daily ritual.

The next challenge was my sports jacket, the one that was supposedly 'identical' to that designated by the school. This only attracted a few facetious comments from the masters. Most memorable was that from my English master. I entered class, resplendent in my sports jacket. He took one look at me, stopped in his tracks and boomed, "Good God Griffin, who do we think we are today... a bookie's runner?"

"Four to one you are right sir!"

My sartorial achievements taught me a great lesson; no matter how strange a predicament or pair of trousers you may find your-self in, turn it into a joke, your joke, and you come out ahead. You might have to live with the catcalls of 'hey baggy pants' for some time, but eventually they tire and you survive.

As in my primary school years, it did not occur to me that the actual education part was essential to my success. While I found some measure of regret for this youthful neglect when I was older, I managed to sneak in some other activities to make up for the academic gaps.

Being modest, I always saw myself as another Field Marshal Bernard Montgomery at El Alamein, or as the young Winston Churchill, whose book *My Early Life* had no small impact upon me. The fact that he wasn't academically minded either was highly attractive to me. Look where it got him. At that time, for me, his escapades in the Boer War were most captivating. With this in mind, and seeking more adventure than the Scouts, I joined the Royal Engineers section of the school's Combined Cadet Force (CCF), and had great fun. I confess it wasn't having to 'bull' my boots to a mirror finish or the drill we had to do that made it so. Neither was being barked at by a boy whose testi-cles had only just dropped sufficiently to eke out the command "Squad..." in baritone, whilst the "Attention!" bit tended to tail off in rather more of a contralto. After 'Basic Training' it all got much more interesting. If today's schools teach the same sort of things, I'd be worried if I still had boys in school. [39]

I signed up for the Royal Engineers course, and over the next few years I learned about building Bailey Bridges and pontoons, and, rather more what we wanted to learn, how to blow them up. I recall, quite usefully, that one pound of TNT, for instance, would blow up one inch of steel. We learned about 'ring mains', detonators, detonator cord (burns at 1 mile a minute) and safety fuses (burns at 1 foot a minute). We used plastic explosives - or PE808 as it was called - which had a smell of almonds. It had a habit of moulding around your fingers when warm, and if you handled it too long it gave you a headache. Now there's a safe activity for teenage boys. We also had lessons in booby traps with press and pull switches, and how to blow up someone sitting on a lavatory seat; in fact, all the things that would be most useful to a young man in his future career.

Chapter 5

#bombs'n'bangs #boysbehavingbadly #allthevices

Anything military always provided a source of excitement, whether it was guns, explosives or just the adventurous glamour of it all. Easy glamour when you didn't actually have to face a real enemy, firing real bullets at you. This could have very easily resulted in my, and others', demise. Often, at half term, there were boys who had to stay at school rather than have those precious days of freedom, mainly due to the fact that their parents were on overseas postings and it just wasn't practical for them to fly off to Germany or Cyprus for just a few days. I felt very sorry to see some of my friends faced with such a situation, so my parents were always happy for me to bring them home. On my part, being at home did not always coincide with half term breaks of my brothers or other friends and after the initial few hours of the welcome freedom, one was again alone and bored. So it was great to have these 'orphans' over to alleviate holiday boredom.

On one half term break I took one of my best friends home, Brett Morrell. His parents were posted with the RAF in Cyprus. [40]

Brett and I discussed how we may do a little demolition one warm and sunny afternoon, of course for scientific purposes only. I had read, and heard, of the interesting compounds contained in weedkiller, and I had noticed that my parents always had a yellow and black tin of this in the potting shed. Supposedly when mixed with sugar, we thought it could make quite an explosion. So that weekend, Brett and I found what we thought was a suitable container, an old Heinz baked bean can, and poured into it, a half and half mix of weedkiller and caster sugar, taken from mother's pantry. We mixed it up and compressed it as best we could.

I had a length of good old 'Jetex' fuse wire from a model airplane propulsion kit. We pushed the fuse into the mix and placed the can in a piece of my prized shrapnel collection - the tail end fin of a German bomb casing that I had retrieved from a local bombsite a few years previously. We felt this might add a degree of fitting drama to the occasion. We agreed on a suitable location for the detonation: behind a low garden wall my father had built a few weeks before. The 'bomb' was placed, with a few rocks around it to target the blast in an upward direction. We prepared ourselves for the anticipated devastation that we were about to unleash upon my tranquil and upmarket neighbourhood in Swanage.

Brett and I decided a good vantage point from which to view the explosion was from a small spinney of trees at the bottom of the garden. The block house at Peenemunde it was not but it would provide us a level of safety from any blast. With great excitement - and no small apprehension - we lit the fuse, rapidly retired and waited. The fuse seemed to burn for some time. We looked at each other. I was hesitant to be the first to cover my ears, but - as we both thought the explosion was imminent - with uncanny synchronisation, we raised our hands to our ears. For a second or two after the sparkling of the fuse had disappeared from view we saw and heard nothing. Suddenly we saw a massive bright flame, like that of a jet engine or a giant Roman Candle firework, which roared a couple of feet in the air for a minute. But no explosion. We liked the flame but were shattered to have not heard an explosion. We mulled it over, like two scientists, analysing what might have gone wrong with the formula, and like good scientists, decided to try again. There was a limited supply of weedkiller, and caster sugar, unless we were prepared to have our cereal at breakfast without sugar, so we only had enough for one more try, which I fear and much to our disappointment, had a similar result. Our experiments were abandoned, probably to the benefit of us all.

Fifty years later, Brett and his wife Ali, stayed with my wife Gan and I in Thailand, Brett having actually followed a military career in the RAF and retiring as a Group Captain. As we reminisced about our school days, we remembered this adventure. "You know what we did wrong, we just didn't compact it enough."

Having both agreed that that was the problem, and with a mischievous smile for which Brett was famous, he said, "Bloody lucky we didn't work that out at the time, as God knows what trouble we might have found ourselves in - even if we hadn't managed to kill ourselves in the process." How right he was, and how crazy we both were then. Nowadays, we would have found the garden surrounded in minutes by the SAS or Special Force officers, and ourselves in court for a possible act of terrorism.

I am uncertain of where my fascination for explosives came from. I was called Patrick, a good Irish name and the Fenians had quite a reputation for blowing things up, however, as long as I can remember, loud bangs terrified me and I would often cower under cushions on Guy Fawkes Night. Maybe it was an unconscious attempt to overcome this fear.

My cousin Tim and I once rode over to our uncle Kenneth's farm in Loxley. We had learned uncle Kenneth was what Aussies would call a larrikin, and he had been blowing up tree stumps to make way for ploughing a new field. We were intrigued by this and he took us to a shed to show us how he did it. He had a bottle which he explained was *Nitroglycerin*, the most powerful of explosives and a box containing something that looked a little like three inch lengths of seaside rock candy but he explained it was *Dynamite*.

We of course wanted to see him use it but sadly he explained, "Sorry lads but I have done all I am allowed to today and any more bangs will curdle the cows milk, BUT, I could give you a little of each to take back and use in the upper paddock at Tachbrook."

We were very excited at the prospect of blowing up the old hen house at Tachbrook, and eagerly agreed. "Now you must promise me you won't tell your parents, they would have my guts for garters, and you must only use a little at a time and stand well clear, OK".

We both readily agreed. "I will put a little of the nitro in this bottle, I need to be very careful as if a drop hits the floor there will be quite a bang. Do you want me to show you?"

"No, no don't waste it, that's OK"

We stepped back just in case, but he successfully decanted a small bottle for us and then put a few of the small sticks in a box padded with straw. These we carefully tied to the back of our bicycles and very gingerly we set off down the country lane on the four mile ride back to Tachbrook. I was very cautious to take a gentle pace, whereas Tim was far more cavalier and just sped off, not seeming to worry about bumps or potholes at all, I was happy that he rode faster than I, as I felt the greater distance between us was better in the event that he suddenly disappeared in a flash, bang and a puff of smoke. As it was we all arrived safely back at Tachbrook.

We have always called Tim's home 'Tachbrook', but the house was in fact 'The Old Parsonage', an enormous Victorian house set in acres of manicured lawns, at the centre of which grew a beautiful holly tree. The gardens had rose-lined arbours and lush flower beds. As children we loved that house. Its very size was half the fun, not least the ability to crawl in what were to us cavernous spaces under the floorboards. We could see the wiring that controlled the Victorian service bells, setting nerves on edge when we pulled one, sending an adult running to the drawing room to find it empty. There was a nursery, to which we were banished on a single command from my uncle. "Upstairs!". There were umpteen bedrooms, drawing rooms and dining rooms, two kitchens, a scullery, a rather grand front staircase and a back staircase that we children were meant to use. There were maids quarters at the top of the house, converted into a granny flat. And yet, the house still only had two bathrooms and three lavatories, the ones with heavy wooden seats and cisterns with long chains set high on the wall, emblazoned with the manufacturer's name 'Crapper', much to our youthful amusement. Somehow, even with a full house at Christmas and other sundry family gatherings, the household managed. Today the house and grounds are no more, long sold and replaced by about fifteen modern houses that would be regarded 'large' by today's standards.

Uncle Douglas had I was once told, purchased 'Tachbrook' for the princely sum of £900, now a mere pittance, but it was the centre of all things social in the village of Tachbrook. Being a doctor, uncle Douglas settled in and was regarded as the Lord of the Manor. [41]

I might also add that his wife, aunty Joyce, was my favourite and often lent an ear to problems that I would never approach my own mother with. She also happened to lend more than an ear in keeping my finances solvent, in addition to keeping Tim and me, in our teens, supplied with Players cigarettes, which were kept in 200s in cartons in a drawer in the pantry.

Now back to our tale. We headed up to the paddock at the top of the garden where a dilapidated hen house remained, a left over from the family's contribution to the war effort for self sufficiency and 'Dig For Victory' campaign, and where some years before, when collecting eggs for my uncle, Tim and I dispatched with a stick a very fearsome prize bantam who I was convinced was about to savage us, much to my uncle's anger.

Very carefully we placed our explosives and with the use of our trusty Airfix 'jetex' fuse set in motion our demolition. We hurried back to a safe distance and waited. The fuse fizzed and then, nothing. We then tried the nitro - surely this would work. The fuse fizzed again and… nothing. We were fast running out of fuse but had enough for one last try with the dynamite, and yet again just the fizz and no more. We hid our ill-gotten munitions in a hole beneath the hen house and feeling very dejected headed back to the house in search of other mischief.

We never returned to try again to demolish the hen house and in time forgot about the adventure all together. It was many years later we were altogether, uncle Kenneth, cousin Tim and I by now in our late teens, and over a pint we recalled this event, I asked uncle Kenneth, "Do you recall the nitro and dynamite you gave us so many years ago, I wonder if anyone has found it yet, I forgot where we buried it. Hopefully no one will get blown up."

He looked at us with a wry smile. "Not much chance of that. You don't think I would give you two silly buggers nitro and dynamite. The dynamite were pellets we fed to the cows and the nitro was nothing more than cod liver oil, but to see you cycle off down the lane avoiding every bump had me laughing for days." Looking back Tim I suspect knew all along but I had honestly believed we had the real thing.

In keeping with my thrill-seeking, I was quick to volunteer to go on Army summer camp. The first one took us down to a decommissioned army base, St Martins Plain near Folkestone. Regrettably, not the most exciting of places. There were several hundred cadets from all over Britain, and naturally we instantly formed social class rivalries. The group camped adjacent to us came from East London, and they immediately took exception to us *la di da* public school boys.

On the very first day they were up and out before the bugler's Reveille was ringing in the air and heading to the mess at the double. We did not realise the dire significance of this. We duly joined the end of the queue, with our mess tins at the ready. Shuffling along the line we had a mug of Cornflakes unceremoniously dumped in one tin, then swamped with a mug of milk. "Can I have some sugar, please". I sounded like Oliver Twist. Public school boys are always polite.

"It's in the fucking milk," snarled the very bored regular from the Army Catering Corps, charged with feeding these contemptible schoolboy cadets.

A large dollop of powdered egg, a rasher of very greasy streaky bacon, and deep fried bread followed. The mug of what I shall politely call tea that came next was the first time I had ever seen it all combined. Readymade tea with milk and sugar all came out of one enormous battered teapot spout. For a split second I wondered what my mother would have made of this item as a substitute for her Georgian silver teapot. A shove in the back to move on soon refocused me on the delights of the repast ahead. No sooner had we sat down to gingerly pick at the food, than the

East End London boys were up washing their mess tins under the constantly running tap and they were off. Why on earth were they being so diligent?

The reason for their expeditious behaviour soon became horribly, horribly plain to us. Following our indigestible breakfast, with stomachs rumbling for a post-breakfast visit to the latrine, we sauntered over to where the signs directed. We stood aghast as - all too late - we discovered the reason for their early start. There in front of us was a line of two hundred boys, juggling uncomfortably from foot to foot as they waited for their turn in the latrine line.

Even for boys accustomed to almost no privacy and communal showers, the army camp latrine presented a whole new challenge to our sensibilities. It consisted of one long eight foot high corrugated iron wall with a trough at the foot of it which was the urinal. The toilet for more serious business was one long building facing the urinal, with half height partitions, and no doors at the front. What I shall loosely call the toilet seat was in fact one long plank, with appropriate holes cut in, under which passed a trough with constantly flowing water to take your excretions away to the sewer. After suffering the latrine, the next day we decided to beat the Londoners at their own game. Those cunning city boys were miles ahead of us, and arose even earlier before Reveille and beat us once again.

We decided we had had enough and needed to put a plan together that would teach this lot a lesson.

That day's exercise consisted of a group of boys playing Kenyan Mau Mau Terrorists, with the rest of us supposed to be tracking them down and capturing them. Somehow, though, the English fields, woods and hedgerows of Kent lacked the sense of being out in the African bush for which we might have hoped. This would have been far more suited to hunting down escaped

Nazi fanatics who had bailed out during the war. So we adapted accordingly, and our squad wandered around seeing what birds nests we could find, and turning over rocks to see if there were any grass snakes or slow worms hiding, neither of which are poisonous but would be ideal to put in the bed of some unsuspecting cadet from East London.

When we failed to find anything of this calibre, we thought of ways in which we could use our 6 blank 303 bullets issued to us for the exercise. In the humane way of boys, the best thing we found to do was to get a small pencil or a straight twig and pop it down the barrel of our rifle, put a round in the chamber, and see what damage we could do to the squirrels' dreys and crows' nests that we had discovered in a small spinney. Having wrought unspeakable damage on the animals' nests, and having expended all our ammunition, we declared it a day and with no Mau Mau in sight headed back to camp.

Still with no solution as to how to avenge ourselves on our problem neighbours, we dressed in our best uniforms and caught the bus into Folkestone, to take advantage of our four-hour pass. Sitting in a local cafe, over fish and chips, we hatched a fiendish plan. We scavenged along the beach and visited a local ironmonger for some supplementary 'ordinance'.

The following morning called for a volunteer, as this mission wasn't without high personal sacrifice. Fortunately there was Perkins, who was always game. At Reveille, we headed to the mess tent, again beaten to the line by the enemy, whilst co-conspirator, Perkins, armed with the ordinance acquired the previous day and with true British fortitude, sacrificed his breakfast. He headed straight to the latrine, occupied the number one cubicle, and sat to wait patiently. It wasn't long before he heard the clatter of East London hobnailed army boots galloping into the latrine to occupy the remaining 19 cubicles.

Once confident that all were comfortably seated and motions were underway, Perkins smoothly activated the plan. Occupying the first cubicle, Perkins assembled the piece of driftwood and cork salvaged from the beach, attached the large candle purchased from the ironmonger's, and lit the candle. He launched it in the flowing trough under the latrine seats, and sent it on its way, like a Viking's burning funeral barge. Perkins stepped out of the first cubicle, followed by a rapid succession of screams, as first one, then another, and another of the East London boys, leapt out of the cubicles, with trousers around their ankles. They clutched their singed backsides and howled. Such chaos had not been seen since Francis Drake's fire ships destroyed the Spanish Armada in 1588. Ah, victory is sweet. Lucky for us there were no serious injuries. Strangely enough, in the way of boys, far from seeking retribution against us they became our good friends. Not only did they see the funny side, but they were full of admiration for the ingenuity of our plan.

The second of my military excursions was a combined small arms and parachute regiment course. Our instructor was a sergeant who had been at Arnhem, so was an instant hero to us all. We stripped and cleaned handguns, Sten guns and light machine guns (the Bren) until we could do it with our eyes closed. It was all worth it when we were then taken to a firing range and practiced our newly acquired skills for real. The para course was tough and the closest we got to jumping out of a plane was a controlled jump from a mock airplane fuselage and then a tower. What fun. What wasn't fun was the traditional end to the course called milling. For some reason the senior officers thought some mindless violence would be just the thing to round off our training as officers and gentlemen.

Milling involved standing toe to toe with an opponent and punching the hell out of him for three minutes. There was no dancing around or ducking or weaving; just a toe to toe punch-up. My earlier experience of boxing had at least prepared me for the inevitable pain. They say being tall gives you an advantage in life; because I was tall, they put me up against the biggest Neanderthal in the group. Tall? Advantage? Bullshit.

This did however bring back memories once again of my pugilistic encounters. A year or so prior to this as a member of the schools Boy Scout Troop I had been desperate to gain a few merit badges, most went for Cooking, First Aid, or Life Saving, which I had, but I wanted something that might command a little more respect, such as Master at Arms, and so in a moment of rashness I suggested this to Anderson the Senior Scout. He thought that this was a little different and researched the manuals as to what I might do. "Didn't you tell me once you had done boxing?"

This was the last thing I wanted to hear, I had in mind shooting or fencing or something that did not involve the possibility of pain. "Er, yes I did but we would need someone else for me to fight and I don't think there is anyone who would be interested." I said this praying I would be right.

"Don't worry I will sort something out".

I tried again. "But boxing isn't allowed in the school."

Enthusiastic reply: "I know but as this is for the Scouts I am sure we can get permission."

And so it was that I found myself in the first and only officially sanctioned fist fight staged at Lord Wandsworth College.

When the day for the big fight came, the willing opponent that had been found was a boy called Stokes, who thankfully was a little shorter than I, so I felt that I would at least have the advantage. A ring had been set up in the gym and seating laid out all around, I was both amazed and a little terrified at the interest that the event had drawn. I wasn't sure who they wanted to see beaten into submission, but I suspect it was quite simply that teenage boys wanted to see blood spilled.

At 2.00pm on a sunny Saturday afternoon we climbed into the ring. I wanted to at least look the part and had managed to borrow from a friend's locker, Chris Utley, a very nice T-shirt that sported the Oxford University colours. Resplendent in my Oxford Blue I found myself face to face with Stokes in the middle of the ring, surrounded by a gym full to the rafters with cheering boys. Anderson, who had been appointed to referee the fight, spoke a few words little of which I heard except for 'break when I say break' and when, I noted not if, 'you are knocked to the mat you will have to the count of ten to stand up' With this over "have a clean fight" - we touched gloves and returned to our corners. The bell rang and out we came, fists raised and ready for battle.

I didn't see it coming but suddenly I felt a searing pain in my nose, which immediately started pouring blood, much to the excitement of the crowd who were on their feet baying for more. The referee paused the fight for a moment as my corner wiped away the blood, and on seeing no permanent damage the referee waved the fight to continue. Stokes was now definitely the hero of the hour, how quick boys are to switch loyalties. I now was far more cautious and realised this was certainly not going to be a pushover. My guard came up as I recalled from my earlier days, I started to bob and weave and pick my moments. He then made the mistake of letting his guard down and in that second I let loose a wonderful right hook which sent Stokes staggering to the ropes. I followed through with a flurry of jabs, all of which were greeted with roars of approval from the audience. It was about now that I regained my confidence. The bell rang for the end of the first three minute round.

The rounds that followed were all rather blurry. We traded punches and the adrenaline rather numbed any pain. The last round was my finest hour. Although both exhausted, we kept the punches coming. I was able to muster one last masterfully aimed right hook more devastating than the first. As my fist connected, Stokes stopped in his tracks and with a strange look of surprise, fell back with a thud onto the canvas and just stared up at me. The count started and after about the count of six he managed to get to his feet. Anderson looked at him but he seemed OK and wanted to get on with the fight, but as he did I noticed he was slower and his punches lacked any strength. After what seemed a long few minutes the final bell rang. Both nearly dead on our feet we stood there awaiting the referee's decision.

Suddenly my arm was thrust into the air.

I was the winner and would now be able to sport my 'Master at Arms' badge on the sleeve of my Scouts uniform. With elation and a new respect from the boys, I staggered from the gym, exhausted, back to my dormitory. It was only then that I realised I had something more to do. The nice bright white T-shirt with blue piping that I had borrowed from Utley was covered in blood. Somehow I had to get this washed and dried before he discovered I had borrowed it. I was left wondering if it was really all worth it?

Back at school, apart from being belted around by oversized bullies, I had many experiences that toughened me up and gave me the unique blend of charm and cunning I needed to survive in the real world. Financial survival was a skill that my father was determined I should master, and I did to some degree. The other skills I obtained however, were many light years away from the style and type of skills that my father had wished for me.

At the beginning of each term all the boys in the house had to hand over their pocket-money to the House Bank. It was overseen by a schoolmaster and administered by the prefects, all above board and well organised. Just the type of scheme to which my father would have given his blessing. However, the handing over of the pocket-money was an event that I feared and loathed, and as a result I held back behind the others. One by one, the boys stepped forward with the worldly wealth endowed upon them by their parents. The schoolmaster intoned the names as he recorded the sums. "Hickman £10, Stuart £8, Peters £5, Jenkins £10."

So the names droned on. Eventually there was no one else so I stepped up and I handed over the money my father had entrusted to me, with many serious exhortations as to how not to waste such a princely sum. The master looked at it, looked at me. "Griffin, 30 shillings."

With 20 shillings to the pound, dear reader, you can only imagine my mortification at hearing my limited means broadcast far and wide. As I have said, my father was not a mean man, but a cautious and frugal one to whom money was something to respect and not fritter away.

This was a lesson that patently I failed to learn. Money to me has been the means to what it has bountifully provided as I have passed through life: the exotic holidays, the company of lovely women, the bright red Ferrari, with scant concern for retirement. But while I am far from a retired millionaire, I'm glad I have lived life to the full and intend to continue doing so whilst I can, being a firm believer that I can't take it with me.

My 30-shilling purse was merely another challenge to which I needed to find a solution. And as happens so often, the solution was in my own backyard… or at least next door.

Boys will be boys, especially when locked away in a fine gentlemen's establishment of learning, a British Public School in the middle of nowhere. Exploring one day, I discovered the back off-sales door of the Chequers Public House near the front gate of the school. This local hostelry was frequented by most of the masters, but only in the front bar. They assumed that no schoolboy would have the nerve to enter. And they were right, but the back off-sales door was something else altogether.

Having worked my charms on the landlord, he eventually allowed me to make a few small purchases. These were mainly in the form of packets of cigarettes called Players Weights, a popular, but cheap brand of cigarettes selling at one shilling and twopence per pack of five. I could then sell these for sixpence a cigarette, making a healthy one shilling fourpence profit on each pack.

In the way that Dorian Gray and countless other ne'er-do-wells have discovered through history, one vice followed hard on the heels of another. Cigarettes could only scratch one of the boys' itches. In a dorm full of thirteen-year-olds heading at full speed into puberty, there existed a healthy red-blooded interest that to date had to be satisfied with images in the odd dog-eared copy of National Geographic containing pictures of scantily clad women of the tribes of central Africa, or the rare book that had something rather raunchy in it which had escaped the eagle eye of the school library's censor.

The route to my dentist in the nearby bustling metropolis of Basingstoke was lined with many small shops. As I jumped off the bus and walked to my appointment, I spied a small newsagents shop with high shelves. Along these shelves were arrayed copies of a number of conveniently A5-sized magazines. They had names like *Spick & Span* and *Health & Efficiency*, and both were packed with pictures of young women in rather strange poses with little or nothing in the way of clothes. In *Health & Efficiency* they were very active, tossing beach balls at each other and generally having a jolly good time by the beach, on the lake or in the woods. I could well see why the magazine carried such a title, as they certainly looked very healthy, and mightily efficient too. The only thing that I couldn't figure out was why in all the pictures, there was a little spot of blurred ink that always seemed to have occurred in their nether regions.

These tomes, at a shilling apiece, were quite a significant investment for me. But my next venture was to produce such a marvellous return on investment that I found myself purchasing them by the half dozen. It seems I had a lot of trouble with my teeth at that time, requiring rather a lot of trips to that dentist in Basingstoke.

At school, I found a hungry and willing market ready to rent the magazines out at threepence a night. I did need to give some attention to quality control, however, as some were being returned in less than pristine condition, annoyingly often with pages stuck together. I found it necessary to introduce a fine for those who damaged the product in such a careless manner. The demand from my captive market never faltered, but I was starting to have increased expenses myself. I found it necessary to employ the well-built services of 'Bunny ', an unlikely name for one of our star Rugby prop forwards. As boys started to lose magazines or not return them, I discovered that they would listen far more intently to Bunny rather than me.

All this activity was merely my training wheels. I then hit upon my finest revenue earner. I started to diversify. One Christmas, for a bit of fun, some unsuspecting relative gave me a present of a small roulette wheel, complete with chips and the marked out felt table cloth. This would complete the trifecta with gambling joining my list of money-making vices.

Even I grew wary that this was starting to get a little more adventurous as far as school rules were concerned. So I put my excellent woodworking skills to the test, and carefully built a false bottom to my Tuck Box. I did a rather smashing job, if I say so myself, which was confirmed by an independent judge. A snap inspection was called of all lockers and Tuck Boxes, following a strange report coming to the ears of the housemaster that something was afoot. They found nothing amiss with my Tuck Box, and life returned to normal. Normal for me meant that, with Bunny at my side, I started my casino.

And what a winner it was. I felt that if only I could hold off graduating, not that there was much chance of that, I could make a comfortable living here for the remainder of my life. I had effortlessly cornered the vice market of the school, and never worried again when it came to deposits in the House Bank.

I was not in schoolboy terms a corporate high flyer, but I was pretty close and riding high. Then things started to crumble at the edges, as they do in all good moral tales and Hollywood thrillers. I was summoned to the housemaster's study.

"Griffin, I have been hearing disturbing things about your activities."
"*Me*, sir?" I found that there is nothing more irritating to a school master than to receive this sort of response
"Of course you, Griffin; why do you think you are here?"
"I have no idea, sir."
"You do know why you are here, and I know why you are here, so don't try to *bluff* me and let's not play *games* as you are *gambling* with your future."

Having alluded quite clearly to me that the game was up, he forced me to do some hard thinking. In some ways I almost breathed a sigh of relief; although I regretted being found out on any of my selected extracurricular activities, this one probably carried the least ignominy if announced to my parents.

"I will not tolerate this House being turned into a den of iniquity. And I will catch you, Griffin, believe me, when you least expect it. I will be there, and when I do, it will be the sorriest day of your rather unimpressive scholastic years spent at this institute of learning."

On returning to the common room, the questions came thick and fast.

"Are you in trouble?"
"Did you get caned?"
"What for?"

I had to think fast, as the last thing I wanted was for the real reason to come out. It would have been the Wall Street Crash for my business empire. "No, the old bugger was having a go at me over my general performance, with mock exams on the horizon."

This seemed to satisfy all concerned. I then set in place my plan to retire gracefully and profitably from the world of gambling. A week later I put the word out that I wanted to get a new bike and needed some cash. It wasn't long before I hooked a buyer. With £5 in my pocket, I reluctantly handed over my roulette wheel to a starry-eyed young man from North Dorm, who had his own aspirations of untold wealth and riches. A week later North Dorm was raided.

One thing I could never figure out was how, although I seemed reasonably skilled at earning wealth, I seemed rather inept at hanging on to it. This irritating quality has remained with me throughout my entire working life.

Chapter 6

#art-lit'n'metalwork #doghouse2dogcollar #potwasher

My next venture in the summer of 1962 had the single most powerful influence upon the rest of my life. Having found my income much depleted and in need of funds to go and see the latest blockbuster movie, *Ben Hur*, currently playing at the Odeon in Basingstoke, I approached Mitham, a boy who was always willing to bail out a friend. He offered me more than I needed, 30 shillings, as long as I promised to repay it at the beginning of next term. And I took it.

Even before the excitement of the chariot race wore off, my mind was turning over how I was going to pay him back. My father had drilled into us another of his favourite adages: *Neither a borrower nor a lender be*. He was unlikely to be my saviour. My brothers? Even more unlikely as they spent money as fast as I did. This led me to a desperate remedy: I had to find a holiday job.

I applied to Mr Jack Scott, a customer of my father's from the bank, who happened to be the proprietor of The Isles Hotel, on The Promenade at Swanage. I was employed as a general kitchen hand, earning more money than I ever could have imagined: £2 10/- a week. [42]

I found my new home amongst the pots with burnt on minestrone soup, dirty dishes and mountains of potatoes that needed peeling. I was in the hotel industry, and in heaven. I was financially independent. Here was something I actually enjoyed, it was fun and the people were lovely. I fell madly in love with a girl, something I made a habit of in my mid-teens. Wendy was an art student also working for holiday money and to help her through her college education. She worked in the restaurant along with an Irish girl named Maureen.

I am not sure why but I have, throughout my career, come across people from the Emerald Isle who have played a large part in my life, as true friends male and female. Their warmth and special brand of humour work magic. They were good friends and many still are.

Both Wendy and Maureen worked in the restaurant along with a couple of other students and as chance would have it one day, one of the students didn't turn up so being short staffed and desperate Mr Scott turned to me as the most likely employee from the kitchen who could scrub up sufficiently to pass as a waiter.

Donning a white jacket, a bow tie around my rather limp collared shirt, I was all but pushed through the door to the restaurant, terrified as if in my first walk on role on a theatre stage, with two bowls of tomato soup in hand. Maureen met me with a smile and an encouraging word, "My don't we look smart today - but best take your *tumb* out of *da* soup before *da* guests see *ya!*" in her lovable Irish brogue. She guided me to the table and in a way that oozed her warm, friendliness and confidence went as far as to say to the guests for whom the soup was intended, "Now Mr and Mrs Lewis *dis* is *moy* new young man, first day on the job *ye moit* say, so be kind to him or I won't be bringing you your pudding!"

They all laughed and after this I was part of the team. Oh how I loved the performance. I learned from Maureen that you could almost get away with saying anything as long as it was with warmth and good humour. I often wonder what became of Maureen, and my love for Wendy was as short as my work placement. These few weeks at the Isles Hotel rather set in place my future life.

With money in my pocket, and the thirty shillings to return to Mitham as promised, I returned to school for the start of a new term in the lower sixth, and all the privileges that accompanied this position.

Sadly, the gods have a way of dealing us cruel blows just when we are most happy and self-satisfied. Amongst the excitement of earning such funds, and the additional freedom that came from being in the sixth form, I quite forgot that the whole purpose of my enrolment in this rather expensive school was to achieve something academic. Before I knew it, the GCE Examinations were upon me. Utterly unprepared, I took my place in the school's gymnasium to hear the words, "You have two hours in which to complete this paper. You may turn your papers over… now."

I sat there like a stone, faced with a page of questions that meant little or nothing to me. I hoped I would get a mark for putting my name correctly on the paper.

My parents by this time, I suspect, had reached the stage where they believed that enough of their hard-earned and frugally-saved resources had been spent on my education at Lord Wandsworth College. With a growing concern that soon I might find myself at another institution that happens to bear the same name, but a far less salubrious reputation, namely Wandsworth Gaol, they advised the school that I would not be staying on for the upper sixth and would depart at the end of the Christmas term. My departure confirmed and the exams over with, the realisation began to dawn that my total scholastic achievement of the past four years amounted to a GCE O Level in Metalwork and English Literature, neither of which would propel me into the professions my father might have hoped for with his large investment of many thousands of pounds. There being nothing I now could do to change this, I felt I could relax and just coast through the remaining weeks. Apparently, however, the academic staff at the school believed I had relaxed and coasted from the day I arrived.

My last days saw one highlight. I was with a few friends, reliving the events of the past few years, whilst listening to the radio in the lower sixth common room, when there was a knock at the door, and a squirt from the third form stuck his head in. "Mr Henderson says you must turn off the radio and make less noise as he is teaching maths to the lower third next door."

"Piss off!" we chorused.

Ten minutes later, the door opened again and without looking we let out another cry of "Sod off!", which trailed off as we realised the head around the door was that of a fuming School Headmaster, Mr Henderson, and in his sternest Highland Scottish accent,

> "It might be your last days but you are still pupils and I still have time to try and drill some discipline into you. Griffin, go to my study and bring back my cane."

I felt a mix of fear for the caning I was to receive and pride in the fact that he had selected me to be entrusted with the task of going to his study to collect the instrument that was about to be inflicted upon us, an honour indeed.

The song playing on the radio at that moment was The Kingston Trio asking *Where have all the flowers gone?* and as I lurched off I heard them mourn, *when will they ever learn...when will they ever learn?* So it was that on the very last day of my school days,

I was to receive the final ignominy of a ritualistic beating in front of the lower third by the Headmaster himself; what a way to go.

It is correct to say that my attitude to life and authority did not fit well in such an institution as the British Public School, and while it produced some of the greatest independent thinkers who helped build the British Empire, such as Burke, Pitt, Wellington, Palmerston and Gladstone, it probably held the seeds of its own downfall in not being able to harness my unconventional ingenuity and survivalist skills.

The following Monday, the term ended. After fond farewells, those of us who were leaving and not returning, in a final show of defiance, feeling like the African-American athletes giving the black power salute at the Mexico Olympics, took out our packets of Players cigarettes and lit up as we boarded the bus that took us to Hook Railway Station and thence on to whatever awaited us in the big wide world outside. After the Spartan existence of those few years, just going home seemed like a pretty good start.[43]

Lord Wandsworth College did not rate too highly, when it came to seeking a job; it was not Eton or Harrow. The only boy of note that I could recall, was a young man called Dudley Philby, known as Tommy. Fortunately at the time, unknown to him or to those of us who shared his classroom, his father, Kim Philby, was to be exposed a couple of years later as a traitor and became one of the most reviled men in Britain, along with Guy Burgess and Donald Maclean, who fled to Moscow whence they never returned. I often thought of what that poor boy might have suffered at the hands of his fellow patriotic schoolboys had it been known when we all studied together.

It was not until the Rugby World Cup in 2003, and Jonny Wilkinson's winning boot, was to suddenly bring forth claims of 'I was at Lord Wandsworth College where Jonny Wilkinson learned to play his rugby...'

They say your 'school days are the happiest days of your life'. I would say, there was nothing to complain about. I had survived, not sure how, but I had. I was often asked by grandparents, aunts and uncles, prior to receiving some welcome monetary gift or other, "Well Paddy, have you been a GOOD boy?" With outstretched hand, I would of course always answer in the affirmative. This as you know was far from the truth. Something else they say is 'confession is good for the soul' and therefore it might have been more cleansing to confess that in my childhood, I was not so much 'A good little boy' but rather 'A real little shit.'

On returning from boarding school my mother had a yearning to leave Swanage and return to the bosom of the Langley Family in Warwickshire and so we moved to the pleasant town of Royal Leamington Spa. [44]

I thought we had been very happy in Swanage, and could only ponder as to the reason for our sudden departure. I was left wondering, was it the result of my youthful exuberance and we were in fact banished, thus making my parents start a new life, with new neighbours and the family in support. I can only now start to imagine just how long-suffering my parents must have been.

When my final school report arrived it was met with resignation by my parents. Even so, they were not ready for the final indictment of my years of study at this expensive seat of learning. I had failed in all my GCE's with the exception of English Literature and Metalwork. This posed the conundrum as to what profession these results might open the door to, apart from breaking into the safe at the local library. The final disappointment flowed from the rapier pen of my housemaster J.M. Merriman.

"A smooth and plausible boy this, I am sure he will do well in his chosen *trade*."

The pejorative adjectives were bad enough, but *trade*! The Griffin and Langley families educated their offspring with a view to finding their place in the professions. A trade was just not an option. My relationship with my parents now took on a different character.

With Lord Wandsworth College behind me, I was now a 'free man' and starting to think that the real world wasn't all it was cracked up to be, compared to what our furtive imaginations created from within the confines of the school dorm. I was devouring my first meal of freedom, a delicious sirloin steak and chips, my favourite that was always served by my mother upon my release. I was certainly not missing the delicacies of the many bland, overcooked school refectory meals, when my father asked what I thought to be a most extraordinary question. "So, what are your plans?"

I had not thought of this at all, beyond of course going to the pub and the possibility that an opportunity might arise in which I might lose my virginity. Preferably with Carol, whose bikini-clad body was forever etched in my memory from the last days of the summer holidays spent on the beach at Swanage. Sadly, even if my father knew of such incipient desires, I hardly think he would have concurred. "I'm not sure, Dad." Less than enthusiastic response.

"Well you can't just sit around the house." It was a statement of fact as well as a question requiring some response, which I did not possess, so I was silent. My father pressed on.

"What about the hotel business? You seemed to enjoy the work you did at The Isles Hotel last summer?"

It is strange how one's life can have its direction set for the next fifty years in such a casual manner. My mind was simply not ready to contemplate anything past my hormone-fuelled images of Carol, a racy passage in the book *Peyton Place*, and Mitzi Gaynor in shorts in *South Pacific*. I wasn't much of a fan of poor old D.H. Lawrence, and when I did discover *Lady Chatterley* it was banned in the UK. It wasn't until 10th November 1960 that it was released and within a year the book had sold two million copies, outselling even the Bible. I did not have one of those two million copies, being locked away at school at the time. I was well into my teens when I did find a copy of *Lady Chatterley's Lover* belonging to my mother that had been carefully hidden. I just could not picture my dear sweet mother reading a *dirty* book. Even though the lawyers had argued in court that it was one of *the classics*, finding the book was a complete surprise to me.

Ironically, my surprise at my discovery of my mother's clandestine copy of *Lady Chatterley's Lover* was but a *frisson* compared to the shock I managed to give her in return. When I lived at home a friend Simon, gave me a set of very dog-eared, grainy, black and white 'adult' pictures. Naturally having tired of these meagre charms, I hid them and in time completely forgot about them.

Years later when I had long left home, there were domestic changes in the occupation of bedrooms, and my mother moved into my old room, as father 'snored'. Even more years later, my mother was having furniture removed from the room and new carpet laid. Just imagine her surprise to find all the carpet layers on their hands and knees in her room chuckling away when she brought up a tray of tea for them. As they hastily leapt up from the floor looking rather sheepish, one young lad was brave enough to say to my horrified mother, "Sorry ma'am, we were just lookin' at your photos that we found under the carpet." She was so well-bred she could not even bring herself to admonish me for it until many years had passed.

My father's mind was utterly focused on setting me on a path to adulthood, responsibility and make me a contributor to society. "If you are interested in hotels…"

The 'if' was again a challenge and was really an 'as'. Unless I could come up with an alternative fast, and I couldn't.

"… I saw an advertisement in *The Times*. The owner of the Old Red Lion Hotel in Stow on the Wold is looking for young public school boys, to learn the hospitality business as a 'general assistant.' The position pays two pounds ten shillings a week and living accommodation and meals are provided." [45]

I was still silent. Stow on the Wold was a picturesque country town in the middle of the Cotswolds, and miles from anywhere; hardly the bright lights and fleshpots I'd had in mind for myself. My father continued to map out my future. "I have actually written to Reverend Burr on your behalf."

Reverend! Oh God this was becoming a nightmare; not only in the middle of nowhere but under the guidance of the Church. My virginity looked as if it would remain intact for some time yet. "He has replied and I am taking you over to see him next weekend."

Thus commenced a hesitant career in hospitality. I did start working for Reverend Burr and while it only lasted for a few months, these months were not without their educational moments. The retired Reverend Burr was straight out of the pages of a Dickens novel. He continued to wear his dog-collar and conducted the hotel along the lines of a seminary. He had three passions in evidence: his collection of silver, a Queen Anne coffee pot in particular being his pride and joy; his hens at the bottom of the garden who provided eggs for the guests' breakfast; and classical music.

The Old Red Lion offered the traveller a choice of ten rooms, all named, unsurprisingly, after classical music composers. The décor remained trapped in a time warp of the 1930s and each room had an electric bar heater in which one had to place six-penny coins to make it work. Our duties each day were to be up at 6.30am, collect the eggs and assist the cook with breakfast. Mrs Riddle was a lovely, plump, jolly local woman, very much in keeping with the Dickensian atmosphere, and very much in the mould of Peggotty the apple-cheeked housekeeper from *David Copperfield*. I, on the other hand, felt I was cast in the role of Pip, and although I did not have *Great Expectations* for my future, Carol was very much yearned-for, but was now as unattainable as Estella.

Each day, breakfast was served and cleared away. None of this took very long, and I find it hard to recall whether many, indeed if any, guests actually stayed. We then cleaned the rooms, and generally helped as required. My duties were soon shared with another public school boy called John, who was quick to tell me his father had only placed him here whilst he awaited the results of his entrance exam into Hendon Police College. John was a charming young man, and was as utterly lost as I was as to why we were here.

The morning was the time we followed the good Reverend around the market and shops of the town, each feeling totally embarrassed to be carrying a wicker shopping basket. Neither of us was presenting the image of the cool, pop loving teenagers of the 60s that we yearned to be; this failure was thrown into sharp relief when we encountered the lovely Phillipa, daughter of the local grocer. Suddenly, John was no longer my good friend but a deadly rival.

The afternoon was spent serving the occasional passing tourist afternoon tea, however as we were now in winter, tourists were few and far between. As a result, we were instead summoned to join the Reverend for tea and to listen to the classics.

I could not help but think that this was not the Ritz, and that this was not how I envisaged the hotel industry. The final straw was when a particularly bad snow storm then cut us off for nearly a week. When the roads were cleared, news came that John had been accepted into Hendon and would be departing at the end of the month. That night, after the customary supper with the Reverend, prayers, and the compulsory 10.00pm bedtime, I crept over to John's room for a chat about my plans to soon follow him in his escape. We had not been long into a discussion of the delightful charms of Miss Phillipa, and the realisation that my chances would double with John's departure, when the bedroom door flew open and there in the doorway in his thick woollen dressing gown stood the good Reverend. He flashed his torch in our direction. We just sat there staring, at a loss as to this dramatic entrance.

"I am not having any of that under this roof! How dare you! What on earth do you think you are up to?" thundered the Reverend.

What on earth was he on about? John and I looked at each other in disbelief as it dawned on us that the dirty old bugger thought he was catching us *in flagrante delicto,* and I believe he was disappointed that he hadn't. The next day I went straight across the village green to the public phone box to call my father to tell him I had had second thoughts on my career and wished to come home.

I suspect that my father had anticipated this. Within days, he presented me with an alternative plan, involving a further attempt at boosting my scholastic achievements by way of sending me off to what was rather in vogue at the time, a special school, referred to as 'a crammer', that focused purely on the academic achievement and not on the character of the student. He felt this might suit my independent demeanour better. And so I headed off to my crammer with the objective of obtaining a reasonable GCE pass in the subjects of Maths, English, French and Art, so that these four subjects might add to my limited success in English Literature and Metalwork, thereby opening up a world other than that of the hotel *trade.*

Chapter 7

#conventgirls #sexdrugs'n'rocknrole #jobopportunities

Westcliff School, on Bathwick Hill, in the relatively large and thriving Somerset city of Bath, was a joy to behold after the confines of boarding school and quiet country town life in the Cotswolds.

This fine establishment of intense academic learning was under the care and guidance of Mr Lambert and his wife, both teachers, who were somewhat in the mould of Mr Chips and his wife. Rather more of the Robert Donat than the Peter O'Toole style, Mr Lambert was a stern but kindly man, occasionally given to making jokes in Latin that - strangely - only he found amusing. However this was more a reflection on the academic state of the boys he now found in his charge.

My time spent here was extremely educational. Sadly, for my father, the nature of the education was not what father had expected, nor that for which he was paying. The cause of this additional failure to reach my father's aspirations was that this particular segment of my education epitomised the era of the 1960s known familiarly and fondly as Sex, Drugs and Rock'n Roll.

Sex: The first of my three deadly sins arrived with the delightful charms of a young woman from La Sainte Union Convent in Bath, a school for young ladies located at the bottom of Bathwick Hill. This was a pure revelation to me, having been confined to a country market town or locked away for so long in an all boys institution in the heart of rural Hampshire. T'was a very clumsy affair on my part, not aided by the large amount of 'dutch courage' I imbibed prior to the event.

I shall be forever grateful to the lovely young woman who helped me in my initiation to manhood. As I have passed through life with all the experiences it has had to offer, especially in the promiscuous period of that time, I have not forgotten, and never will, the name of that kind and accommodating young woman. Nor will I ever forget the experience of the night in question, however strange and sobering it is to think that she would now no doubt be a respectable grandmother, her offspring regarding her as the epitome of moral rectitude: why does each generation imagine *they* are the only ones to have any fun?

One of the alumni of that time, who went on to become an MP and a rather flamboyant TV personality, Ann Widdecombe, reportedly stated in an interview many years later *"There was no sex education,"* she said of La Sainte Union. *"The school had no attitude to sex, and neither did we."* A sentiment I have difficulty agreeing with, as my memory of convent girls was that they had a very highly developed attitude towards sex, and to quote David Aaronovitch, the journalist who wrote the article in 1999:

> *'Indeed, they understood with a sickening precision, the exact point at which a dalliance became a mortal sin. Is it possible that the adolescent Ann Widdecombe misread the hearts of her fellow pupils?'*

With that I must agree.

Drugs: My second arena of the trio of misdemeanours, I have to admit, was only that of tobacco, and although there is so much said about the taking of drugs in the 60s, I knew of no one who did. I am sure there was a particular social set, amongst them the rock stars of the day, and a lot more ordinary people by the 70s, but for most teenagers in the 60s it was rather a myth. Unless you were part of the sophisticated London club scene, none of us would have had any idea as to where to obtain such things in our sheltered provincial towns around England.

Rock'n Roll: Any lack of the other two deadly sins, we made up for with rock'n'roll, as we had it in spades, and what a time we had. Next door to the aforementioned La Sainte Union Convent was a small 'Community Hall' that had a little stage and accommodated, at most, about 150 in the audience. Many of the headline acts of the time played here. The first I saw was The Shadows, but a more entertaining act and one way ahead of his time, was Screaming Lord Sutch. He was a wild character who appeared on stage sporting bright green hair and for some reason only known to himself, a toilet seat around his neck.

Naturally, later in the decade, he stood for Parliament in my own local, true blue, seat of Stratford on Avon. He contested the seat vacated by another iconic name of the time, Mr John Profumo, better known for his scandalous association with 'model' Christine Keeler. My younger sister campaigned for his Lordship, much to our parents horror, but even with her help it was not sufficient to gain enough votes to win him a seat in The House of Commons. (See Appendix A for more on the eccentric Lord.)

It was also at this Community Hall that I saw a group heading the bill who were rapidly gaining popularity, The Beatles. The first time I had seen them perform was as a supporting act to teenage star Helen Shapiro, in Coventry. The fame of The Beatles had not as yet reached the level of superstardom that was to follow in the next few years. The profile coverage of the band members was in its infancy, and hence I did not appreciate the opportunity I was presented, when walking through Bath on the Saturday afternoon of their performance.

As I crossed the street, I was surrounded by a group of girls asking for my autograph. In response to my totally bewildered "why?" I heard "Aren't you John Lennon?" I have often pondered how I might have turned that situation to my advantage. At the time I was baffled as to who he was or how such a mistaken identity could have occurred. I have since cleverly assumed it to be due to the fact that we both had a prominent proboscis and I sported what became known as a Beatles haircut, being naturally a man at the height of fashion trends at the time.

The show that night was incredible, with a packed audience of 150 or so, all sitting on green canvas tubular chairs laid out in neat rows, with those who couldn't get a seat, gathered in their hundreds, standing outside listening through the open windows. It is amazing to imagine such a small intimate concert, when in the next few years The Beatles would be playing to tens of thousands packed into arenas around the world.

It was around this time that fortune favoured me further, when my cousin by marriage, became involved with a new pop TV show 'Ready Steady Go'. This relationship gained me great favour, as well as the promise of entry to the show.

More of life's lessons that I learned in Bath proved very worthwhile. My fellow scholastic chums included a rather timid boy called Adrian, a devout Roman Catholic, who received a lot of ribbing about his faith. We never meant it unkindly, however I felt sorry for him as he was quite alone in his beliefs. This spurred me into seeking ways in which I could come to his aid, ostensibly for altruistic reasons, but really there was nothing I enjoy more than a good debate against all odds.

I descended to the library, a place rather alien to me, and then set off to the local RC Church where I found lots of pamphlets on the subject as one might expect. Amongst these I found a tract on the differences in the beliefs between faiths and the term 'Transubstantiation'. A wonderful word, that, once thrown into the argument, soon had all the antagonists backing off either for fear of showing their ignorance, or simply because it had become all too deep and as such boring and time to move on.

Little did I realise how much this was appreciated by Adrian, who asked me to visit his church and receive thanks from his priest for 'defending The Faith' against such odds. Unfortunately my mild interest in a good debate turned into a situation beyond my expectations, as it appeared Adrian had rather over emphasized my religious zeal and the priest thought I was a true candidate for conversion. I spent the next few weeks being stalked by this tenacious priest bent on saving my soul.

My other lesson was at the expense of one of the foreign students. Mohammed was Persian, as Iranians were then known, and a very wealthy young man who had monthly 'pocket money' more in line with the annual salaries of his fellow students' fathers. We made our pilgrimage to the small and famously quaint Nash cinema, named after John Nash a foremost architect of the Regency era, which still boasted wall-mounted gas lighting, the service of tea in the interval, and the provision of two front rows of wooden benches at sixpence a ticket. Most incongruously it was screening the most unlikely blockbuster action movie for its turn of the century setting: a new film about a secret agent called James Bond, which you may have heard of: *Dr No.*

Dr No changed our lives. We all left the cinema that day with grand aspirations of our future careers in MI6. For most of us this amounted to, at best, changing our brand of cigarettes to a Turkish Blend and, if we could afford it, a gunmetal cigarette case, if indeed one could be found. More impressively, it also cemented a need in us to be stylish and suave. These qualities had not hitherto suggested themselves to us as part of our development. Dr No also instilled in us a newborn interest in books; we devoured any of Ian Fleming's novels that we could get our hands on.

For Mo, as Mohammed was known, the transformation certainly didn't stop at a few ciggies and assumed suavity. A few weeks later and to the undying amazement and envy of his peers, and not least the faculty, a sports car was delivered to the school gates. A Triumph Spitfire, the latest in stylish British sports cars. Apparently he had wanted something grander, but as a seventeen year old for some strange reason could not get insurance. So he settled for the Triumph, whose insurance premiums matched the cost of the car. This turn of events then led to seeking out further ways we could channel James Bond, and we alighted on Chemin de Fer, his favourite card game of chance at the tables of Europe's casinos.

Bath had one club that allowed gaming and this was where Mo headed, chancing his luck with much of his pocket money that, once expended, was soon magically replaced. One evening I was invited to join him, although I had little left of my two pounds term allowance. Upon arriving, thankfully no one enquired as to our age and Mo was even greeted as a VIP and I, as his friend, likewise. A very attractive hostess, sporting an outfit not too dissimilar to that of a Playboy Bunny, offered me a drink. As I refused, and seeing me fidgeting with the few coins in my pocket, she gave me a kind smile and whispered "it's OK, they're free". I was still recovering from this news when another similarly-clad hostess offered me a tray of nicely cut sandwiches and a few little biscuits with what I assumed was caviar on top. This was truly the James Bond lifestyle. I was way out of my depth.

At that moment a chair became available at the Chemin de Fer table. "Come on," commanded Mo. "I'll show you how to make money."

I stood behind him, watching a few of the others lose more than I could imagine anyone could afford. Mo suddenly called "Banco!" I was terribly impressed as he had truly taken 007 to heart. I am further convinced of Mo's transformation, as his pile of chips grew, and furthermore absolutely amazed when the brightly coloured ones with 25 engraved on them started to pile up. The seat next to him being vacant and he invited me to sit down. Suddenly I hear "Go on you have a go".

"But I haven't enough money..." I whispered weakly.
"That's OK, take these". Ten chips worth around £100 were pushed in my direction.
"I can't... I can't pay you back..."
"That's fine; I'm giving it to you."

I took a deep breath, coolly lit a cigarette, and drew a card from the shoe.

From that moment on I found myself in the role of Bond's villain. With each hand my pile of chips diminished with the speed of light. With ever increasing panic I drew more strongly on my cigarette until it was consumed almost as rapidly as were my chips. From that evening I have never gambled since, even in the bright lights of Las Vegas many years later.

You may had well be wondering about my academic studies, which were after all the purpose of this sojourn. You might well guess that they have not progressed as my father would have liked. At the end of my year I headed home to await the arrival of that manila envelope from the Cambridge Board of Studies with the results of my 'efforts'. Unfortunately it was only too fast in coming.

My father handed me the ominous looking communication with a look of resignation. "I'm sure your efforts will have paid off".

I knew he would be disappointed. As I tentatively drew the single sheet of paper from the envelope, I was proved horribly correct. My dismal academic efforts were indeed reflected in the dismal results.

Maths – Fail
English – Fail
French – Fail
Art – PASS

I do not know why this failed to impress my father. I bade farewell to a career in banking, or indeed to any other 'profession' that came to mind. My 'chosen trade' loomed again on my horizon. With that conclusion cemented into place, we set off in search of how best to secure my entry into one of England's better luxury establishments. It was 1963.

I would like to think that I had grown up a little, and that my entry into the hotel industry was due to my own charm and personality. Regrettably it was not so, and was again due more to the efforts and contacts of my father. I have found this to be the case many years later as an employer, receiving phone calls from concerned fathers whose children have been gifted with social skills, charm and personality, but lacking in the academic field.

My father through his network of friends and contacts from the bank, arranged my first interview with the very progressive chairman of Forte Hotels, Mr Charles Forte himself, later to become Lord Forte, having eventually built a hotel empire from his original 'Milk Bar' in the Strand in 1935. As the day approached for the interview, my mother coached me in the hope I would not make a complete fool of myself or embarrass my father. Included in her sage points of advice was the fact that I should not smoke at the interview even if sanctioned to do so, and "If asked for your view of 'coloured' people working in the restaurant, it is best to offer the opinion that the English public are not quite ready for this and it might be more appropriate that they remain behind the scene for the foreseeable future." I didn't give it a second thought, as then I knew no one who was coloured, and the rationale of this was over my head. This was no doubt the popular view at the time.

The day arrived for my interview, and my father drove me to London and dropped me off at the front door of The Cafe Royal in London's West End, where Mr Charles Forte had his office. As I stood there, alone, before the large and heavily gilded entrance looking at a doorman in his full livery, I found my feet stuck to the pavement, unable to move.

"Can I help you sonny?" the doorman asked kindly.

Suddenly I came to life. "I have an appointment with Mr Forte at 2.30"

"Yes sir." No more sonny. "Inside the doors and ask at the desk".
"Thank you".

I walked into the palatial surrounds of the Cafe Royal and even further out of my comfort zone. I was then confronted with my next challenge: which desk? I saw a large brass sign that read 'Reception'. With a little more confidence, I addressed a smartly dressed young woman.

"I have an appointment with Mr Forte at 2.30pm".

She was not as impressed as the doorman seemed to be. "Yes, if you care to go to the Concierge desk, they will assist you".

"Oh, OK, thank you." Confidence slipped back once again.

Across the marble lobby was a group of uniformed concierges who looked even more intimidating and did not appear to exude warmth and understanding, as I assumed was their *raison d'etre*.

"Hello," I said, rather timidly, to one of the men who was assessing me as I spoke, coming to the conclusion that this young man before him, rather uncomfortably attired in a new suit, was not one to impress and unlikely to reward him with an appropriate gratuity for any service he might be about to request. "I have an appointment with Mr Forte at 2.30," I said yet again.

Looking down at a list in front of him he said "Mr Griffin?" I almost looked over my shoulder for my father, having never been addressed in my life as anything other than simply 'Griffin'. After a moment's hesitation I confirmed I was indeed that personage.

"Kindly sit over there." The encounter was over.

I sat down on a large armchair; leaned back, no, best sit up. I crossed my legs, no best uncross them. Tried to look comfortable and at home. Leaning back again, I suddenly found the back of the armchair was further back than I thought and nearly found myself in a prone position. Quickly recovered the upright position and hoped no one saw me. Decided sitting upright was the best position. I fumbled for my cigarettes; better not.

After a few minutes a slightly older woman came out of the lift towards me. "Mr Griffin?"

"Yes" I eagerly replied. "I have an appointment with Mr Forte at 2.30pm."
"Yes I am aware of that, please come this way."

With which the conversation was at an end. My first interview was becoming more stressful by the minute and I felt my palms started to sweat. Oh God no, please no sweaty palms. My mother had told me to make sure my hands were dry and that I give a firm handshake, and don't smoke, even if you are offered a cigarette. The trouble was the more I thought about it the worse it became. Don't smoke. How I longed for a cigarette. Into a lift and up a few floors. Why do people say nothing in lifts but just watch the numbers or look at the floor? It was at this moment I vowed that in future I would always engage people in conversation in lifts. What could they do? They were trapped.

The lift shuddered to a halt and the doors opened. I followed the woman along the corridor having given up on attempting small talk. She opened a door to an office. "This is Mr Griffin," she said, addressing a woman even more senior in years than herself. "He has an appointment with Mr Forte at 2.30"

"Take a seat over there", the elder woman gestured to a chair in the corner.

As I sat there listening to the click of the typewriter, I ran through the instructions my mother had given me. As I did so, I felt the cigarette packet and lighter in my pocket pressing against my leg. So near and yet so far.

2.30 came and went. Maybe the meeting has been cancelled, thank God. But then a door behind me opened and another woman entered the office. "Mr Griffin? I believe you had a meeting with Mr Forte at 2.30? I am sorry, he has been delayed but will see you now. Please come with me."

My heart was suddenly in my mouth and my stomach was churning. I followed her down the corridor and into another lift. As the doors closed, I smiled nervously, and said "Weather has been rather strange lately, must be all that nuclear testing." What was I saying?

The secretary looked at me, rather startled. Then she gave me a big smile and with a maternal tone said "First interview? Don't worry you will be fine".

We entered a large oak panelled office, with a leather topped desk placed in front of a big picture window. Behind the desk sat a rather corpulent man, bald, with cold and piercing eyes. I saw a wolf sizing up his prey. In the window was the silhouette of a diminutive man, who turned as I approached the desk, and with a rather heavy accent Mr Charles Forte warmly greeted me,

"Mr Griffin, I am so pleased to meet you, your father wrote to me about you."

"How do you do, sir?" I quickly rubbed my palm on the seat of my trousers and proffered my hand.

He took it and I firmly shook his hand. "This is Mr Jack Bottel, who will have a chat with you, I unfortunately must go off to another meeting."

With this my encounter with the man who was to become one of England's great hoteliers, was over, and I was left with the wolf. Mr Bottel gestured to a seat in front of his desk, picked up a silver box, opened it and offered it to me. " Cigarette?"

"Er. No thank you sir."

I recalled my mother's instructions. A close call but I overcame the temptation. I do not recall many of the questions he asked but he was aware that my brother was attending Westminster Hotel School, the leader of only a handful of hotel schools in Britain at the time. He seemed more interested in him rather than what I had to offer. The interview was not one of my finer moments and yet again my father was faced with disappointing news.

Over the next few weeks, I had a number of interviews, among these was with Ind Coope Hotels, owners of the Leofric Hotel in Coventry, one of the first hotels to be built after the Second World War and a symbol of Britain's recovery. The company was more into small hotels than the grand luxury style I had in mind. All 'good experience' my mother would say encouragingly.

Just when I thought my father was running out of friends and contacts, he came home one evening and announced, "Today I had lunch with a client at the Manor House and ran into Selby, the general manager; he mentioned he would be happy to see if there was an opportunity of a position as a trainee manager with The Grand Hotel Eastbourne Company, of which the Manor is part. I have arranged a meeting with him on Wednesday."

I arrived for my interview at The Manor and met Mr Selby, I said little and listened a lot as to how tough the hotel business was and how only one in ten trainee managers taken on ever complete the four year training course. If I were to join the company I would need to 'try out' for six months at the Manor and, if successful, I would then transfer to the company's flagship, The Grand Hotel in Eastbourne, one of England's finest hotels.

On the following Friday, I received a call from Mr Selby. "Hello Patrick - can you come to the hotel on Monday, at 11.00am and meet two of the company's directors. If they are happy with you, I can see no reason why you won't be joining us".

I prepared for my meeting with the directors, with my mother running through again and again all the things that she believed I should or shouldn't say, and how to say them with my best public school accent. As it turned out, I was again required to say very little. I was introduced to the two directors, Mr Beattie, who ran The Grand Hotel and Mr Platt, the company secretary. Having established that I was not an academic, I managed to convince them of my enthusiasm and my personality.

Mr Beattie asked "Why are you so interested in joining The Grand Hotel?"

At last - the question I had been rehearsing over and over again with mother. "Well sir..."

I had only got so far, when Mr Selby cut in. "I think I might be able to answer that a little better. Patrick is from a good public school background and his father is one of our leading bankers; he has an uncle, a leading surgeon; and another a lawyer and the Warwickshire Coroner, all of whom are good customers of the hotel."

I wasn't sure that was accurate but in any event this was far from the answer I had prepared and one I felt rather indignant about. Was it not me who they were to employ, not my father or uncles? It seemed, however, to be an answer that satisfied them, so I said nothing further. This became the first lesson I learned in business - it was not what you know but often who you know, and something I believed to be innately wrong, but I soon learned it was simply a reality of life.

So it was that the letter arrived confirming my start with The Grand Hotel Eastbourne Company, at The Manor House, on Monday 5th August 1963. I would initially be paid the princely sum of three pounds, ten shillings for a 48 hour, five and a half day week. My initial position would be in the hotel's kitchen and was that of 'plonge' ...whatever that was. [46]

Chapter 8

#chefswhites #safesex #meths'n'alchohol

The day that I was to enter the workforce eventually arrived. My mother had taken me to a supplier of workplace clothing, as recommended by the hotel, to equip me in the appropriate uniform for working in the kitchen, for her very much a novelty. I was required to wear a set of 'whites' and was dutifully equipped with two sets of a white double breasted jacket, checkered trousers and a chef's hat, which I thought was quite fun. I had always loved dressing in uniforms.

On Monday morning, I was up early filled with a mixture of excitement and nervous apprehension of the unknown. I dressed in a shirt and tie, my smartest sports jacket a pair of my cavalry twill trousers, and the accepted uniform for an ex public school boy. I placed my kitchen uniform in a bag, and headed downstairs where my mother had prepared a good breakfast. "Best to go to work on a full stomach, dear", and then added, "...although no doubt after a while in the kitchens of the hotel, my cooking may not be good enough..."

"Mother, nothing will beat your home cooking."

This seemed to please her, although I had no idea why.

I was not sure who was more nervous that morning, me or my mother. With some emotion, she wished me luck and gave me a big hug, with which I mounted my bicycle and pedalled off down the road for the two mile ride to the hotel. I arrived and, wanting to create the best impression on my first day, had my first moment of panic as to where do I go? No one had given me instructions. I pedalled up to the main entrance of the hotel. As the squeaky brakes of the bicycle brought me to a halt, the heads of two departing guests turned, as did that of the porter, who was struggling to fit a large Louis Vuitton suitcase into the small boot of an MG sports car. I waited astride my rather less than impressive mode of transport, with my carrier bag over the handlebars, for the porter to complete his task.

This done, he glared at me and with a less than friendly tone "What the hell do you want?"

Not to be intimidated on my first day I cheerfully replied "I am starting work today in the kitchen. My first day".

"And your last if you arrive at the front door again."
"Sorry, I didn't know, where should I go?"
"Go around to the back of the hotel; you will see the back door of the kitchen and to the right is another door; that is where you can change. I suppose then you can just go to the kitchen and ask for the chef."

At that moment another guest appeared at the door and the conversation was over.

I turned my bicycle and went in search of the changing room, but this encounter had made a dent in my initial confidence. I found the door, knocked. No response so I cautiously entered. I thought I had arrived at the wrong place as this was a boiler room, but then I spotted some pegs on which some clothes hung, and beneath this was a bench with an array of shoes beneath. Not exactly what I had expected for a luxury hotel, but what *was* I expecting?

There was no one around so I took out my uniform, and then something struck me: how exactly should it be worn? My only previous experience was with a Scout's uniform, my school uniform and my Army Cadet uniform, all of which had detailed rules and regulations. This I pondered for a moment, and seeing my 'whites' as overalls I decided to don the checked trousers over my cavalry twills and my white jacket over my shirt. I thought I might discard the tie, which I did.

Kitted out in my uniform and carrying my chef's hat, I rather tentatively headed for the kitchen. As I entered it seemed to be a hive of activity. At first no one noticed me, then one of the chefs did, and within a few seconds it seemed that all went quiet and all eyes were on me. "Is the Chef about?" Hesitantly.

"Are you the new kid: the 'trainee manager'?" asked one of the chefs with something of a sneer in his voice that caught me off guard.

"Er...yes..." I responded even more hesitantly. I supposed that was what I was, although my starting role was that of 'plonge', which still meant nothing to me.

At that moment, an elderly, very tall and dignified man sporting a Lord Kitchener moustache entered the kitchen. He looked very impressive with a hat on his head, a 'toque' as I learned to call it, that was two feet tall and sat starched and perfectly vertical on his head, adding even further to his impressive six foot plus frame. Immediately the hive of activity re-commenced. He had not said a word but just glanced in their direction. This was obviously The Chef.

He looked in my direction. I am not sure whether it was a look of despair or sympathy, but it was not an initial look of warmth and welcome. "Griffin?"

"Yes sir"

"Don't call me sir. Call me Chef. Come with me."

I dutifully followed him into a glass-partitioned office from which he could survey his realm. In a small office beside him was a very gaunt, elderly moustached man, bent over some papers which he seemed to be reading with some difficulty though a pair of thick spectacles. This was Mr Gee, the 'kitchen clerk'. The Chef pointed to a chair. "Well now why are you here?"

This threw me as I thought that if he didn't know, how was I to know? "Er, well I want to be a hotel manager..."

"A hotel manager? Not a chef?"

I immediately realised that I was on dangerous ground here. "Er, well," I saw his eyes narrow, "...but I realise that to be a manager one must fully learn how to be a chef, as the food is what must make a hotel what it is, it must be the most important department in any hotel." With this I saw a softening of his look and a very slight smile.

"Right. I am glad you realise that. Let me tell you a thing or two"

At this point I could not help but notice over his shoulder and through the glass partition, the elderly Mr Gee had not moved but forming on his nose was an enormous dew drop, of which he seemed totally unaware. Chef continued, "I have to say I am not keen on trainee managers; they take up a lot of time and then they move on. Right now we are short staffed and I wanted someone who wants to be a chef and has some idea".

I was partially listening but intrigued at the dew drop that by this time had grown even larger.

"Unfortunately you will also find that some of my chefs may feel the same, most are ordinary lads and haven't been to a posh school or live in a big house in the best part of town ..."

The dew drop was now at a point where it had started to gain a momentum of its own.

"...so you may find that they are not so keen to have you working with them; they are good working class lads."

I was certain it was about to drop any second now.

"...So I suggest that you understand where you stand and do not behave in anyway that makes them think that you believe you are better."

There it went! Gravity having taken over, it was heading south. To my amazement a white handkerchief appeared as if from nowhere, at such a speed that would have shamed a chameleon shooting for its prey. It safely caught the dew drop and Mr Gee settled back into what seemed like his previous comatose state of inactivity.

"Do you understand what I am saying? If you don't work with these lads you will learn nothing."

With no further distractions I focused on what was being said. "Yes sir, I mean Chef, I do understand, but I really do want to learn and I am sure I will get on with all of them." I was somewhat perplexed at the lecture on the class divide.

"OK, I will introduce you to the lads, and to Murphy, who you will start off working with... and for goodness sake put on your *toque* and always wear it in the kitchen, although you will look a little ridiculous until it gets its first starched laundering."

My confidence now totally destroyed, and with my *toque* hanging over my eyes like a Frenchman's beret, I headed out to face the foe with Chef by my side. God I wished I was back at school.

As we entered the kitchen, I realised that the man beside me was a god. Everyone snapped to attention as he approached. They barked an instant response to any word he deigned to speak in their direction. He was in total command. We navigated around a vast gas stove at the centre of the kitchen, whilst around the walls were workbenches. I discovered that these areas were known as 'corners', and the individuals each had their own titles. "This is Mehmet, my Sous Chef'.

"Hello," was the response in a strong Cypriot accent. I offered my hand which he took with hesitation, after Mehmet had wiped his own hand on the cloth neatly folded into his apron, wrapped around a rather corpulent belly.

"Get Mr Griffin kitted out with an apron, neckerchief and a rubber."

The latter item of apparel confused me for a moment until I noticed a cloth tucked in his waistband, OK a dishcloth. I refocused. "Yes Chef," snapped the reply.

"And then introduce him to the rest of the lads. He will be working with Murphy on the pot wash".

Pot wash? I thought I was a plonge. Maybe that's what a plonge does? Ah, so that's what it means. Well at least that can't be too hard. It was at this point I started to feel the immense heat of the stove with all its burners going at full power. In fact, it started to feel as if I was beside a blast furnace. Beads of perspiration gathered on my forehead, not only due to the stress of the situation and the heat of the stove, but also to the sheer amount of clothing I was wearing.

I suddenly realised that this was yet another error of judgement on my first day. I should have discarded the cavalry twills, the shirt and any other unnecessary garments. By this time, I was flushed and rivulets of perspiration ran down the back of my neck. My discomfort did not go unnoticed by the lads around me, who naturally regarded it with huge amusement. Of course, they were all dressed in the uniform as it was meant to be worn - in the heat of a kitchen that reflected the pre-war times in which it had been built and air conditioning was a thing unknown.

With nothing further to bark, The Chef turned and retreated to his bunker. "For the time being I will give you my spare apron as I haven't time to take you to the laundry, and here is your rubber".

With that he tossed me a cloth similar to that which he had neatly tucked into his waistband. So that confirmed what a 'rubber' was; I was immensely glad to have cleared that up. I put on the apron and no sooner had I tossed the rubber over my shoulder, I realised I had made yet another mistake in the omnipresent eyes of the kitchen staff. "NEVER do that again. Everything has its place and a rubber should be neatly folded and tucked into your waistband. If ever Chef catches you with it anywhere else you will be for the high jump."

I could almost hear the mutters of *"He won't last long", "who is this stuck up prick", "who does he think he is?"*

"Come on, let me introduce you. This is Brian, he's the Chef Garde Manger, he works over there in the Larder; this Phil, he's the Chef Patissier; this is Alec, he's the Chef Saucier and this is Stewart..."

And so Mehmet introduced me in a whirl of names and indecipherable job titles that meant nothing to me other than what common sense would help me work out for myself. Together they formed what the hotel called The Kitchen Brigade. "...and this is who you will be working with..."

"Hello *der.*" A heavy Irish brogue.

And so I came to meet Murphy. With his warm voice and heavy Irish accent, I was delighted to once again find an Irishman and the first smiling and non-judgemental welcome since I stepped into the kitchen. "And what would your name be?"

"Griffin." I replied just as warmly and gladly.
"Well *dat's* a good start and is *dat* what I should be calling you?"
"Well actually at home I am called Paddy."
"Paddy? *dat's* even better, *den* you must be Irish, Paddy Griffin."
He mulled it over and repeated it a couple of times. "And what part of Ireland would you be coming from?"

Having at last found a friendly face and a warm welcome, I was desperate not to disappoint him, but with not a drop of Irish blood in my veins, that I knew of, and having never set foot on the Emerald Isle I fumbled for the right thing to say. "Well, I fear I haven't been to Ireland, but I know my parents are very fond of it, so I think there may be something in the past ..." What else could I say to keep his friendship? I knew nothing of Ireland, but then inspiration came to me, and I heard faint voices singing *It's a long way to Tipperary...*

"Actually I think one of the family in the past came from Tipperary."

At this, his eyes lit up. "Well who would believe *dat? Dat's* not far from where I was born." I was now his mate, and as close to a fellow countryman he would find in this steaming kitchen. No less did I welcome his friendship. "Well now, let's get you sorted out. But first we are going to have a tea break, and I *tink* it might be best if you popped back to the changing room and got rid of the shirt, or you might be melting."

This done, I returned to my new friend, who said, "Don't worry about the lads, they are a nice bunch. I *tink* when they heard that a trainee manager was to join *dem*, a son of one of the guests who is a friend of the boss, and from a posh school to boot, they thought they were going to get a kid *wid* a silver spoon in his mouth who wasn't wanting to work or mix with *dem*. You will get some flak I'm sure but just hang in *der* and don't let it get to you. They will come around soon enough. Now, let's get some work done".

He shepherded me to the back of the kitchen. I faced two huge sinks and an ever growing mountain of cooking pots. So it was that I started to scrub and clean an endless number of pots and pieces of culinary equipment. To make it worse, they all had strange sounding names that were totally alien to me. I learned to hate minestrone soup; each time it was cooked, there remained at the bottom of the pot a thick burned on layer of pasta and vegetables. How could they always cook soup and burn it? As I applied my scraper to clean the endless pots, the steam, the grease and heat ensured that I had perspiration running down my face and neck in a way I had never before experienced.

No sooner was a clean pot placed on the rack but there it was again on the mound of pots, as if it had never been cleaned. Throughout this suffering I survived my first day, thanks to the help and encouragement of my new found friend and 'fellow countryman' Murphy. God bless him. He taught me about surviving the first days in a job, which strongly influenced how I managed my staff in years to come. Gradually I learnt that this was what training was all about - it was not simply how to get burned minestrone out of a pot.

Murphy, it turned out, was a man of education and I wondered how he came to find himself in this pot-washing role. He never gave me a complete explanation, but I gathered that after a troubled marriage, he seemed to lose interest in the corporate world and steadily drifted into this sort of work where responsibility was minimal and life fell into an unchallenging routine.

This kind of routine involved all the basic jobs within the kitchen domain and a few others in which no one else was interested. I welcomed a break from pot-washing when he asked me to join him in another of his motley tasks: polishing the silver flambe lamps, or spirit stoves, used in the restaurant for such culinary delights as Steak Diane and Crepes Suzette, which were highly fashionable at the time.

One of Murphy's other duties was sorting the empty bottles from the 'bottle basket' behind the bar. Following a banquet, there were multitudes. I wondered why he chose not to share this job with me, although I was more than willing to assist. One day I discovered the hard way the reason behind the exclusivity of this job. Following a very busy morning in the sweltering heat, and having washed more than the usual Everest of pots, I lamented to Murphy, "My God what I would do for a drink right now, I am absolutely parched."

He understood my situation all too well, and, with a furtive look over his shoulder, reached beneath the draining board of the sink and pulled out a cider bottle. With a whisper he pushed it in my direction. "Here have a swig of *dis*, it should help and will certainly put hair on *yer* chest."

I looked at the bottle with apprehension, but it looked innocent enough. I enjoyed a glass of cider, although I was a little more concerned about sharing the bottle than the cider. However, he meant well and I reasoned that alcohol would put paid to any germs anyway. Any hesitation was soon put to one side when, with a further look over his shoulder, Murphy chided "Go on quick before anyone sees you."

With this I took a large swig and quickly passed the bottle back. Within a second, the expected sweet taste of cool thirst-quenching cider turned into a gagging burning sensation. I thought I was going to throw up all over the recently washed pots. I managed to suppress this reaction and swallow, coughing and spluttering as I did so. "Wow." Pause for breath. "What the hell was that?"

Murphy gave me a knowing smile. "Told you it would put hair on *yer* chest."

"Put hair on my chest? More likely take it off. What was it?"

"*Dat's moy* little secret" is all he would say.

Although I'd only had one mouthful, I was starting to feel a little woozy and lightheaded. I was certainly more relaxed, although my gulp had done nothing to assuage my thirst. Apart from cider, a few beers and a vodka or gin with orange – to take away the taste – I'd had little experience of alcohol. What I had just consumed was a new world to me. I tried to work out what it was, as it had such a mixture of tastes and a rather metallic aftertaste. It seemed so familiar, but I just couldn't place the taste. Murphy was tight-lipped. I vowed not to partake again, and to rely on simple water from the tap in future.

A few weeks later, I got a horrible clue as to what was in the "Murphy cocktail". Following a very busy lunch when we'd had more than the usual number of Steak Dianes and Crepes Suzettes, a very irate, hot and flustered *maitre d'* barged out from the restaurant, cursing and swearing, and his anger was without doubt focused in our direction. Oh no, what had we done? "You bastard Murphy! If you touch my flambe lamps again I will flambe your balls and serve them to you!" What was he on about? I had cleaned and polished the lamps as instructed and Murphy had refilled them with methylated spirits. "Two of the lamps ran out in the middle of cooking, you stupid sod. The meths is for cooking, not for your fucking consumption!"

Ah, so that was it. Murphy had not only taken a shine to the lamps, but to the meths as well. Suddenly the cloud lifted in my mind. Oh my God. That metallic taste was meths. Thankfully it had been much diluted with what I was to discover later were his other ingredients that constituted the 'Murphy Cocktail' in the innocent-looking cider bottle.

The daily emptying and sorting of the bottle baskets in the bar produced a never ending elixir for those in need of alcoholic refreshment. A bottle in the restaurant, once empty, was relegated to the bottle basket. I discovered then, and it did not change in the years to come, that the basket was a treasure trove. Each and every bottle, whether it be wine, spirits or sherry, always had a little bit of liquid left in the bottom. It was these last drops that were carefully harvested and added to the cider bottle, imparting colour, body and variety to the 'Murphy Cocktail'.

During those early years, I grew close to a number of friends from Ireland, all of whom were warm, friendly and kind. Murphy was one of these, a wonderful man with a heart of gold.

His friendship while I was starting out in my first job, filled as I was with fear and trepidation for the unknown, taught me that vital skill of empathy towards any new starter in a job. He also taught me empathy towards those in the toughest working conditions, something which is seldom experienced by contemporary management. I've had a soft spot for the Irish wherever our paths have crossed over the years. They are wonderful people who have those essential qualities required by the hotel business: a great gift for enjoying life and seeing its humorous side.

Those first few months at The Manor House Hotel set me on a steep learning curve. Having never been regarded as the brightest light in my academic studies, I was delighted to discover that all things are relative. The lads I now found myself working with were an interesting bunch, but still very much from the other side of the social divide that was so apparent in those years. Most were from working class families and all were educated at the local school, leaving as soon as they had reached the age of fifteen. Like me, none was a gifted academic. I therefore soon discovered the meaning of the saying 'amongst the blind, the one-eyed man is king.' I took full advantage of this, and I will have the good grace to say I am a little ashamed of it. After all, it was a very new experience for me. My academic history also gave me a level of respect and prestige I had never before experienced.

The sous chef, Mehmet, I discovered did not have the same authority and respect as that of The Chef. Mehmet was a bully, who shouted and abused anyone who did not do his bidding. Naturally he was thereby disliked by most of the lads, in particular the apprentices, who were indentured employees with few rights or redress. We trainees felt we were similarly cruelly enslaved, except that we didn't have the extra burden of the indenture which bound the apprentices to their place of work.

Having always been a believer in natural justice, and having experienced more than my share of bullying in the past, I was finely tuned to the unfairness of Mehmet's treatment of the boys. One day, I could not bite my tongue any longer. A young lad was busy trying to whip up a load of eggs for hollandaise sauce over a hot steaming *bain marie*, a job hated by all, and his task was not made easier by the fact that he was so short he could hardly reach the top of the pot over the boiling water. Predictably, he received a verbal roasting from Mehmet for taking so long, which ended in a cuff to the back of the lad's head, sending his hat flying. "Cut that out Mehmet," I heard myself saying. "He's doing his best."

"You can fuck off, you public school shit", came the heavily accented reply. "If you want trouble, I will fucking give it to you," waving a large kitchen knife.

Silence reigned and all eyes in the kitchen were now on the two of us. God, what do I do now? Pride and principle kicked in.

"I can certainly say what I like," I retorted in my best public school accent. There was no going back now if I was to have any standing amongst the lads. Mehmet started towards me, still brandishing his knife.

"Do you know what you are doing?" I continued in my most authoritative voice, stifling the quiver. "You have already broken three laws and if you advance one step further I will have you on a common assault charge. You do realise my uncle is a lawyer in this town?"

The combination of some legal jargon and my elevated social position, for which he had been so quick to denounce me, had the required effect. He stopped in his tracks. He looked around and, in the way of all bullies, turned on the lads who were still standing in stunned silence before the events unfolding. "What are you lot looking at, get back to work before I report the lot of you to Chef."

It was over.

After this incident, I glowed in a new light of stardom and suddenly found I had lots of friends, who started asking me what I thought about anything from the rights of workers to which horse would win the Grand National.

Sadly, in my youthful pride, I abused my new found status as the academic in the kitchen, and to this day have always regretted it. As I worked in the pastry department one day, doing some rather mundane job of sifting a hundredweight sack of flour into a storage bin, a conversation started on school days and favourite subjects. Having nominated mine as chemistry, and knowing I was on safe ground as none of the others had studied it, I thought it made me sound good even though I did not like it. One lad said he loved the English language and that he had prowess in this field. I immediately felt the need to retain my position as the educated *prima donna* of the kitchen, so I set about testing him on his expertise. "You were good at English, were you?"

"Yeh I wuz", he said with confidence.

"Good at spelling, were you?"

"Yeh-eh," he replied, but with rather less confidence.

"OK then, how do you spell the plural of knife?"

"Nah, that's stupid," he defended.

"No, go on, spell it."

"Why should I?"

Sensing a victory here, I pushed further, although I was a little puzzled as to his level of panic. I went in for the kill. "You do know what the plural of a knife is, don't you?" I was rather hesitant now and feeling awful that I had pushed him so far.

"'Course I do. It's the '*andle* bit, *innit*."

With this, I quickly changed the subject and asked if he could show me how to make the pastry he was working on, which he was very happy to do, back in his comfort zone.

I was not sure if I would last but I was enjoying working life. There was little employee protection and one could be sacked on a whim so I felt some security when the Assistant Manager, Mr Naylor, came into the kitchen with some papers. "Here you lot, you get it soft nowadays, it seems we now have to give you a contract to tell you your hours and pay conditions, so get your copy and sign." [47]

We complied obediently with hardly a glance as to what we were signing, but it had to be better than nothing. When he left we had a closer look. "What cobblers, I would like to see the day we only work 48 hours a week" one of the lads blurted out.

The conditions were by today's standard laughable but it was a start, and at least we now 'may' get sick pay should we be injured at work, although 'at the discretion of the management.'

We actually worked at least twelve hours a day in reality although our official shifts were from 9.00am to 2.30pm and back again at 5.30pm until 10.00pm. Such hours did not fit in with the social life of my friends of old, so I fell in with the lads from the kitchen. We spent most of the time wandering the streets of Leamington or making a cappuccino last three hours at the local Espresso Coffee Bar run by one of the new post-war Italian immigrants to our shores, Giovanni.

We listened to the latest records on the JukeBox, cigarette in hand, chatting up any young woman who dared enter our realm. The lads were particularly good at this, somehow possessing a confidence that I lacked. I learned fast, however, and started to plan what conquests I might achieve from this bevy of new girls to whom the lads introduced me. I knew of course that they would not meet with my mother's approval, mainly being shop girls, and some others who were more glamorous were, without fail, hairdressers.

One such young woman I was convinced was going to fall for my worldly charms, and such was my confidence I felt I really should be prepared. The lads advised me to acquire some condoms, but I had no idea as to how. "Doesn't your dad have some you can nick?" came one suggestion. The thought filled me with horror. My father... condoms! Why would he have any? Surely he wouldn't. He and my mother... At this point, it all became too terrible a thought to contemplate, and I forced it out of my mind. There must be another way.

"Well you could buy some; the gents barbers in Regents Street sells them, and they have a little hatch by the entrance so you don't have to go in."

Armed with this information and encouragement from the lads, this was my only option. I walked past the barber, and checked the hatch. Sure enough, there it was as described. I walked back, hesitated, and walked on. What if someone sees me? *Come on you can do it*, I urged myself.

Steeling myself, and focusing on the possible rewards for my endeavours, I turned and walked back. As I approached the hatch, I took a deep breath. A sign commanded me to 'Ring Here for Service'. Before I could back out, I pressed the bell.

BRRRRRNNG! My God it sounded like a fire alarm. I was sure it could be heard all down Regents Street. A woman turned as she passed and I could read her mind: *I know what you are up to.* I felt my cheeks burn bright red. I counted to five and if the hatch didn't open I would take off. On four, the hatch flew open. "What can I get you sir?" an elderly man asked. I could read his mind as well, *dirty little sod, I know what you're here for.*

"Er, um, a packet of Durex, please," I can still feel the heat in my cheeks.

He looked at me with a rather bored expression, having seen it all many many times before. "What size?"

Shit, I don't know, no one told me they came in sizes. Now bordering on panic. "Large or standard"

"Er, large please." I had no idea.

"OK." Surprised look on his face.

Suddenly, behind me a voice I recognised all too well, "Hello Patrick, how are you, parents well?" There standing inches away was Mr Hewitt, a bank colleague of my father's. Oh God please go away before the barber arrives back at the hatch. My invocations worked, as by divine intervention a car horn sounded. "Hurry up dear, we'll be late, oh, hello Patrick"

From behind me, "Here we are, sir." I did not turn around but stood frozen to the spot, as Mr Hewitt got into his car.

"Here you are, sir," the barber repeated, giving my jacket a tug. I did not move and tried to ignore the barber's impatient calls. After an eternity, the gear was engaged and with a hearty, but knowing smile Mr and Mrs Hewitt drove off.

Once the car was out of sight, I quickly turned to grab my purchase and make a fast exit before anyone else I knew walked in on my guilty transaction. "That will be 12/6." I nearly choked; that was a quarter of my weekly wages. "Sorry how much?"

"12/6, that's the cost of a large box of Durex, you did want a large box of 36, didn't you?" I thrust the money into his hand, turned and made my escape as fast as I could.

Unfortunately, Margie and I broke up the next week. But at least the stress of my adventure was not completely in vain. In true form, I managed to sell the packet of 36 condoms individually to the lads for sixpence each, thereby clearing around five shillings on what I'd paid.

Chapter 9

#grandhoteleastbourne #theclassdivide #eccentricenglish

My life as a trainee progressed well and I enjoyed my new found friendships with the lads of the kitchen. I came to understand that I had had a most privileged upbringing and certainly a very different one to my colleagues. Even if I could not do the five declensions in Latin, this just did not matter in my new world. My mother, always concerned that I should remember my social and business standing as 'management', was keen that I should not become too involved with the other boys who were, as she saw it, of a distinctly different social standing. She started subtly to reinforce the differences. I was rather surprised when, on leaving for work one day, she asked "What do you do in the afternoons when you have your break?"

Faced with this loaded question, I was not sure how much I should tell her, so I answered with the teenager's usual non committal, "Not much."

"Well, why not bring your friends back here for tea, and you can play in the garden".

I was mightily taken aback. Tea? Play in the garden? These ideas were totally out of keeping with our testosterone-charged adventures at Giovanni's espresso coffee bar. With absolutely no way to extract myself from this invitation, which in reality was a direct command, I agreed, knowing that I could always say they had to work overtime.

As the morning shift drew to a close, I pondered my mother's invitation, and realised that she would no doubt have loaded the oven with scones and cakes. I felt trapped. What do I say to these tough working class lads who now looked on me as one of their own. "What shall we do this afternoon?" I asked. This was the daily standing question as we had to fill the three hour break between shifts from 2.30pm to 5.30pm.

"Don't know," came the general response.

"My mum wondered if you would like to come back to my place?"

I thought *mum* was better than *Mother*, but then I thought it sounded ridiculous to say my mother was inviting them. While still grappling with this, I was shocked to hear the sudden enthusiastic response. They all wanted to come, although a couple of lads had other things to do.

So eight of us all headed home to meet my mother for tea. As we entered the gates of our house in Northumberland Road, a rather grand suburb of Leamington Spa, I noticed a sudden air of nervousness envelop the group. This fell to complete silence as we entered the hallway. "Cor, it's posh, innit, and big," came a comment, something that I hadn't even considered, having lived in large houses all my life.

At this moment my mother appeared from the drawing room. "Hello, boys," and I introduced them. For their part they greeted her with utmost respect and politeness. For me it was all over the top; each greeting took on the formality of a presentation to The Queen. "Run along out into the garden and play and I will call you when tea is ready."

God how embarrassing. But none of the 'boys' seemed bothered, they were rather enjoying their visit. We went down into the small orchard at the bottom of the gardens, and messed around.

I was surprised to see them all playing as if in a second childhood, and I played along.

"Boys, tea is ready, come along." I heard my mother call in the distance. With immediate obedience to the royal command we all dutifully filed back to the house.

"Wipe your feet," and, having obediently done so, entered the French windows into the drawing room.

There before us was a table resplendent in sandwiches, cakes, scones, cream and home-made jams. "Sit down where you like," with which she handed out plates and napkins. "Do help yourselves as there are far too many this afternoon for me to look after alone", which seemed to me to imply that today was the maid's day off. "Tea?"

"Yes please," came the chorus of responses.

"I do hope you like the scones I have made, cooking for trained chefs like yourselves is rather a daunting task"

A masterly comment. Then the final touch: "India or China...with milk?" My mother started pouring from the large silver teapot into the fine bone china tea cups, all the time chatting happily to the 'boys' with the warmth and friendliness that rather belied her real purpose for the visit, one of highlighting the class divide.

The afternoon turned out for me to be a resounding success, and set me up as the unquestionable leader of the lads. On our return to work, they were full of praise for my mother and what a lovely lady she was: "Not stuck up at all". Those who hadn't come were regaled with stories of the house, that rapidly became a mansion, and the gardens that seemed to gain the proportions of an estate. The silver and china tea service was only available to royalty.

The visit was talked about for days and confirmed my distaste for the English class system, still prevalent in the 1960s. This would regularly be referred to in the newspapers, and often with some humorous rebuttals. My favourite came some years later from the rapier wit of Prince Philip when he commented ...'*People think there is a rigid class system here, but Dukes have been known to marry chorus girls. Some have even married Americans'*. This rather snobbish view was reinforced a few weeks later when, after a number of staff went down with flu, the deputy manager, Mr Cairns, asked me to assist in the restaurant as a commis waiter for a busy lunch. This was exciting, as I would be out of the heat of the kitchen, and would get to wear a smartly laundered jacket, shirt and bow tie, as well as a long apron that reached to my feet. The job was not a difficult one; all I needed to do was to ferry the food from the kitchen to the waiter who served it to the guests. I loved the job, and, apart from the ribbing I got from my friends in the kitchen who saw me changing side to join the enemy, it was a lot of fun. So excited was I that I had been chosen for such duties, I couldn't wait to get home that afternoon to tell my mother of my promotion.

As I entered the house, I heard voices, and recognised my aunt Constance's rather distinctive voice. It had a certain style about it, like a cross between a duchess and a BBC newsreader. She was my mother's eldest sister and the matriarch of the family. As I entered the room I was bursting to impart my news. After the usual kisses on cheeks and greetings, they sat quietly and listened to my news. Far from the joy and congratulations I expected, there was a silence only broken when mother said in very controlled tones, "Did Selby ask you to do this?"

"Er, yes. Well his deputy did." I was shattered by the lack of enthusiasm.

Turning to aunt Constance, my mother said "Selby assured me that Patrick would not be working in any public areas." And, as if to utterly deflate my moment of glory, followed up with, "What would your father have said? What if he was entertaining someone at the restaurant? Good God, what was Selby thinking, I will have to call him."

My mother was now in full swing, when dear aunt Constance stepped in. "For goodness sake Hilda stop worrying. Even if there was someone in the restaurant who knew Patrick, who on earth ever looks at the waiter?" With this defining statement and appreciation for her elder sister's wisdom, mother relaxed, and settled back into her chair. Aunt Constance, in a final act of pacification, said "Have another cup of tea dear?" With which the matter was dismissed.

I, for some reason, was never asked to assist in the restaurant ever again.

My final discovery of this trial period was that trainee managers had no rights whatsoever. We were expected to do whatever was asked, no matter what. The theory was that it would be 'educational'. Managers, after all, are 'jacks of all trades', and naturally need to have knowledge of all the arcane mysteries of a hotel's operations, including, of course, the sewage system.

Mr Selby appeared at the front of the kitchen. "Chef, may I borrow Griffin for a while, I have a job for him." This was not really a request, but a courtesy extended to the Chef de Cuisine. He was one of the few employees extended such a privilege. It was, and is, custom and practice that even the General Manager sought permission of the Chef to enter his kitchen domain. I have dutifully continued this practice to this very day, which says a lot for the fear and awe with which chefs are viewed.

I followed Mr Selby out to the carpark. I saw the manhole cover was off one of the drains, and next to it sat a pile of drainage rods. Curious and innocently expecting to see a plumber down below, I gingerly looked down the twenty-foot hole. It sported an iron ladder attached to the wall, but I saw no plumber. I recoiled as a wafting aroma of sewage assaulted my nostrils.

"We have a problem," said Mr Selby, rather redundantly. "The drains are blocked, it's backing up into the guest rooms, and the plumber can't get here for a couple of hours."

What was he expecting me to do? He read my mind. "I want you to get down there and stick the curly worm rod up the bottom pipe to clear it." To illustrate his point perfectly, just at that moment there was a gurgling noise and a jet of effluent shot out from one of the upper pipes that fed the main drain manhole.

"What down there ...?"
"Yes. Now, this is just one of the sorts of problems you will be faced with when you become a General Manager, so it will be good experience for you."
"But I could get covered in ..."
"Shit, yes." He completed my horrified sentence. " Don't worry, I will be here and if I hear the gurgle, I will call you in time for you to get out."

Always a willing volunteer, in fear of nothing and mostly thinking of the Brownie points I could get for this sacrifice, I descended down the ladder armed with the rods. I did so not realising the Brownie points might not be all I expected them to be. I started to push the first rod into the pipe, connected the next and pushed it further. After about the fourth rod, a call from above echoed down the hole, "Come on up, quick!"

As I reached the final rung of the ladder, I heard the gurgle approaching. Grateful to be clear of the hole, I waited and watched as almost instantly more effluent spewed out of the pipes.

Taking a deep breath, I descended yet again. After only attaching a few more of the rods, I heard "How are you doing - have you reached it yet?"

"Not as yet; what has caused the blockage?"

"Bloody women,"

I was surprised to hear Mr Selby grumble. Why would a woman block the drains? "They try to flush things down the toilet instead of putting them in the bin provided," he continued to grumble. What things? I was no more the wiser, as such things were not a topic of discussion at home nor in the dormitories at school. I thought we had discussed all possible things to do with the opposite sex there.

I descended back down the hole, now more confident in my skill at this task. I quickly put two more rods together and pushed hard. Eureka! I had reached "It". Twisting and pulling at the rods, I felt movement. "Griffin, come on up... Now!"

I was on the verge of success. "Hang on, nearly done it."

"NOW!" came the urgent command.

"Done it!" I announced victoriously.

"Quick! NOW!" I could now hear the note of desperation in his voice.

With that came the horrible realisation that the joy of my victory may be short-lived. I rapidly ascended the ladder, desperately taking the rungs two at a time. I was looking up at the sun's rays shining down the shaft, ready to welcome me back to their bright cleanness. Concurrently, I was working out the odds of getting to the top in time.

As if to mock me, there was a roar and the bright sunlight overhead was obscured by a shower of dark liquid. With no other option, I pressed myself as close to the ladder as I could, kept my head down, and prayed it would fly over me. Regrettably this was not the case. With wringing hair and a soaked back, I crawled out of the hole into the sunlight. Naturally an audience had gathered around the hole, and my eruption out of the hole made them take a sharp step back.

"What about the rods?" asked Mr Selby, with heartlessly little concern for my predicament.

Not wishing to ruin my hard-earned credits in this wholly selfless venture, I controlled my initial desire to tell him where he could next stick his rods. Instead, I obediently returned to the reeking pit and retrieved the plumbing drain rods. "Well done, Griffin. I suppose you will need a bath now. I will let you use a guest bathroom and get you a new set of 'whites'." As if this was reward enough for what I had done.

Surprisingly though, I was rather excited at being able to use a guest bathroom and this added to the 'flush' of success I achieved in saving the hotel from the flooding that was threatened by the blocked drain. I thought this was likely to be the greatest and filthiest test I would face in my climb up the hotel management ladder of success, but this was not to be the case. I would find many more such showers would descend on me during my career.

What this test did do, however, was to convince the powers that be that after three months I had proved that I had the grit and determination to stay the course. A week later I was called

into the office to be told that the following month I would transfer to The Grand Hotel in Eastbourne to commence my training
for management in earnest. The weeks went by quickly. Soon
I was packed and ready to go, but not without the parting words
of counsel from Mr Selby. "Griffin, you have started well, and may
you continue to do well. Sadly, it doesn't always work out."

I started to tune out of yet another boring adult lecture, but
then suddenly I was listening. "For some reason," he continued,
"the boys who I have sent down there have been ruined. You
know that Eastbourne is the biggest vice den outside Rome?"

Did he say 'vice den'? I thought it was full of old people waiting to die. My mother had described it as 'such a nice town,
very gentrified', having visited there once when she was a child.
Neither of these latter descriptions boded well in my book,
as 'nice' and 'old people' did not correlate to a vice den in my
extensive experience.

With new found enthusiasm for my future in Eastbourne and
one brown suitcase in hand, I farewelled my parents on Platform
One of Leamington Spa Railway Station, boarded a third class
carriage on the train from Snow Hill in Birmingham bound for
Paddington. From there I crossed London to Victoria Station
for my onward trip to Eastbourne. Hopes were high for what
I eagerly anticipated would be the pleasures of this den of vice,
and a career that I was sure would surpass the success of the
man I regarded as my inspiration, Cesar Ritz.

The train pulled into Eastbourne station on a dark and damp
November evening, I handed in my ticket as I passed through the
gates. The station was an ornate structure reflecting the Victorian
era in which it was built. A couple were sitting in the station's
cafeteria as I passed, an uncanny resemblance to Celia Johnson
and Trevor Howard in a scene from *Brief Encounter*. As I stepped
outside into the night air the streets seemed empty and I was

pleased to see a taxi standing vacant nearby. As I hopped into the back seat I confidently said, "The Grand Hotel please".

He looked at me in his mirror. "Would that be the Compton Street entrance laddie?"

"I am not sure, why?"

"Well you don't want to piss off the doorman and porters when they realise you are not a guest and they won't be getting a tip."

"OK, and thanks, the Compton Street entrance it is."

"Right laddie, the back entrance it is," came the broad Scottish reply.

How did he know I wasn't a guest? Was it my rather worn pre-war suitcase given to me by my father, which now contained my worldly possessions, or was it my new £10 John Colliers suit?

We arrived in minutes at the 'back entrance' where I alighted the taxi, suitcase in hand. No sooner paid, and my friendly driver was off. I watched the lights of his car disappear into the distance and turned to face two enormous mahogany and glass doors.

Somewhat hesitantly I put my weight against one of the doors, wondering if it would open, it did with ease and I found myself suddenly in a lobby looking up an ornate marble staircase with a red carpet running from top to bottom. Bloody hell, if this is the back entrance, what is the front like? [48]

As if the staircase hadn't intimidated me enough, what I saw through the glass doors of the lobby almost had me turning on my heels in search of my Scottish chum and his cab. After a few deep breaths to settle my anxiety, I planned my next move. As I peered through the thick bevelled glass of the doors, I saw a bevy of tailed-coated waiters in bow ties, serving coffees, brandies and liqueurs to the guests sitting in a lounge dominated by a large flaming fireplace. The guests were animated in soft conversation and totally oblivious to the waiters who were trying to place the glasses in front of the right guest. Some guests looked almost soporific, leaning back in their well padded arm chairs, with the ash from their cigars falling on the carpet beside them like a recently erupted volcano. In the corner I watched a quartet as they tried to gain some interest from their audience, with little success. I recall the piece they were playing was Barber's *Adagio for Strings*, one of those haunting pieces of music. I didn't know the name of it until I saw the movie *Platoon* many years later.

I rather timidly tapped on the glass, trying to attract the attention of one of the penguinesque waiters. I was utterly ignored. Eventually, I thought there was nothing more I could do than to actually venture into this sanctuary of hedonism, for it surely was so. With the hotel's printed tariff quoting a daily charge of £4 17s 6d., one night cost more than I would earn in a week. [49]

No sooner had I got the door a matter of inches open, than the handle was grabbed from the other side and I was faced with one of the waiters assuming it may have been a guest about to enter. His eyes focused on me for a second. "You no come in here," was his definite statement.

Why not? "You no come in here!"

He repeated in his strong Spanish or Italian accent, this time with a little more authority. It was at this moment that a more elderly man appeared at the door, equally resplendent in his tails. Never quick to make judgements, Charlton was the head lounge waiter and personal butler, as I was to learn later, to the Managing Director of the Hotel, Mr Dick Beattie, who I had met at my interview. More softly and in a kindly manner he said, "May I assist you young man?"

As I explained I was a new trainee manager who was due to start tomorrow, his expression relaxed. "OK, best pop over to the concierge desk ahead of you, they should be able to help you;

be quick but don't run, and leave that suitcase here." I felt an immediate bond with this kindly man.

As I crossed the lounge I could not help but feel the eyes following me. I tried to avoid any eye contact but just looked up and around me. I could already understand why it was called 'The Grand Hotel'. The plush carpet underfoot, the large fireplace and the enormous chimney breast that seemed to go up several floors. A minstrel's gallery where no doubt musicians played in years gone by. And wonderful plasterwork on the walls and ceiling tower above me. All very 'Grand' and very awe inspiring to a young man new to such interiors. So this was to be my new workplace.

I appeared before the concierge; he was mature, immaculately dressed in his frock coat, bearing the emblems of 'crossed keys' on his lapels. These meant little to me at the time but I was later to discover that they were the emblems of a highly respected association that bonds all concierges across the world. The 'Union Internationale des Concierges d'Hotels' or better known as 'Les Clefs d'Or'. Little did I know then but in forty years hence, I would be humbled by an invitation to join their respected ranks as an Honorary Member when I was awarded a 'Diploma d'Honneur' in 2006.

He nodded at me. His name was Ron Marion, but no one in those days wore a name badge. Guests were not interested in those who served them. Ron had started at the hotel in 1947 as so many of the staff had. "You must be Griffin, the new trainee manager."

Somehow I felt it was not said in an admiring way but more in a way that indicated that 'trainees' were regarded with some disdain. Public school boys who had failed to meet the prescribed standards of academic achievement to enter 'The City'. Instead they use their class and education to enter into a senior role that the average employee in the hotel had spent their lives building up to. And these employees were expected to instruct us in the ways of their profession, only to then find us as their superiors, like a young naval midshipman of the Nelson era. Although the accepted way of the class-bound times in such an establishment, it understandably caused angst, certainly amongst those work colleagues, of a similar age doing a similar job. "These are the keys to your room, you are over in St Vincents along with the rest of the trainees."

I wasn't to appreciate the full meaning of this for a few days and the extent of the difference between 'us and them'. "I will have one of my boys take you across."

With that a young page boy appeared from nowhere, sporting a very smart uniform with an array of brass buttons on his chest and a pillbox hat on his head. He looked no more than twelve, but must have been older. "Come this way." With which we backed-tracked on my steps, the page boy grabbing my case, and headed for the grand entrance at the rear of the hotel and across the street into a large car park in the middle of which sat 'St Vincents', a large Victorian house that was to be my home for the next few years.

"Here we are." The page boy almost tossed my suitcase through the door. It landed at the feet of a boy of similar years to myself, who reminded me of a school prefect and whose role was not too dissimilar, being the most senior of the trainees.

"Griffin? Welcome to The Grand. You will find everyone is known by their surname here, but we tend to use first names around the house. What shall I call you?"

This I almost had to think about as I had only really been referred to as 'Griffin' for a major part of my life. "My family call me Paddy, although my name is Patrick." The latter observation seemed somewhat fatuous in afterthought, but went unnoticed.

"Mine is David, David Dickinson, I'll take you to your room and you can settle in. Sorry but the stewards' room is closed now so if you are hungry you may need to go to the Saloon Bar for a bag of crisps or something. We are going down there soon."

Thankfully he then added, "But maybe you are too knackered and may just want to settle in?" This I agreed with, and followed him up three flights of stairs to my attic room.

"What time are you starting in the morning?"

"I have no idea." I responded with some hesitation, assuming someone would tell me.

"Oh no one has told you: typical. You are starting in 'room service'. I will take you across and introduce you to Morris, the head floor waiter. Be ready in the morning at about eight. You do have a pair of dress black trousers and a white shirt I assume? The uniform jacket and tie will be given to you."

"Yes." I was nervous about their condition after their journey. But the shirt was 'crease proof' and I could put the trousers under my mattress for a pressing overnight.

By this time we had reached my room. "Settle in and I will see you tomorrow." An afterthought, "The bathroom and lav is over there - don't hog it as you share it with five others on this floor." He turned and headed back down the stairs. So here I am. The Grand Hotel and the start of my training in a style of luxury that I hoped would give me the lifestyle I deserved.

The knock on my door to herald the start of my first day came with David, standing resplendent in his morning suit, the official uniform of the trainee working in the offices at the front of house.

He cast a casual eye over me in my black dress trousers, polished black shoes and white shirt. "OK you'll do, let's go."

The cold air hit me as we walked across to the hotel which
rather took my mind off the nerves of the first day. We entered the
hotel as I had the day before via the Compton Street entrance,
an honour I had not appreciated as a privilege accorded to trainees. All other staff had to enter via the staff entrance where they
clocked in; again a rule not applied to trainees and a privilege
afforded only to senior and management staff, the relevance of
which I did not appreciate at the time. It was only later I realised
that when the seventy hours we trainees worked in a week was
not rewarded in our pay packet, the training and management
status was meant to be regarded as the reward in itself.

At the time my official weekly wage was £4 per week, about
£38 in today's money. This was 'live in' and so should be man-
ageable for the frugal, which of course I was not. It was to be
many years before I felt I received the benefits and rewards for
the effort and hours I worked, which really only fell below sixty
hours a week at the quietest of times.

I followed David, or should I say, Dickinson, through the
doors into the service area of the kitchen, behind which there
was a hive of activity by white clad chefs in tall hats, and the
smell of cooking wafting across the hotplate that ran the twenty
yard length of the kitchen. I was immediately reminded that
I had not had breakfast, but was too nervous to ask about this
on my first day.

We reached the gate of the lift, that I think must have been
there since the hotel was first built. David threw back the metal
gates and we stepped in, pressed the button and with a jerk
started to ascend, arriving at the second floor in what seemed
like a few minutes. Throwing back the gates we were faced with a
scene of five uniformed waiters sitting around a table, polishing

cutlery and glasses with a pall of cigarette smoke hanging over them as they sipped at cups of tea and coffee. This didn't look at all like an onerous way to start my day. "Morris, this is Griffin, your new trainee."

The first week was one of being measured and outfitted with the uniform for my role as 'Floor Waiter'. The uniform was proudly proclaimed by management, as being designed by Hardy Amies one of the Queen's designers. Although regarded as modern and stylish it was disliked by all those who had to wear it. It was an unexciting soft grey man-made fabric popular in the 60s but with no real style or cut. It was considered as 'a one cut fits all' and for the older professional waiters, of which there were many, they felt no dignity in wearing it, when compared to the crisply starched jackets to which they had been accustomed.

The Head Waiters, Morris, Atfield and Pritchard, had flatly refused the modernisation and were allowed to retain their starched collars and tails. Such was the disapproval of the planned updating of the staff uniforms no further changes occurred and the starched collars and tails remained for most staff. Sadly, however, not for me. With an exceedingly thin frame and long arms I was to remain in an outfit with sleeves that hardly passed my elbows. I was regularly referred to as the orangutan. This did not really upset me, being accustomed to being ribbed at school so often about my anatomical defects. All I desired was to be cool and fashionable. No doubt this contributed to the substantial sums I spent in my latter years at bespoke tailors to ensure I represented the desired image of the urbane Englishman.

My training was 'monkey see, monkey do', and to tell the truth it continued in this manner for most of the years at The Grand. At the time there were not the laws and regulations that were to follow in the years to come. The only real legal issues that affected the day to day operation of the hotel were that of the Liquor Licensing Regulations and the Health Inspector. Departments of 'Human Resources', 'Sales and Marketing', 'Public Relations' were not yet acknowledged as a requirement for the British hotel industry, and any formal training was still in its infancy. It was only being offered in the Hotel Schools of Switzerland, the USA and a few colleges in Britain, such as Westminster, the one attended by my brighter brother Bob.

The real focus was still on guest service and the hands on experience offered that was handed down by the older masters in service at the traditional luxury hotels like The Ritz, The Dorchester, The Savoy and Claridges, together with a few luxury hotels outside London, like The Grand Hotel. (For more information on The Grand Hotel see Appendix B.)

I spent much time in my early days polishing the cutlery, china and glasses. I then laid up trays and trolleys, for the service of breakfast, lunch, afternoon tea and dinner to the rooms, each service being laid in a different way and for tea with different fine china. I also accompanied the experienced waiters in servicing the residents' suites, of which there were a number, each with their specific needs. Often there were shortcuts to learn; for example Lady Prince always wanted a jug of fresh water. A beautiful crystal jug was covered with an equally beautiful Belgian lace doily, with no such thing as bottled water and minibars. The work in changing the water, which was often untouched from day to day, was seen as far too much effort and was handled more simply with a pencil giving the water a quick stir. This washed away the bubbles that accumulated on the inside of the jug giving the impression of a fresh crystal clear supply of water.

Sometimes it was actually the guests cutting corners. A retired Scottish clergyman, whose residence at The Grand was courtesy of an endowment by a late and kindly parishioner, regularly entertained guests in his suite. The popular drink of the day was sherry, whisky with ginger ale, and most of all gin and tonic, the clergyman's beverage of choice. These beverages were displayed on an antique sideboard with glasses, mixers and a bucket of ice, replenished at lunch and early evening. The requirement was for a bottle of Tio Pepe sherry, one Harvey's Bristol Cream; two bottles of Haig Whisky, and three bottles of Gordon's Gin.

The gin required special attention. Each bottle was marked with a small number on the label: 1, 2, or 3. Bottle 1 was the gin as delivered from the cellars of the hotel. The bottle marked 2 was carefully mixed with fifty percent water. Bottle 3 had only one third gin, the remainder of the bottle being topped up with water. At first I did not understand the need for this until the clergyman, explained to me one day, and as only a Scotsman could justify, "Well my boy, with most of my guests wishing to partake of my hospitality to some excess, and with no regard to me being an impoverished parson of limited means, the first or even the second Gin and Tonic is acceptable and poured from number one, but when they exceed this they do not fully appreciate the real quality of what they are imbibing and thus the second bottle and by the time they start on their fifth or sixth glass they are far too intoxicated to appreciate what they are consuming and thus the third bottle." I have to say I was impressed with his thinking and respected this canny clergyman from that day on.

There were other residents who had their finicky ways, such as the departed Major with whom I began my story. None however were more eccentric than the rather infamous Mrs Benson and Mr Myers.

One day I was called to attention by Mr Morris. "Griffin as a young and well educated public school boy I have just the job for you that should be of no problem, and will help with your experience and broaden your knowledge of life as you climb the management ladder."

"Thank you Mr Morris," I responded with some hesitation.

I had by now already learned that such an introduction was normally followed by a challenge that none of his team of 'real' waiters wished to accept. I had also learned that on the other hand, it was best to volunteer for any mission as they were unavoidable and by accepting you did at least gain 'Brownie points' that could be cashed in to your advantage at a later date. "Mario, as you know, is taking a holiday to visit his family back in Italy and will be away for six weeks and I want you to take over some of his resident guests."

I almost let out an audible gasp. "Not Mrs Benson?"

"Yes I am afraid so. But you will be fine, she loves young boys like you and anyway you will earn a little extra to boot."

Of all the guests in residence, Mrs Benson in suite 112 and her brother Mr Myers, whom she looked after in their adjoining suites, were renowned throughout the hotel for their demanding and eccentric ways. "I am sure you will impress her," As if to reassure me. "She wants to meet you, so best we get it over with." I had no choice in the matter so accepted my challenge as a *fait accompli* and followed Morris out of the pantry in the direction of Mrs Benson's suite.

Morris gave a hard knock on Mrs Benson's door. I waited for the reply. A further knock, again no reply. Morris cautiously opened the door. We entered a corridor that led to a further closed door at which we stopped and Morris knocked again, this time also announcing "Good morning Mrs Benson, Morris here."

A muffled, "Enter Morris."

As we gently opened the door I got a faint whiff of lavender. It took a few moments for my eyes to become accustomed to the darkness, although it was morning and a surprisingly sunny day. The curtains were partially drawn and the room was in semi darkness. It was filled with furniture unlike that which filled the other hotel rooms, but every item belonged to a previous century.

There sitting in a high backed chair was Mrs Benson, her gaze was firmly set on me. In that moment I realised that she resembled my fearsome grandmother who had terrified me in my childhood. She was dressed in a gown that came to her ankles in the Victorian style, heavy laced shoes, and an amber stone necklace. It struck me as she sat there she was actually not like my grandmother but more like Miss Havisham from *Great Expectations*. She was something of a recluse, and had not left her room for many years. "Madam, this is..." Morris was about to introduce me but was cut short.

"Come forward young man." Mrs Benson interrupted with no greeting and in a rather husky, gruff voice and perfunctory tone. "What's your name?"

"Griffin madam." I replied addressing her in the same manner as Morris, stepping slightly forward with my hand outstretched. "How do you do?"

She visibly recoiled at the sight of such a forward gesture, from a lowly waiter. "Where were you educated?" she responded as if challenging me.

"Lord Wandsworth College in Hampshire madam."
"Oh a minor public school I assume; never heard of it. And your father, what does he do?"
"He's with Lloyds."

This seemed to relax her a little. "In the city?" I was not able to reply as she continued to cross examine me. In any event she seemed content with this assumption. I am sure she would have been disappointed had I told her it was the commercial public bank, Lloyds Bank in Coventry and not Lloyds of London.

"So you are to replace Mario." It was a statement and not a question. "I believe that servants should be rewarded for good service, I will pay you threepence for breakfast, and sixpence for lunch and dinner."

There was a pause and I heard a slight cough from Morris.

"Thank you madam," I quickly responded.

"I demand absolute cleanliness at all times, so you will ensure that you thoroughly wash your hands should you use the lavatory, something young boys are not known to do." I was somewhat taken aback at such an instruction. "That's all, Morris will tell you your duties." With this we were dismissed.

We left her suite and Morris looked at me as the door closed behind us. "Well that seemed to go OK; but what were you thinking about by offering your hand? You are a waiter for God's sake. You never touch the guest, let alone shake their hand as if you were their equal."

My aunt's words to my mother that afternoon after my venture in the hotel restaurant came back to me: "Who on earth looks at a waiter?" Such was the role I was now to play, which I now took on board and regarded as a bit of theatrical fun and took no offence.

Over the next few months, Mario choosing not to return, I learned my duties and found that Mrs Benson took up most of my time which seemed acceptable to the rest of the team, who were happy not to have drawn the short straw to be looking after this demanding guest. It left them to look after the other guests who were, I later discovered, far more generous with their gratuities than the residents. My routine in looking after Mrs Benson and Mr Myers was the same every day, but was never short of its moments.

Mr Myers, Mrs Benson's brother, was equally eccentric; we believed that he was a member of the Myers Rum family from which he accumulated his wealth but that was never confirmed. He was a keen horseman and owned a horse which was stabled in one of the 'Martello Towers' that were built along the South Coast to repulse the possible Napoleonic invasion. The horse, George Henri, was very old and slow and was brought to the front of the hotel each day by the chauffeur, Wally Hawes, whose main duties were to care for the horse and the car, a magnificent 1930s Rolls Royce. On occasions Wally would take Mr Myers for a gentle drive back and forth along the Eastbourne seafront. This in itself was something of an event as he insisted on bringing a small valise suitcase on each trip in which we all speculated he carried a set of clean underwear.

Wally was not permitted to exceed 20 miles per hour, which was to be his downfall. Some years later he parted company from Mr Myers when after much frustration at the speed restriction and other demands placed upon him, he decided enough was enough. Having to maintain such a speed he was constantly abused by other motorists who backed up behind him as he crawled at the designated snail's pace. After much horn honking and 'V' signs by irate motorists, the final straw for Wally was to be passed by an elderly woman in an Austin 7, who appeared most out of character for a woman of her years; at last being able to pass, she smiled and to Wally's amazement gave a one fingered salute. Such things were most out of keeping with gentrified Eastbourne. At this moment Wally lost it and gave a similar gesture in return, whilst putting his foot to the floor and bringing the graceful yet aging flying lady to a speed, a *'Spirit of Ecstasy'* that she would not have experienced in years. In doing so Wally left the Austin 7 in his wake.

Mr Myers, having first recovered from the G-forces that had propelled him back into his seat, scrambled to lean forward whilst shouting into his communicating device for Wally to "stop immediately". Naturally Wally ignored this. Being now in for a penny and in for a pound, he decided to see just how fast the magnificent machine would go. He sped along the seafront at a pace not seen before, enjoying the exhilarating experience of speed. Mr Myers was by now hammering on the glass window partition that separates master from servant, with ever increasing indignation demanding a stop to this madness. It was at this point Wally was reaching the end of the road known as 'King Edwards Parade' and turned sharply into South Cliff. He hurled the car into the curve and almost took the corner on two wheels, throwing the occupant in the rear against the door with the centrifugal force of this manoeuvre. Wally then accelerated back towards The Grand and home, with Mr Myers gesticulating madly, convinced Wally was trying to kill him. As the erstwhile chauffeur sped back in the direction of the hotel, pedestrians crossing the road jumped for their lives, and others looked on in amazement as the Rolls almost left the ground on entering the gates of The Grand Hotel.

Upon coming to rest before a stunned liveried doorman, Wally exited the car, dropping the keys in the palm of the doorman. "Sod it I resign." was Wally's only comment. Mr Myers, although somewhat pale and dishevelled managed to regain some composure as he lifted himself from the floor to the seat at the back of the car, and awaited the doorman's arrival to assist in his dignified exit from the car. "Can you park the car for me? My chauffeur is a little unwell and I do not think he will be returning". That should have been the end of Wally's fifteen years of service.

The build up to this event occurred over many years where his duties were somewhat difficult and on occasions demeaning to say the least. As mentioned another task was to collect the horse and bring him to the hotel entrance where Mr Myers had had the hotel's carpenter build a set of 'mounting steps'. Wally was required to hold the horse whilst Mr Myers mounted and then walk beside him as he progressed along a similar route as that which the Rolls Royce followed. He was armed with a small coal shovel, a hessian bag and a handful of carrots. In the event that the horse decided he would stop, Wally was required to tempt the aging horse into a forward motion with the carrots to continue his exercise. In a similar manner as the drives in the Rolls, speed was not an option and nothing more than a gentle walk required.

It was also Wally's duty to collect any droppings from the rear of the horse with the shovel and place them in the bag he carried. This was always of some amusement when viewed by the locals and tourists, watching the horse and master, followed by his man in chauffeur's outfit of cap, buttoned jacket, jodhpurs and knee high gaiters pass by. No doubt this did not sit well with Wally, who must have been horrified at the lack of dignity for a man who had been in service man and boy. [50]

The excellent manure was, on return to the hotel, deposited on the rose beds at the front of the building, and certainly added to the beauty of their colourful display. Mr Myers never ceased chiding the hotel for not discounting his bill for this supply of nutrients to the flower beds that he so generously provided.

As a final note, it appears that on his death, one condition stipulated within Mr Myers will was that his horse be put to death with nitrous oxide, better known as laughing gas. I believe this request was not allowed by the local vet, and the horse was advertised in the Horse & Hounds for sale at the princely sum of £500, and by all accounts was put out to pasture for what remained of his days.

I faced my first day with Mrs Benson with some trepidation, not least because of the stories I was now hearing about this reclusive woman. She was paranoid about cleanliness and demanded that every glass, plate and piece of cutlery was spotless, hence I spent much of my day simply polishing every item that was to be delivered to her suite.

My shift was adjusted to fit in with my duties and dear Mrs Benson. This allowed me to arrive in the morning at 8.00am in time to serve her breakfast at 8.30am. I worked through until 1.30pm and was then off until 5.00pm and worked until her dinner was cleared; if the dinner service was quiet I would finish my shift at around 8.00pm.

The first task was to check the tray was properly laid and all items spotless. Breakfast consisted of two three-and-a-half minute boiled eggs, four slices of rye crispbread, and a pot of Earl Grey tea. Meals were only delivered to Mrs Benson's suite.

The time came for delivering the breakfast. Sharp at 8.30am I knock on the first door of the suite. No reply; there never was. Knock again, after which enter and approach the second door and knock again. "Come in Griffin". I enter to find Mrs Benson, dressed as on our first meeting and in the same high backed chair, but this time with a small table on casters in front of her. "Put it here." She indicates to the table.

I obey. "Good morning" I say as I position the tray carefully before her. No acknowledgement of my greeting, just a stare at the tray and silence. She then takes each item on the tray and holds it up to examine it, carefully returning the item to its place once checked. Then the egg spoons.

"These are dirty. Take them away," she stated in her usual gruff voice. This was patently rubbish as I had paid particular attention to ensuring they were spotless.

"I am sorry, I will do it immediately." I depart back to the pantry.

"What's the problem?" Morris greets me as I entered.

"The bloody spoons," I answer.

"Ah she's winding you up as the new boy. Best get back fast before she decides to find something else."

"But I need to get new clean spoons..."

"Rubbish; there is nothing wrong with the spoons; go on off you go."

So clutching the same spoons which I placed on a side plate I return to the suite. I enter, she takes the spoons, closely examines each.

"In future make sure they are clean."

"I am sorry madam I will take greater care in future". I assume this is the end of the matter and I am about to leave.

"The eggs are cold, get me fresh ones."

I am about to protest but wisely think better of it. I take the eggs and return for the second time to the pantry where again Morris was waiting, this time with a smile, in his hand a silver bowl with four eggs.

"Eggs cold?"

"Yes, the silly old cow."

"Best get back; don't let her get to you, she's just trying you out. Be ready for the tea being cold".

As I enter her suite for the third time, eggs in hand, I immediately take the initiative. "Mrs Benson, your eggs" and without hesitating "Your tea must be cold can I replace it?"

Surprised, she stares at me. "No thank you, it is perfectly acceptable".

I gather from this that it was a request about to be made but having beaten her to it she was not going to give me the pleasure of pre-empting her. I am about to depart when I sense it would be a mistake and I should wait until I am dismissed. I stand there as she carefully peels the shell off two of the eggs and lightly butters two of the crispbreads, pours a cup of Earl Grey tea and then picks up a small bell that was on a little table beside her chair.

We wait; after a minute, the door from the adjoining suite slowly opens through which an elderly man in slippers and heavy dressing gown appears. "Morning dear."

No response from Mrs Benson. He moves forward, picks up his cup of tea and boiled eggs and crispbread and with no further sound shuffles back through the door from whence he came. So that was Mr Myers, I assume. I am now dismissed to return the pantry where once again Morris waits, teapot in hand,

"Here you are lad, she's really giving you the run around on your first day".
"That's OK she is fine."

Surprised, Morris says, "She always asks for another pot of tea when she is in this mood."

"No, she is fine."
"Are you sure?"
"Yep fine," I reply somewhat smugly.
"What happened? How did you get out of it? She has never sent a new boy back only twice."
"Well after you told me there would be something else, I thought it could only be the tea, so I got in first and offered to replenish

it, and she was so taken aback at losing the upper hand, said no."

"Bloody hell that is brilliant. You will go far my lad, well done."

As this exchange occurred the other waiters were listening and all chimed in with their congratulations, as it seemed I was the first to get one over on the truculent woman. Feeling rather pleased with myself I returned to polishing the glasses and plates and my other duties, such as stirring Lady Prince's jug of water, watering the gin of our resident clergyman and preparing myself for my next bout with Mrs Benson.

Lunch was served to Mrs Benson at 12.30pm. I first met Wally, the chauffeur, when he delivered a packet of frozen Birds Eye broad beans for Mr Myers' lunch. I was required to boil these for four minutes and place them in a bowl. At 12.25pm the 'ding' of the dumb waiter rang, a small lift that came directly from the kitchen below to the room service pantry. As I opened the lift door, there on the shelf was a silver salver and under a cloche were four grilled double lamb cutlets ready for delivery. Placing them on the prepared tray, I was off for my next visit to Mrs Benson.

As I entered, following the previously established procedure, I found Mrs Benson sitting as for breakfast behind her table. I placed the tray before her and she proceeded to check each item for cleanliness. To my surprise nothing was said. Once done, she just sat and looked at me. What was to happen next I wondered, starting to panic, then I realised: remove the cloche that covered the cutlets. Seeing my hesitation she now appeared rather pleased; she now had the upper hand.

She closely inspected each cutlet, holding it by the little paper frills we'd put on the ends of the bones, *papillotes* as they were known, a ridiculously fussy affectation of the time.

"They are too greasy; wash them."

"Wash them?"

"Yes, wash them," she replied as if it was a perfectly normal request. "There under the tap." Her bony finger pointed in the direction of a small hand basin. I picked up the dish of cutlets and rinsed each of them under the tap as instructed.

She then placed two washed cutlets on each of the plates. She rang her bell and after a moment Mr Myers appeared again, this time dressed in a pair of riding jodhpurs and a hacking jacket. I stood back as he proceeded to position himself in front of the table.

"With or without?" Mrs Benson enquired

"With." came his reply. She handed him a plate and taking his bowl of broad beans, he once again retired. I was once again dismissed.

"Did you have to wash the cutlets?" Morris greeted me with a statement rather than a question.

"Yes," I replied, now ceasing to show any surprise as to this woman's requests who I was fast coming to believe was completely batty.

"But what on earth was the 'with or without' question she asked of Mr Myers?"

"No idea; we have never worked it out."

Dinner was served at 7.15pm. Two Dover soles, grilled, and a bottle of Malvern Water.

At 6.55pm, the dumb waiter went 'ding' and I collected the silver salver for delivery to Mrs Benson. Having inspected the tray, cutlery and glasses, she turned her attention to the silver salver. On this occasion I had removed the cloche with something of a flourish. The two soles were carefully examined, first by prodding the flesh and then carefully lifting the eyelid of one of the fish. Her gaze once again fell on me. "These fish have never seen the Straits of Dover in their life, take them away."

This comment had no response that I could think of, so I complied and headed back to the pantry. Morris was there to greet me. "What's wrong with the fish?"

"Seems they have never seen the Straits of Dover."

He took the silver salver, carefully swapped them over and placed them under the grill for a couple of minutes. He handed them back to me and sent me back. Surely she will know they are the same ones? We couldn't have ordered and cooked two fresh fish in this time?

As I entered the room and placed them before her, she did not even take a cursory glance at the 'new' fish. With an impressively deft movement she just removed the flesh off the bone and placed it on the two plates. Again, she rang her bell to summon her brother, who dutifully appeared, this time in his pajama trousers and a velvet smoking jacket. "With or without?"

"Without," and he returned to his suite without a further word.

These meals never changed; they were served every day. As time went by the relationship warmed between us. This was unheard of. I feel she rather enjoyed being waited upon by a young Englishman rather than a foreigner. It was not that she was racist, but I feel that she was not keen on those with whom we had been at war only a few years before. I suspect that she lost her husband in the war.

On one occasion, I felt the relationship was at a point where I started to have small conversations with her. Strangely, this was instigated by her on one occasion when she asked at breakfast one day what Corn Flakes were. I explained about the variety of cereals that were now available in supermarkets. This naturally raised the question "What are supermarkets?"

I was amazed that she genuinely appeared to have little knowledge of the developing consumer market. After I explained some of the ways of the post-war world and the 1960s in which we lived, she seemed fascinated with my tales and would ask questions and raise topics each time I served her meals. On one of my weekly visits when I stood before her to receive my remuneration, most weeks amounting to 12 shillings and 9 pence, I mustered the courage to ask "Mrs Benson, forgive me asking, but why don't you occasionally venture out of your suite? I am sure you would be fascinated to see a little of the outside world."

I had rather expected to be admonished for stepping above my station but surprisingly she seemed to consider my question. After a short pause she looked at me. "Who would accompany me? A lady such as I could not venture out alone."

In a moment of madness I replied "Well I would be happy to if you like."

Again a pause while she reflected on the suggestion and I regretted immediately what I had just impulsively proposed. "No I don't think I could as I don't have any shoes to wear outside."

Again, I was determined to challenge her further, "I am sure you must have some. If not, then why not venture out to buy some".

"I will think about it".

I was about to leave when she called me back. "Before you go can you pass those to me". She was pointing to the mantelpiece above the fireplace. I went over to see what she was referring to and apart from two silver picture frames and a pair of silver candlesticks, there was nothing other than three small rocks that I first thought were meteorites that as children we had on occasion found with great excitement.

"These?" pointing to the rocks.
"Yes, bring them to me." Holding them in the palm of my hand I offered them to her. She made no attempt to take them from my outstretched hand.
"Do you know what they are?"
"No Mrs Benson, what are they?"

She now looked me straight in the eye with something of a smile. "They are my gallstones." I was stunned and almost threw them to the ground. I somehow managed to take the few paces to return them whence they came, with a weak "Really?" Once returned, I did wait no longer and retired from the suite, almost breaking into a run back to the pantry.

"That fucking woman is crazy," I vented as I scrubbed my hands under the tap.
"What's the problem?" Morris enquired.
"She gave me her gallstones? Can you believe it?"
"Ah, the gallstones," came his knowing reply.

Morris then went on to explain how she had been diagnosed with a gallstone problem a few years earlier, and required an operation to resolve the problem. She didn't want to go to a hospital for this operation and came to an arrangement with the management to have the procedure carried out in the hotel. A nearby suite was converted into an operating room and her Harley Street surgeons arrived from London to carry out the required procedure, the trophies of which were now displayed on her mantelpiece for all to admire. Having now heard the tale I was not holding out any hope of her now venturing out to purchase a pair of shoes to enable her to discover what the outside world had to offer.

It was therefore with great surprise that a few days after this event, I entered her suite and she announced that she had summoned her cobbler from London to travel to Eastbourne, and measure her for a new *last*, from which a new pair of walking shoes may be made. I was astounded. Was I to achieve something that no one else had even attempted? What would the outcome be? What responsibility now rested upon my shoulders? A few days later the cobbler duly arrived and I was called in to meet him, a little Jewish man who seemed delighted to meet me, the boy who had managed to arrange such an unexpected commission.

The weeks went by during which I asked about the progress of the shoes, thinking that she may well have had second thoughts and cancelled the order. Eventually a package was delivered to the hotel and the idea that the reclusive Mrs Benson might at last be seen about the hotel had become something of a talking point. I received a call from the concierge desk asking if I would care to deliver the parcel to Mrs Benson. I agreed and went down to collect it. I was met with some mixed comments from the desk, most fearing that I might have opened a can of worms by encouraging the woman to now start appearing in other areas of the hotel, creating mayhem with other members of staff.

Parcel in hand I delivered it to her suite. "The shoes have arrived. Shall I open the box?" I asked somewhat excitedly and presumptuously.

"No; place them over there and I will do it later."

The days went by and each time I entered I looked to see if the package had been opened but as yet the brown box was just sitting there. It was after about three weeks that I eventually saw the brown wrapping paper had been opened and the lid of the box was on the floor below. I was not sure whether to comment but eventually I could not resist. "How are the shoes?"

"Uncomfortable." With this single word, the episode of the shoes and the planned adventure of leaving her room came to an end.

There remained the final question that had to date eluded me. What was the significance of the 'with or without'? On my last delivery I positioned myself to one side when Mr Myers was summoned, where I might have a better view of the quiz set before Mr Myers each day. As Mrs Benson posed the question I noticed that her hands were beneath the table with a finger pointing up towards one of the plates. I then realised the game that was played out at each meal, as there may have been a question as to which plate held a slightly larger portion than the other. By pointing unseen, it became pot luck as to which meal would be given and therefore avoided any question as to who would receive the larger or smaller serving. A rather child-like game that they had no doubt played for years.

Now with the secret discovered I left the suite with some satisfaction. I would be unlikely to see such people come my way again as such guests were a dying breed. They left a rather empty space behind them, as a bygone era passed away.

Chapter 10

#coffins'n'corpses #cooks'n'kitchens #arsnic'n'oldlace

I n the 21st century, there is now immense enthusiasm for food and cooking. Menus sport colourful and exotic dishes. In the 60s, however, menus were the complete opposite: bland and unexciting. The one thing that seems not to have changed dramatically is the choice of food served for afternoon tea: cucumber or smoked salmon sandwiches, scones with jam and clotted cream, sweet cakes and, a favourite, Battenberg Cake. This was only supplemented at holiday times when the hotel became full of Jewish guests down from London. It always amused me that it was the time of the Christian holidays when the hotel was at its busiest with guests from the Jewish community; at the time this phenomenon raised eyebrows in some circles. Macarons were all that were requested during these periods, and the pastry department could hardly keep up with the demand.

After serving afternoon tea with macarons to one of our Jewish guests in his room, I retired from his presence and headed off duty. Unfortunately I forgot to pass on this order to the waiter on duty to enable him to clear the tray, and I left for my afternoon break. It was not until the following morning that I took a call from the switchboard who could not get a reply from the man, and his sister had some concerns. Could I go and check that all was well?

I entered the room only to find a small frail man lifeless in an armchair with macarons around his feet and crumbs all over his chest. Apparently he had choked on the biscuit, which caused his demise. By now such things no longer horrified me. This was the fourth death I had encountered and it was a completely normal outcome when so many very elderly guests visited the hotel. I called the switchboard and reported the sad 'departure' of the guest. This call then set in motion a well-rehearsed routine that we all understood.

Management were advised, calls were placed to the hotel doctor, the police and finally to the undertaker, who were accustomed to handling such events at hotels in Eastbourne. Such was the routine of these events, that we had a particular room service trolley slightly longer than normal that would accommodate the tin box that would accompany the undertakers when they arrived. They would remove the body, discreetly tucked under the tablecloth that cloaked the tin box with the corpse hidden beneath, as it was wheeled along the corridor out of sight of any passing guest.

This particular morning, being a very busy breakfast service due to the holiday, the lift was in high demand to deliver the trolleys and trays to the rooms, most of them laden with hot cooked English breakfasts of bacon, eggs, sausages, tomatoes and fried bread. This was a substantial meal and one preferred to be taken in the room by the guests who were of the Jewish persuasion, rather than in the restaurant. This enabled those enjoying their bacon and eggs to avoid offending the sensitivities of those of their faith who might be slightly more observant of the dietary requirements. Ironically, there weren't actually *any* who were so assiduous, apart from the occasional rabbi who dropped into the hotel.

I reported my macaron fatality to Morris. "Have you called the switchboard?" he asked as he busily sorted the next tray to be delivered.

"Yes all done."
"OK, then get this tray up to 308." And so the life of breakfast delivery continued.

The orders kept arriving and departing. It was about an hour later that I entered the pantry to find Morris pressing the lift button repeatedly, with increasing frustration.

"Who the hell has hijacked our lift? Where is it?"

At that moment the grinding of the motor and wires could be heard as the lift appeared. As the gates were pulled back, there stood the undertaker, the tin box and the trolley. Morris lost his cool, something very rarely seen.

"What the bloody hell are you doing using my lift at this time? It's breakfast and we are sodding busy getting food to the living. Your guest isn't going anywhere nor would he care if his breakfast were cold, whereas all my other guests would. Now get that bloody thing out of my lift."

With a look of stunned surprise the undertaker quickly removed the trolley, the box and himself from the lift. Not addressing anyone in particular, he asked, "Where is 214? Can anyone let me into the room?" As I was the one to discover the body and had no breakfasts to deliver, I volunteered and he collected his sad cargo. He arrived back at the pantry and the door banged as it was pushed open by the trolley followed by the undertaker, looking somewhat nervous. "Can I use the lift now?" he asked as Morris also re-entered the pantry.

"What is that bloody thing doing here, you're not using my lift until the breakfast rush is over."

The undertaker looked nonplussed and equally frustrated. "What am I meant to do with it then?" he asked, with an edge to his request.

"Stick it over there out of the way and come back later to collect it," growled Morris.

Angrily, the undertaker pushed the trolley to one side and left, muttering imprecations and something about telling the manager about the lack of cooperation. It was at this moment that the phone started going crazy. I answered it and heard the agitated switchboard operator.

"For God's sake what are you guys up to, I have had Mr Goldberg on the phone going ballistic as he hasn't had his breakfast yet, and he and his kids are due to be picked up soon by friends to go out for the day."
"Leave it with me and I will get it to him ASAP."

I found the docket for six English breakfasts that should have been delivered half an hour ago. I shouted the order down to the kitchen and asked for it as soon as possible, and thankfully they were quick to respond. At that moment Derek, one of the new waiters appeared. "Derek, thank God, can you lay up a large trolley for six for Mr Goldberg in suite 132?" The phone rang again with a call to deliver some more butter to another room,

"Griffin, you're free, take it up and get back fast, we're starting to lose it."

The butter was delivered and I returned, bumping into the undertaker as I entered the pantry. "OK you silly buggers, where is my trolley, who's hidden it?" We looked at one another and with rising horror and panic I said, "Where's Derek?"

"He has taken the breakfast up to the Goldbergs."
"On what and how long ago?"
"You must have passed him seconds ago."

Morris started to tap into the panic in my voice. At that moment we both looked at the undertaker and then at each other and in unison cried "Fucking Hell!"

"Quick get down to 132 as fast as you can."

I was out of the door before he had completed the sentence. I took the fire stairs three at a time. The door to the first floor swung open with a crash and I sprinted down the corridor to see Derek knocking on the door. As I arrived out of breath, Derek looked at me with confusion. Mr Goldberg threw open the door.

"About bloody time too." He was not happy with the delay.
"I am sorry Mr Goldberg," Derek announced. "Can I set the table up for you?"
"That's OK, just leave the trolley and we can eat it off here."
Mr Goldberg and Derek started to guide the trolley into the suite.
"Er, I am sorry sir, we couldn't do that, allow us to lay it up for you," I interjected.
"That's OK, we're in a rush."
"It will only take a second, that's why I was sent down too," I added.
"Oh alright then if you must, but hurry up and get on with it."

During this exchange Derek was moving the trolley back and forth totally confused and bewildered as to what was happening. With the table laid we then attempted to leave. "You can leave the trolley behind and clear it when we go out". Derek started to leave, when I shouted "I am sorry sir, we are so busy I am sure you understand, that we need the trolley to serve other guests..."

"Oh all right take it with you but don't expect a tip. Now please just get out so we can finish our breakfast."

As we pulled the trolley back into the corridor, Derek looked at me, and asked with irritation "What the hell was that all about?"

I said nothing but lifted the tablecloth draping the trolley to reveal the large tin box. There was a sharp intake of breath followed by "Oh shit." No further conversation was necessary on the walk back to the pantry. We mused on what might have been the outcome had we not retrieved the box, and if Mr Goldberg had been curious about its contents. I aged a number of years that day.

We also had a pet policy that was extended to our guests. Englishmen have always been known for their love of animals; after all, at that time it was illegal to beat your dog and yet quite acceptable to beat your child or wife. *Spare the rod and spoil the child* was regularly quoted and often enacted. It would be regarded as utterly unacceptable by many of the women to leave the pet pooch at home whilst they enjoyed a luxury five star stay at the seaside, even at the daily charge of 7s 6d. To leave the husband behind would be a different matter altogether.

The hotel would attend to every pet's needs as carefully as that of their masters and mistresses. There was a special menu for both dogs and cats; one with fillet steak prepared in different ways, bones and dog biscuits prepared by the pastry department, the other with River Tay Salmon on offer. Obviously pets in the room could also lead to possible hygiene problems, and to assist with this a special letter was carefully worded to handle such situations:

'Dear Mrs Hamilton Smith;

I hope that you and Toby have settled in.

I am pleased to offer Toby his own special menu which may be ordered through our room service and delivered to your suite at any time during the day.

Whereas I am certain Toby is an exceedingly well trained and well behaved member of the family, it is understood that within his strange surroundings, accidents may happen. In such an unfortunate event, I am pleased to have supplied you with a soda syphon. This should, in case of such an incident, be sprayed liberally over the offending area, after which please immediately call the housekeeper, who will take appropriate action to ensure all is returned to normal for yours and Toby's comfort.

To further assist, our concierge is happy to assist with Toby's daily exercises if you should require.

If there is anything further you or Toby require, please do not hesitate to advise me.

Yours sincerely
The General Manager'

Needless to say that such calls to the housekeeper were handled but never welcomed, even by the most ardent pet lover on the staff.

Another lovely Irish woman crossed my path at this time. Her name was Hanna, she was in her late forties, and coincidentally bore the same surname as myself, Hanna Griffin. The surname brought us together in a way that would otherwise never have occurred between a trainee manager and a chambermaid. She was a large and very jolly woman and would often stop me in the corridor for a little chat.

One morning she told me of something that had occurred the previous day and was fearful that it might lead to her dismissal from her job in the event that the guest complained. The man in question was a fairly regular guest at the hotel, who also had a reputation for shocking the female staff who were servicing his room. Once he had appeared before a young woman who was cleaning his room, with nothing more than a towel around his waist. With his hands on his hips he pulled in his rather wide girth, allowing the towel to fall about his feet. "Oh dear." was his only comment, with no effort made to retrieve his towel, he just stood before her nude. The young and innocent Irish woman screamed and ran from the room, the guest laughing in her wake. As you might imagine this became a talking point amongst the chambermaids, and hence a more mature maid was appointed to service his room on future visits. This task fell to Hanna.

On the morning in question the guest had called for house-keeping to deliver some additional towels, and Hanna set forth with them. On arriving at his door she found the daily paper awaiting his collection. Picking it up, she knocked on the door. "Come in," he called, and Hanna entered. He was lying in his bed. "Ah, my paper."

It was at this point that Hanna noticed that his hands were beneath the sheet, and the sheet was rising up and down with some speed around the region of his waist. Being aware of the man's proclivity to shock young women in a certain manner, she assumed that this was now his intention. Without a second thought she dropped the towels and in one fell swoop, raised the newspaper and brought it down with the force that only an Irish woman of her stature could, upon the rise and fall of the offending action taking place beneath the sheets. This stunned the man, who let out a yell, both of surprise and no doubt pain. "You dirty old bugger," chided Hanna.

He slowly raised his hands up from under the sheets holding a pair of spectacles. Hanna realised he had been polishing them on the bed sheet in anticipation of reading his newspaper. Both were embarrassed and Hanna departed the room without a further word. I assumed the chap set about, with some discomfort, reading his paper.

After a few days and with no summons of Hanna to the Head Housekeeper's office, all seemed to be forgotten. From that day the story entered the annals of humorous guest anecdotes from housekeeping that would not be forgotten.

At another time, a young chambermaid, who was rather well endowed, found that due to her physical attributes the buttons on her uniform were constantly challenged at their maximum pressure point. Custom dictated that chambermaids carried a master key which, like a watch chain, was attached to the uniform and hooked to the top button. The protocol was that any staff entering a guest room would first knock on the door, awaiting a call to enter, if not heard would knock a second time and once again if not acknowledged, would place the key in the door, cautiously open the door and clearly announce 'Housekeeping'.

One morning whilst delivering something to a guest's room, the young woman obediently followed the custom, and on not hearing from the guest, put the key in the door ready to enter the room. Having just placed the key in the lock, she was startled when the guest at the same moment suddenly threw open the door. The key was firmly in the lock and attached to the chain and also to her uniform. As the door was pulled open, it popped the buttons from the top to the waist of her uniform, baring her torso to the surprised guest. At the same time the door pulled her almost into his arms. Our only regret was that none of us witnessed this exposure, other than the surprised and, as we thought, very lucky guest.

My training in room service was now coming to an end and I would move to more general waiting in the restaurant and banqueting. Another trainee had arrived to take over my former duties. I had enjoyed my time with Morris and the team, and certainly had some eye-opening experiences in my repertoire. As my grandmother would say from her Lancashire roots "There's nowt so queer as folk". In fact, my whole career was proof positive of this adage. The class system was very much alive; if you were poor, you would more than likely be locked up and regarded as a criminal or a nutter for certain behaviour, but if you had money and position, you were simply regarded as eccentric.

Apart from occasionally returning to the department to help in times of need, I said farewell to Morris, Atfield, Pritchard and the team, all of whom had played a fundamental role in my initiation to the rich tapestry of life in the hospitality industry.

I found myself back in the kitchen, under the watchful eye of Les King, who - for an executive chef - was a remarkably likeable man. Perhaps the toupee sticking out from under his tall chef's toque gave away a little of his dignity and made him more approachable. [51]

The kitchen was an area to which I had hoped I would not be required to return, but trainees went where trainees were told. Then, as now, 'trainee' was the title given to an underpaid and overworked employee who had no option but to comply with management demands. In this case, Signor Chero, the breakfast chef was returning to his homeland, and left a space behind that a trainee was expected to fill, as cooking breakfast was a simple job. As this task took up only a small part of the day there were more jobs that could be allotted.

My duties were explained and I spent a few days learning the tasks of the breakfast chef. Simple enough; grilling trays of bacon, sausages and tomatoes. Frying, scrambling or poaching eggs. There was rarely a demand for anything more exotic, except to add a sprig of parsley as the plate left the kitchen destined for the guests in the restaurant, this was when all meals were served and the cost saving strategy of the buffet breakfast was yet to be accepted.

The great thing about working in the kitchen was that one never went hungry. We enjoyed the same food that was served to the guests who were paying seventeen shillings and sixpence (or 75 pence) for the *Table d'Hote* menu, consisting of seven choices, or even more should they venture on to the *a la carte* menu which included caviar at one guinea or twenty one shillings. Ordering *a la carte* was rarely allowed to happen, in fact actively discouraged, as both waiting staff and the kitchen hated deviating from the prepared routine of the 'TDH' menu. [52]

Trainees were given a tough time from the chefs, but not as tough as that doled out to the young apprentices, who were naïve and without any knowledge or experience. They were always very young and sometimes not very bright. All were terrified of the chefs and the discipline and the pressure in the kitchen. Some of the 'pranks' played on these young men included being sent down to the pastry department for what they understood was a measuring scale. On asking for a 'Long Weight' they got the usual answer from the patissier, "I'm busy, go stand over there." After about ten minutes, during which the apprentice was becoming more nervous at the displeasure he would incur from the chef who had sent him on his errand, the patissier would look at the lad and growl, "OK bugger off, you have had your 'Long Wait'". It was only as they ran off that they would shamefacedly realise they had been the brunt of a very old and hoary joke.

At other time apprentices would learn the art of 'chopping flour' (where sieving would have been the answer); suffer being sent to the larder with a tray of egg shells with a request to get them filled; having to confront the fishmonger and tell him the blue lobsters he'd delivered were ruined by sea spray as they should be red... and the final indignity, during the holidays with many Jewish clients, being told to cut the balls off the matzah, as they were needed for a special soup. The apprentice would invariably be asked if there was any other part of the matzah that could be eaten, as it seemed a waste if it was only the balls that were eaten. The idea was pinched from a much published story attributed to Marilyn Monroe when married to Arthur Miller.

The other job I was entrusted with was that of The Aboyeur. On being told this I was completely baffled. "What the hell does an Aboyeur do?" I asked.

"He shouts," the chef replied. I realized that I had found my true forte: a job where I could shout at people... and they couldn't shout back.

The restaurant of The Grand Hotel was simply known as 'The Restaurant', and no attempts were made in those days to create something more marketable. The closest one came to such names within a hotel would be something like 'The Savoy Grill'. 53

What we lacked in creativity for restaurant names, we made up for in the staff titles. The *Maitre d'Hotel* who supervised the restaurant, was not a man to cross, either as a member of staff and even more so a guest. I say 'man' without hesitation, as this was an unwritten law; women most certainly were not seen as suitable employees within a restaurant or cocktail bar. I argued about this with a number of general managers as I climbed the management ladder. I believed that often young women were far more suited to such work and were most certainly appreciated by the male guests, who were in larger numbers. By tradition, women were seen as only suitable for reception and housekeeping duties, and certainly not management! I am proud to say I had a hand in changing this later in my life. [54]

Other eloquent titles for the staff included *chef de salle* for the head waiter, of which there were several, each with responsibility for their own section of the restaurant. The *chef de vin* or *sommelier* was the wine waiter. Next down the chain were *chefs de rang*, waiters, and finally *commis de rang*, or busboys, as Americans call them. They were the lowest of the low and were the runners, cleaners and polishers for the *chefs de rang*. Naturally this was the role that I would fill. On my first day I was issued with a long starched white apron and retained my Hardy Amies jacket. I was introduced to the *maitre d'*. "Put your hands out; cut your nails and get rid of that filthy nicotine off your fingers and come back when you have done it."

Not a good start.

I found a pumice stone and scrubbed off the offending nicotine. In keeping with the fashion at the time I was a heavy smoker, an addiction that was not yet seen as a disgusting habit. I returned to the restaurant and stood before the *maitre d'*, hands outstretched for inspection like a naughty schoolboy. "Make sure you come to my restaurant smartly dressed, clean with perfect fingernails, and polished shoes. I am surprised at you, a trainee manager. What sort of example do you think you were setting?"

I was duly admonished. He then smiled; "Right let's get you sorted; Mr Stapley, meet your new boy." Bill Stapley was a head waiter, he had started at The Grand in October 1946 when I was eight months old and in nappies, and by his look I might be still wearing them. As quickly as I had been passed down the line from the *maitre d'*, so the head waiter passed me down to the *chef de rang*, Giovanni. Not mister, just Giovanni.

It turned out that all the waiting staff were Italian, the preferred choice, or Spanish, who were now more available as the Italians were all departing to set up their own restaurants. " 'ello, what's your name?" Giovanni asked in a thick Italian accent as he approached me.

"Griffin."

"A trainee manager eh? You won't last long."

Another indication of the contempt in which trainees seemed to be held. I had some understanding as to his feelings. Waiters in those days were highly skilled and it was seen as a career after many years of training; yet young men like me, 'trainees', came with an expectation to learn his skills in a few months only to then become a manager and possibly his boss.

This contempt was not helped by the cultural and class divide. Trainees never mixed off duty with any of the general staff; and even on duty we had little contact. We had our own restaurant, 'The Stewards Room', we never ate with the rank and file in the 'Staff Canteen'. We had our own bedrooms in a separate house, and were never expected to sleep four to a room in the hotel's basement as the regular staff did. We also had other privileges not extended to general staff. It always sat a little uncomfortably with me; but I accepted it, as that was the way it was. After all, most of them were foreigners, I supposed.

Working in The Restaurant was very different to room service. It was harder and less fun, with little chance to get to know anyone, guest or staff. I walked miles each day and spent much of the time just cleaning up after Giovanni, doing the polishing and laying of the eight tables for which we were responsible. Endless pieces of cutlery, glass and china had to be laid with great precision. "Go get me some teaspoon," Giovanni ordered.

I trotted off to the silver room where a team of three spent the day washing and polishing all the hotel's silver, that I always had to polish again. "Can I have some teaspoons please," I politely asked

"...'ow many?" came the reply in a heavy Greek accent.

"Oh, about twelve," I guessed, having failed to establish this.

"...'aven't got any," he replied. Obviously untrue as there was a box beside him with dozens of new shining teaspoons.

"But you have them there," thinking he may not have understood me.

"...'aven't got any," he repeated, without looking up.

I tried a third time only to receive the same negative response. I returned to Giovanni to be greeted with "Where are my spoons?" As I tried to explain he interrupted, "Just go back and get them." Yet again I tried to no avail and very nervously returned to try and explain my lack of success. Again, I got little sympathy from Giovanni. "Are you bloody stupid or something? If you can't look after me, I ain't going to look after you."

I started to learn the system. Although there was a gratuity of 12% added to hotel guest accounts, it was normal that many guests, especially those from 'outside', tipped the waiters individually in cash. From these tips the waiter would pay the head waiter a percentage who ensured he had 'good' and 'generous' guests directed to his tables. The head waiter in turn paid the maitre d' a percentage to ensure these guests were shared equally. Last of all were the commis who were looked after with a very small percentage, providing they looked after their bosses: the waiters. This is what it appeared I was failing to do. "Are you looking after the guys in the silver room?"

"Er no, I didn't realise I had to; anyway, how do I do that?"

Looking at me as if I was completely stupid, "My God you are stupid. Don't you know anything? If you haven't got money, you smoke, yes? Then give him some fags. Now go get my spoons!"

I felt into my pocket for a packet of my Players Cigarettes. Armed with knowledge I returned yet again to the silver room. I was greeted shortly with "Wot you want again?"

"Er sorry I meant to give you something."

"OK wot?"

I offered out my half full packet of Players. "You trainees always have good fags," with which he emptied the lot in his shirt breast pocket. I was about to protest as they were all the cigarettes I possessed and had little money to buy more until payday, but then thought better of it. "Can I have some teaspoons now?"

"OK what you want?"

"Twelve teaspoons if I may."

He looked in his box of spoons and counted out. "OK, 'ere you are."

Back in the restaurant I handed my hard won silver over to Giovanni. "Why you take so long?" was the only comment I got for my efforts. All I had left was my concern for the future and how to satisfy my nicotine craving until my next pay packet was handed to me.

The next few months were not enjoyable. Although I may have become fitter with the miles I walked each day at the beck and call of Giovanni, I was not a great fan of exercise and it left me unimpressed. I was however given a little more responsibility: I was allowed to serve coffee and on occasions allowed to help guests maintain the standards expected of guests who dined with us.

It was the *maitre d'* who spoke with me on one occasion. "Sadly our guests of today do not have the breeding they once had, so it is up to us to assist them through the trials of the correct etiquette as to manners, and even the process of using the correct implement with which he consumes his meal." Thus it was that on the odd occasion I found it necessary to, most tactfully and discreetly, as the guest was about to commit the great sin of taking up the wrong knife or fork, to gently take the offending implement from his hand as he picked it up with some nervous uncertainty, and quietly whisper, "I am sorry sir, would you care to use this fork, as I have noticed the one you are holding is not as clean as it should be."

This was most often met with a grateful smile and rarely questioned. It was often followed with a hesitant look in my direction for confirmation of future cutlery choices as well. The service of coffee was quite a ritual. On one occasion a rather sweet elderly lady asked for tea in preference to coffee after her meal. I felt a little churlish in my standard response. "I am so sorry madam, only coffee is served after the meal; however should you prefer tea I am happy to arrange for it to be served to you in the Lounge."

Somewhat nervously she replied "No, of course, coffee would be fine".

In the summer, with no air conditioning to meet a rare hot English day, a busy Sunday lunch could be quite overwhelming with the heat, not only for ourselves but the guests as well. On such days, it was not unusual for a guest to remove his jacket. This was regarded as the ultimate act of poor breeding, as an Englishman should always bear himself with style and dignity under situations of utmost discomfort. Was it not Noel Coward who sang *Mad dogs and Englishmen go out in the midday sun*? Even in the tropics an Englishman would always wear his jacket. On such occasions when this rule was transgressed, one would stand behind the guest who had placed his jacket on the back of his chair, take the offending attire and clearly hold it up for all to see and announce "May I assist you on with your jacket sir?" It was said as a command rather than a request, and never questioned, with the guest meekly obeying the 'request'.

It was all part of showing who was really in charge; any indiscretion by a guest was rapidly pounced upon to enforce our rule and authority. Far from our positions being seen as servile, we were in fact in total command; we were the real masters.

While working in the restaurant I met another man of interest. One day Giovanni pointed to one of our tables. "'Dat's Bodkin Adams." he said as if it was meant to mean something to me. I was a little puzzled, and his presence was indeed causing something of a stir amongst the staff and a few guests who gave furtive glances in the direction of his table. He was having lunch with one of the hotel's elderly ladies in residence. Was he a famous actor or politician? He looked more like a politician. He was short, rotund, bald and wore a pair of wire spectacles. Later in the steward's room I asked the chief concierge, who was of a rank to eat with us, who Bodkin Adams was. [55]

Turns out he was the infamous Dr John Bodkin Adams, a popular medical practitioner who was loved by many of the elderly ladies of Eastbourne, some who were residents of the hotel. He was a keen game shooter with an impressive collection of guns. Although he had started his initial house calls on a motorbike, he now had a number of rather special cars, including a Rolls Royce and an MG sports car. He was known for his 'bedside manner', his warmth, Irish charm, and his kindness to his patients became legendary.

A number of his patients died apparently from natural causes, and left him bequests, having rather surprisingly changed their wills. It was not unpredictable that the deceased woman's family members started to question these bequests and soon whispers started to do the rounds that he may well have hastened them to their graves with drugs he prescribed. The police investigated. Eventually he was charged with the murder of a Mrs Morrel who had left him the Rolls Royce and some silver.

Later Dr Adams was also charged with the murders of Mr and Mrs Hullet from whom he also received a large bequest. It became the talk of the town and he was tried at London's Old Bailey in March 1957. Due to the loss of some evidence, the suggestion of trying the wrong case, and a brilliant defence, he was found not guilty of murder. He was however later found guilty of falsifying cremation certificates, was fined and struck off the medical register.

It was some years later that, having regained his license in 1961, he was allowed to practice again, and was visiting a patient at The Cavendish Hotel in Eastbourne where I was by then in my position as deputy manager. He was a very likeable, charming and pleasant man and on his death in 1983, he was still considered by the police as being responsible for at least nine murders for which he was never convicted. In later years the press always made reference to him when other infamous practitioners in death came to light such as Dr Harold Shipman.

Chapter 11

#ladiesnight #cash'n'creditcards #cups'vs'buckets

The Grand hosted many prestigious events with a number of banquet rooms and as trainees we were often used to assist with their setup and service. Once I was instructed to set up for a VIP Masonic banquet. A new trainee and I were charged with the setup of the tables, which were to be a top table and three sprigs, rather like an 'E' shape. The tables to be set up were in those days rather old trellis tables about ten to twelve feet in length with legs at each end that folded to allow for easy storage. We set them up, covered them with starched tablecloths and laid out the cutlery according to the menu.

Being a Masonic ladies' night this was quite an extensive menu with a number of courses, and wines for each course. All the fine silver was laid out with careful measurement between each setting. The wine glasses were set according to which region the wine was from, with a Hock being served in a brown stemmed tall glass, and a Mosel being served in a green stemmed tall glass, which was frowned upon by some of the more traditional sommeliers on staff. The Claret, or Bordeaux, was served in one glass and the Burgundy in another.

With a dinner of this style most of our wine glasses were on the table. A large ball of string was then produced, rolled out and stretched to form a sort of horizontal 'plumb line'. Each glass down the length of the table was lined up against it to ensure all were perfectly aligned. This done, all that remained was to lay out the Masonic Lodges' 'family silver': a number of candelabras and epergnes that were displayed with pride upon the top table and each of the three sprigs,. Next we aligned the chairs and called the housekeeper to place the flower displays. The tables looked amazing, although loaded under the weight of all that was displayed. We were now free until our return to duty at 6.30pm to serve at the banquet.

We returned that evening and were given our stations, blissfully unaware of the terror that would shortly strike us. The pre-dinner drinks were served and the Masons and their ladies found their places. The liveried Toasmaster, resplendent in his red tailcoat, called upon the guests by way of three measured raps on the table with his gavel.

"Please be upstanding to receive your Worshipful Master, his good lady and their honoured guests." The top table filled up with due ceremony to the rhythmic applause of the remaining guests. Once all were seated, the Toastmaster yet again struck the table with his gavel. The Worshipful Master again rose, calling upon one of the lodge members of the clergy to say grace. The Toastmaster yet again struck the table. The speeches were endless and the Toastmaster continued to control the evening's speeches with his heavy gavel strokes.

It was after the main course was served that the terror began. The Toastmaster, in an attempt to bring to order and command the attention of a rather noisy room with guests all speaking loudly simultaneously, no doubt aided by the volume of wine consumed, gave a particularly heavy rap on the table with the gavel. I watched as, in slow motion, the long table near me started to move, gaining momentum as it collapsed. Rather like the fall of standing dominoes, the end sprig collapsed upon the knees of the seated guests and as it did so the glasses, plates and silverware cascaded like a crystal waterfall to the floor. The noise was deafening and then the room fell silent. The guests were in shock. The waiters rushed forward to assist guests and to reset the tables. I was still rooted to the floor.

"Give me a hand!" demanded one of the head waiters, as he struggled to bring the table back to its vertical position.

In doing so I could not help but notice how in his final movement to regain control of the table he - with one firm movement - slotted into place a bolt that locked the legs in place. Obviously. My eyes met those of my fellow trainee who had assisted with the setting up of the tables. Our gazes were full of panic, but he shrugged his shoulders and grimaced as we both realised neither of us had appreciated the purpose of the bolt. All the tables were just balanced upon the legs, awaiting a further nudge to set them in a domino collapse around the entire room.

The table was rapidly reset and apologies extended, glasses refilled and the dignity of the evening restored. My colleague and I however winced on every occasion the Toastmaster banged his gavel; we prayed for the speeches to cease and the evening to end. I felt my hair turning grey and a growing need to throw up, which I did in the lavatory the moment the last speech ended.

My absence was not noticed and thankfully the domino effect was attributed to the out of date tables. New banqueting tables were purchased from a company aptly named Lock'nline, much to the delight of the banqueting staff. I'll never know if anyone knew of our ineptitude, but this incident gave me confidence and broadened my comfort zone. If I could survive this, then anything that followed surely could not be as terrifying.

We also had conferences, especially in the winter months on which the hotel survived, one of which was for The London

Rubber Company, better known at the time for their production of the brand name Durex, which was the universally used
noun instead of the generic 'condom'. At the time these were
the main preventative for unwanted childbirth, the contraceptive pill being in its infancy. As with all consumer products,
marketing and sales were vital. This conference was for the
benefit of the company's sales force, with the planned launch
of a new product.

The room was laid out with chairs and displays, and at the
rear of the room was a large table with pamphlets and information on a new condom. I and another trainee followed the
organiser to carry boxes up from the store; although there must
have been twenty or more large cartons, they were quite light.
We made several trips and the organiser went about emptying
these boxes on the table, building a sizable mountain of what
we suddenly realised were individual condoms in a variety of
coloured packages. I nudged my colleague and naturally we
grinned in a most childish way. We couldn't help it then but
burst into laughter when the organiser turned to his young
woman assistant and asked "What do you think of Johnny's
display?"

He realised his *double entendre* when the young woman
blushed furiously. I can only assume that Johnny was head of
marketing and it was his idea to create the mountain of condoms to cause a reaction, appreciating the naive innocence of
the times and how the mountain would cause a stir. The impact
of the display of thousands of colourful condoms was unfortunately a little misjudged. It wasn't until the opening of the conference the following day that a major problem was revealed. On
entering the conference room that morning the organiser found
that his Himalayan mountain of condoms had diminished into a
much less impressive hill.

I could understand his annoyance as the impact would be lost and quite probably the hotel staff were to blame for the theft of several hundred condoms. In reality his biggest concern was the fact that these condoms were for display purposes only and were not tested. As a result, a most memorable letter was sent to every employee of the hotel, on the subject of birth control. We were advised that should we be in possession of any of the illicit items or offered them for sale, then we should not use them as they cannot be guaranteed to be a safe contraceptive. The irony of this theft was the fact that most of the staff were from staunch Latin or Irish Roman Catholic backgrounds. It was never recorded if the Eastbourne birth rate spiked nine months after The London Rubber Company's conference was held at The Grand.

The best bit of knowledge I gained in banqueting was through my task of providing feedback to management. This was simply done by being first to the cubicles in the men's toilet prior to the rush after any meal and before the commencement of the usual speeches. Safely ensconced behind the locked door of a cubicle, I sat quietly with a pencil and notepad, as the male guests attending the banquet crowded in to relieve themselves so they could sit in comfort for the lengthy speeches that inevitably followed dinner.

I was always amazed at how openly the guests spoke of their dining experience whilst standing next to one another at the urinal. There was not a course, a flavour or a wine that was not critiqued, along with the service, and not excluding the attributes of those of the service staff who were on the rare occasion young women. I duly recorded all the necessary comments about the food and wine.

From banqueting, I moved to assist in the lounge where I met, for the first time since my arrival, the kindly Charlton who ruled it as his own territory. Charlton was at least fifty, and was a man who had experienced a lifetime in private service. Prior to the war I believed he'd been in the service of The Duke of Devonshire, although he never made reference to it. Apart from ruling his empire in The Lounge, he also prided himself on being the Personal Butler to the hotel's Managing Director, Mr Dick Beattie. He carried out this role with great dignity and gravity, although none of us really understood quite what his duties entailed. Charlton was known for his style, sharp wit and boundless knowledge. Such was his reputation, he was held in respect and awe by management, staff and guests alike.

The hotel was crowded with the Jewish community at certain times of the year, who, in contradiction of the stereotype, were always generous, and senior staff vied for their attention. Such was the ubiquity of the guests of this faith that, with all good humour, whole areas of the hotel were renamed. The swimming pool was known as The Sea of Galilee, the Sun Lounge was the Gaza Strip.

One of our regulars who was very fond of Charlton, and who was always ensured his spot in the lounge, was a man called Jack Cohen. He was the charming founder of the Tesco Supermarket chain. The name, we understood, came from a combination of his wife's name, Tess, to whom he was devoted, and his name Cohen, hence *Tes-co*. Many years later, in my retirement, I moved to a small town in a remote part of Thailand, where to my surprise I found a Tesco supermarket. I believe that neither he nor I could ever have imagined his name would reach so far around the globe in the years ahead. Charlton was standing beside the restaurant entrance one day when Mr Cohen - later Sir Jack - engaged him in a chat as he was wont to do. "Tell me Charlton, you must be one of the only Gentiles here; you must feel a little difficult with so many demanding guests of our persuasion."

Charlton said nothing for a moment, and then replied, "I had not appreciated that fact sir, but it is not one I consider difficult."

Mr Cohen was not prepared to accept his diplomatic answer. "Come on Charlton, how many years have I known you, talk to me, tell me how you really feel?"

Again Charlton replied with the utmost diplomacy. Again Mr Cohen would have none of it. After receiving a further chiding, Charlton looked Mr Cohen in the eye and said "Well sir, I have to admit that on occasions I do feel like I'm one of the crowd in a crowd scene at the crucifixion." For a moment there was silence; other members of staff, myself, and a few guests who were nearby had heard the conversation and looked on with horror as to what would happen next. Mr Cohen looked at Charlton and after a short pause, burst out laughing. Only Charlton could get away with such comments.

One evening, also on a public holiday weekend, a group of teenagers, one the offspring of a very wealthy and influential guest, and a few of his friends, came into The Lounge and, with a click of their fingers summoned Charlton. "Charlton, get us six coffees, will you, old chap?" This was followed up as Charlton was about to depart with another click of the fingers. "Charlton, and please don't bring those piddly little cups but larger ones."

Charlton stopped in his tracks. He was prepared to have over-looked the young man's ill manner of address, no doubt wishing to impress the friends. This last request however, was taking it too far. He turned slowly and gazed upon the young man. Such a stare would have terrified the most hardened guest, and so the young man immediately realized his error. "I am sorry 'sir', but do I understand that 'sir' and his friends do not wish to take their coffee in coffee cups?"

The young man was by now feeling very uncomfortable and regretting his attempt to take on the formidable Charlton.

Without hesitation Charlton, realising his advantage, continued, "Would 'sir' wish to have his coffee in a teacup, or," (slight pause) "in the next size up - a bucket?" He did not wait for an answer but simply turned and left the boys in stunned silence.

He was an amazing character in the hotel and was answerable to no one. There was little he did not know and was often the father figure to many of the trainees who sought advice from this sage fountain of knowledge.

I was next tried out in the Saloon Bar, a casual bar where beer was the main beverage. It is a beverage with which I had become well acquainted as this was the bar that, as a privileged trainee, I was permitted to enter as a customer. It also had a small side bar that was the domain of all other staff. The Saloon Bar was a job sought after by all the trainees, for the perks of free beer and cigarettes that were provided by the barman, Mac, a kindly but wily old gentleman, who officially ran the Saloon Bar. He paid these dues as 'silence money' due to the many fiddles and scams that he had running, most of which I had no idea about. My knowledge of such things came later when I did my training in the hotel's American Cocktail Bar, where the real fiddles were performed by the masters.

The Saloon Bar was quite popular with actors who were performing at the Devonshire Theatre, located a short way down the road. Amongst those who performed there I was told was the actor Connie Booth, 'Polly' of Fawlty Towers, who assisted her husband John Cleese in writing the famous TV show. So many of the events that occurred at The Grand were similar to those in Fawlty Towers that some were convinced that the ideas were generated out of stories heard and retold in The Saloon Bar. The hit TV series truly mirrored the life that we lived in those days.

The cellar was interesting; it was deep in the hotel's bowels. The chief cellarman was Ted Thwaites, another character, who had lost his toes to frostbite in the last war, or considering how old he looked it may even have been the First World War. As a result he used to shuffle around the cellar with difficulty, and it was the trainee who did all the lifting and carrying. The cellar was on two levels with the 'dispense' up a further steep flight of steps, connected with a small lift that was operated by a rope. Nearly fifty years later when I returned to visit my old friend Jonathan Webley, the long serving general manager, I was told that the lower level of the cellar had to be closed as a fire/health and safety risk, but such is progress, there were no such sensible concerns in my day. [56]

The dispense was under the control of Mrs Reed. Dear Mrs Reed was a maternal figure to all the trainees, always wanting to help and if ever we were short of a bob or two she would be only too happy to help us out. She very rarely accepted the money to be returned even when willingly offered. She had a room in St Vincents and often we would watch from our windows as she returned home at night after a late banquet, the route taking her from one side of the road to the other. She claimed that she never drank; her evening walk back, however, most certainly indicated otherwise. It may have been the interpretation of 'drink' that caused the confusion. In my time helping her in the dispense during busy banquet functions I admit I never saw her drinking from a glass. She did have a most particular habit however; after pouring any spirit or liqueur, she would tip the measure into the palm of her hand and lick up the drops that were left over, this I am sure would have amounted to a substantial amount over the course of the night, which no doubt accounted for her somewhat haphazard walk home.

She had a heart of gold; she was a war widow who worked to supplement a meagre war pension. She had a son who appeared from time to time in a magnificent cream Jaguar XK150, with red leather upholstery, to the envy of all trainees, and that we believed she had bought for him. She had no other kin and as her only family he took full advantage of this situation. It was this good nature of hers that made her care for the trainees as if they were 'her boys'. I look back with some guilt and shame that we were not more grateful for her kindness.

One evening I was called out from behind the dispense counter by the Deputy Manager. "I want you to help on the banquet tonight, have you a dinner jacket?"

"Yes sir I have."

He turned to Mrs Reed. "You can manage without him for a while, can't you?" It wasn't a request but a statement. "He can help if you really get busy; and make sure that the waiters are checked and only get another bottle of wine when they return an empty one. Tonight is all to account so I do not want them getting pissed at our expense."

I had already learned that events like this were a joy to management; there was little chance of the customer ever knowing for sure the number of bottles consumed. The number was always loaded, thus supplementing the management's drink allowance and also delivering the surplus expected by the stocktakers who were due shortly.

"Why are you still here? Get going and change and see me back here in ten minutes."

I was back in time sporting my dinner jacket for the first time on duty and intrigued as to what was to be expected of me.

"OK Griffin, I know that these bastards are knocking off the wine, I even caught one the other night with a bottle hidden in the tails of his jacket, so watch out for that one. They are clever buggers and there is no end to the schemes they get up to. It will be a great experience for you."

I realized that this was another reason that many staff held us management trainees in contempt; having been working alongside them learning their job, we were now spies for the boss and were here to catch them in their errant ways.

"Watch that one in particular, he always seems pissed by the end of the evening and yet I have never been able to catch him with a bottle."

In my smart dinner jacket I took up my position near the service exit in the Grand Ballroom. I watched the suspect wine waiter bring in three bottles of wine to be served and carefully place them in an ice bucket he had prepared earlier. As the evening wore on the empty bottles were placed inverted in the ice bucket as was the way. Once the three were empty he would leave the room with the ice bucket and the empty bottles to replenish the ice and swap the empties for full ones.

All seemed fine. But as the evening passed, I could not help but notice he started to show the early signs of intoxication. I checked with Mrs Reed that all was well and that the system was working with empty bottles being exchanged for full. I returned to my station. Obviously the guests were getting into the evening with two of the three wine bottles already consumed and inverted in the ice bucket. As I wandered around assisting where I could, I asked 'my' wine waiter if he needed assistance, and was rebuffed with a clear response that he was fine and needed no help.

I stood for a few minutes beside his ice bucket watching. How was he doing it? I noticed the ice in the bucket had already melted, and asked "Are you sure I can't help, shall I get more ice?" With an indignant, aggressive, tone he said, "Go help someone else, I'm fine and will get my own ice." I was rather put out as, after all, I was offering to help. It was then that I noticed a strong fruity smell of wine, the popular Hock called Blue Nun was being served. I was puzzled as to why the smell was so strong where I was standing and then I realised. The crafty bugger. I had worked out how he was getting his free wine.

I returned to my station by the door and watched. As he went around topping up the glasses of the guests at his tables I noticed most only received a small drop. After a few such top ups, the bottle he was serving was returned to the ice bucket and in a deft movement turned upside down into the ice bucket. With the empty bottles in the bucket, he headed to the door to replenish both wine and purportedly, ice. I followed him out and into the glass pantry which held the ice machine. Unaware I was behind him, he took the bottles out and then immediately placed the bucket to his lips and gulped down what was meant to be water from the melted ice, but was actually wine. Far from being empty bottles inverted into the ice bucket, he had only served about a third to the guests and then emptied the remains into his empty ice bucket for later consumption.

He hurriedly downed what he could of the wine from the bucket, and tipped the rest into another bucket concealed behind the machine. Gotcha! He turned and suddenly noticed me, realised his fiddle was discovered and became very sheep-ish. "You're not going to bust me are you?"

His tone was very different to the aggressive way with which he had spoken to me earlier. I was then faced for the first time with a management decision: should I keep quiet and have this waiter indebted to me, or tell the manager and impress *him* and maybe get some brownie points? "I will think about it, but for now get back to work and don't let me catch you doing it again".

He looked at me with a faint smile of gratitude and headed back with the empty bottles to exchange with Mrs Reed and bring back an ice bucket that now actually contained ice. I tipped out his bucket of ill-gotten booze down the sink. As I walked back to the ballroom, I felt the interesting feeling of power and authority. If this was what management was about then I think I might enjoy it, although I was yet to fully understand how it was to be balanced and dispensed with fairness and in everyone's interest. This fundamental issue faces any young manager learning about authority. Some handled it well and others did it simply to benefit their own egos. I like to think I fell into the former group.

My move to the American Cocktail Bar followed quite soon after two barmen were dismissed following poor stocktaking results: it was suspected that they had been bringing their own bottles of spirit into the bar and taking the proceeds of the sales from the cash draw, which wasn't difficult as cash registers were seen as rather too noisy and vulgar for the cocktail bar. They may have got away with it, but had not caught on to the fact that the hotel stocktakers had started to discreetly mark the bottle delivered from the hotel's cellar, and therefore could easily recognise any bottles that were not so marked.

I started as a *commis* with the main task of washing glasses, stocking shelves and clearing tables. I was soon proficient at these tasks and seemed to impress Mr Rogers, the head cocktail barman who then allowed me to serve the drinks and learn to make a few simple cocktails. I was rewarded with a few packets of cigarettes, and I was somehow convinced this was acceptable and a justly deserved perk of the job. I then started to notice some of the other perks. The barmen dismissed this and insisted that as far as the management was concerned it was all acceptable, as all they were interested in was achieving a surplus in each of the monthly stock takes. To achieve this, the barmen had to revert to certain ways.

The ingenuity was astounding. I confess this was something I fell into and over the years, no doubt partly due to the personality and charm of some of the barmen like Pepe and a lovable Irishman Jimmy O'Shea and just accepted it as a perk of the job. It was not until the advent of computerised stock control that such practices were to become unacceptable due to being detectable. I realised that they were not a perk, but, in reality, dishonesty and theft. Back then, due to low salaries and difficulties in control, they were accepted by management, as long as such fiddles were shared equally between the employee, management and company. The problem was only acted upon when staff become too greedy and deprived management or the company of their share.

Some of the methods used were not acceptable, whilst others were treated with a blind eye. The idea of placing a sixpence into the base of the spirit measure to reduce the standard measure poured was not a good idea as it was too easily discovered, whereas to place the ice in the glass prior to pouring the spirit into it was acceptable, as this was done with skill and a skilled barman did it faster than the eye could see. The measure – which by law should be a 'brimming measure' – was far from being so and was tipped into the glass well before the measure was filled. The fact that it was over ice meant the spirit could never be measured with any accuracy. On the other hand, things like the watering down of alcohol was an absolute no-no, as one of the inspectors' tools of trade was a hydrometer that would be used to detect a watering down of the alcohol.

Another method of inflating the stock was to collect the remains of wine from bottles after a banquet. The white wine would be used to top up things like Noilly Prat, Dry Vermouth and such like, and the red wine would augment the Dubonnet, Campari and Sweet Martini. This was quite profitable, but great care had to be taken to ensure that the proportions did not dilute or change the main drink, which was often used in a mix of other drinks. This task therefore only fell to the specialist - the Head Bartender.

All the ploys were done in a way that, should the Weights and Measures Inspector decide to pay a surprise visit, then it would be almost impossible to find them out. One trick to which staff were accustomed was when a guest requested a straight gin and a whisky with no ice or mixer, or for the mixer served separately. This was an obvious giveaway that the 'guest' was an inspector.

Apart from my bad education of fiddles in the bar (which would serve me well in later life catching others), I also learned to be a good listener, albeit with difficulty and quickly forgotten. Often the reason guests came and sat at the bar was simply to chat and pour out the problems that life had imposed upon them.

One such guest came in most days and simply ordered a bottle of Krug Champagne, one of the most expensive bottles on our list. He would just chat: weather, cars, ex-wives, politics, but never religion. We would open the bottle and fill his champagne glass, he would then produce a beautifully ornate swizzle stick. It was like a propelling pencil in gold, he would twist it and five wire prongs would emerge from the end. He'd dip it in the glass and swizzle it; the bubbles in the champagne would froth up and almost half would flood over the saucer shaped glass onto the counter, which we then mopped up. It all seemed an unbelievable waste of such a fine champagne, but then he was a millionaire and it seemed to amuse him. The bottle was never finished so was shared by the staff. This was probably when I gained a taste for champagne - but only the very best.

In regards to staff, it was always rather difficult to control the theft of smaller items like tea, sugar and general food items which could be smuggled out in pockets. In any event this was not regarded as theft, but simply another perk of the job. The role of the Goods Received Clerk, who was located at the staff entrance, was partly seen as security to check on staff entering and leaving the building from the vantage point of his desk behind a large window. In my brief time spent in learning this job, I only came across one incident that I confess I secretly admired. The clerk was on a lunch break, most deliveries had arrived and it was rather quiet. As a result I was left ticking off invoices on my own. Harry, one of the pot washers in the kitchen, came past my window, and seeking anything that might relieve the boredom, I greeted him with a cheery wave. "How are you doing?"

"OK", he replied, but then I noticed he was limping a little. "What's the problem, have you hurt yourself?" Pausing for a moment by my window, he pointed down to his foot. "Dropped a bloody great pan on my foot this morning, think I might go and see the doc". Still limping, as if dragging his injured foot behind him, he headed for the door.

My concentration being broken from the boredom of invoice checking, I stood up for a stretch. I went and stood by the open door of the office. Harry had by now gone from sight and I pulled out my packet of Players to enjoy a smoke. As I looked down to light my cigarette, something caught my eye. At ground level I noticed a piece of kitchen string one end of which disappeared around the corner of the staff entrance, attached to the other end of the string, progressing slowly towards me down the passageway, was a large plucked frozen turkey. I watched in fascination as the turkey came ever closer. As it slowly passed by my feet, I stepped out and started to follow the escaping fowl. It reached the door and then, as if to make a break for it to freedom, it shot at some speed out of sight around the corner. I followed round the corner in hot pursuit, attempting to grab the parson's nose in the process. At that moment I came face to face with Harry, pulling desperately at the string in an attempt to pick up the bird and hide it under his coat, whilst at the same time unravel himself from the length of string that was still attached to his left ankle.

The limp now explained, not a word was spoken, he picked up the turkey and, with a very sheepish grin, simply handed it back to me as if it had accidentally just got caught up around his ankle as he left the building. I untied the string from the bird as he untied the string from his ankle. He then rolled the string up and handed it to me. This done, there was a moment's silence as we looked at each other. I wasn't sure what my responsibilities were in terms of catching an employee in the act of turkey theft. Seeing my hesitation, he took it as a sign that, as I had now retrieved the turkey, all was well. He said "Thanks mate" and turned and went on his way. Harry never returned to work at The Grand.

It seemed if you were confident enough you could get away with anything. Such as televisions and some rather nice antique furniture. Two men in brown warehouse coats and a clipboard came to the concierge desk. "We are here to pick up the TVs in the lounge and replace them with new ones; any chance one of your guys could give us a hand?"

At first the concierge hesitated, not happy to have tradesmen in his lobby. Picking up on this expertly, the brown-coated workman added, "The sooner we can get them the sooner we will be out of here."

Seeing the logic in this, the concierge turned to one of his porters. "Bill, give them a hand and do it quickly." With which they headed off in the direction of the TV lounges. As they carried the TVs from the lounge through the heavy doors of the Compton Street entrance at the rear of the hotel, an assistant manager, it was reported later, most obligingly held the door open. "Thanks, mate," the men said with a cheery smile as the TVs were stacked in the back of the van, and carefully wrapped in blankets.

About two hours later an elderly guest keen to catch up on the cricket came to the desk and asked where the televisions were. The concierge looked at Bill the porter who had assisted the tradesmen with their removal. "Didn't those guys return with the new TVs?"

Bill started to realise that something may be amiss. "No, they said they were bringing them as soon as they got back to the shop to drop off the old TVs."

The panic began. "What about the paperwork? What was the name of the shop on the van?" All Bill could say was, "I don't know."

The guest looked on with interest. "Looks as if you may have a problem."

And truly they did. They were fortunate in the part that the assistant manager had played a role in holding open the door, as blame was now equally proportioned between staff and management. The TVs were indeed replaced that day with new ones; the only problem being that they had to be paid for. In those days, there were limited communications systems in place to prevent such incidents; such heists were rare, and people with the confidence and audacity to do such things were not commonly encountered. These confidence tricksters were surprisingly held in some mythical regard at the hotel, and were always a good talking point to teach the staff a valuable lesson.

Thinking about it now, it is impossible to comprehend the level of trust that existed between a business and the customer. Trust was still the accepted norm in all business dealings. Bills were either paid in cash, or more often than not, by a personal cheque. There were no deposits taken and any such suggestion would have been received with horror and taken as an insult to the guest of a five star hotel. A guest could check in for a week, wine and dine, enjoying the finest food and beverages and all the services the hotel had to offer, only to pay the bill on their departure from the hotel. No identification was sought; bank cards or credit cards did not exist, and nor for that matter did any form of photo identity. It was all down to a matter of trust, and, in the event that the guest failed to meet their financial obligations, the police would take it up as a criminal offence. In later years it was to become a civil offence as moral absolutes changed with the advent of more serious crime.

I recall when I was in 'Cashiers' one day, an American asked "Do you take credit cards?"

I was totally at a loss as to what he was talking about. "I am sorry sir, but I do not believe we do. What is it exactly?" With a look of surprise and disbelief he tried to explain, producing a silver and blue plastic card with the words 'Diners Club' emblazoned on it.

"In the US everyone is getting these cards, we use them to pay for everything from hotels to clothes in the stores and most things when shopping. We just sign a slip and pay Diners Club when they send me a bill at the end of each month."

I looked at it in sheer bewilderment. "So how do the hotels get their money?"

"Diners Club pays them," he replied.
"But when?" I asked
"I think the following month when the bills are balanced," he replied, now losing interest in the subject and wanting to get on his way.

This fascinated me, how the world was changing. A plastic card? I explained what I had just been told to the Front Office Manager, who naturally sneered, "Typical Yanks. It will never catch on over here; we just don't do things like that." So much for his wildly inaccurate prediction.

But in the meantime, we continued accepting guests on trust. My moment of doubting my belief in the trust of my fellow man came when a young man checked in. Apart from being a little too cocky, in my limited experience at the hotel he just didn't fit in. Something was not quite right. I asked the concierge what they thought, as the porter had taken him to his room and carried his suitcase. "Seemed OK and he had a bloody heavy case, so he doesn't travel light."

The alarm now raised, we kept an eye out for him. That afternoon he came past the desk, with a cheery and rather familiar tone, "I'm off into town".

As we watched him depart, alarm bells rang again. Guests who stay in luxury hotels do not normally tell the staff of their movements, as if they needed to explain their actions. Once he was out of sight, we set our plan in motion. Mr Edwards, the new assistant manager, and I headed for the guest's room, instructing the concierge to telephone the room with three rings, giving us time to get out if the guest returned unexpectedly. Upstairs, we saw his suitcase and I lifted it. It was indeed 'bloody heavy'. "That's strange." Edwards was looking in the wardrobe.

"There's nothing in there", I observed.
"Exactly. Don't you think he would have unpacked by now, he's been here for a few hours. Go check the bathroom and see if he has his washbag or toothbrush there".

I checked and sure enough the bathroom was empty. "He is a con man," pronounced Edwards with confidence. "Help me with his case". To my surprise he pulled out a set of suitcase keys that the porters had collected over the years. It only took a few minutes to find one that fitted and popped open the locks. As we lifted the lid, there to my amazement were six London telephone directories wrapped in some towels bearing the logo of another five star hotel in Brighton. We smiled at each other. "Well spotted, Griffin, we have caught the bugger. At least he was a little more clever than the first one I caught."

Edwards's first con man had not used telephone directories. He had decided to screw the case to the floor, in the event that management were to check for the weight of a suitcase. Sadly for him the trick was discovered when the side of the suitcase had ripped off when it was lifted by a rather well built chambermaid when cleaning. Such events all contributed to our greater knowledge of human nature that eventually resulted in today's 'no trust policies': no guest crosses the portals of the hotel without paying in advance for all likely expenses – and more – that might be incurred. Good business, maybe, but a sad reflection of the decline in standards of morality and honesty in our society today.

Chapter 12

#starencounters #teatottlerDJ #suntrapofthesouth

It was 1965. Eastbourne's internal clock was set for half a century earlier. The buildings fitted this period and most of the residents were still alive from that time. For whipper-snappers like me, the real excitement was that Eastbourne was going to be the backdrop for the movie, *Half a Sixpence*, and that the star of the movie was Tommy Steele, the English Elvis Presley (although to my mind the boy from Bermondsey with the London Cockney accent never quite made it). It was a really BIG event – especially when he was booked to stay at The Grand for the weeks of filming. We all desperately looked forward to having a film star at The Grand.[57]

The only thing that could possibly top this was the announce-ment in the *Eastbourne Gazette* that a few hundred extras would be required for crowd scenes. The buzz went around the hotel staff like wildfire. All the staff had visions of a bit part opening their way to Hollywood careers as movie stars. Sadly, however, not only was this vision held by The Grand Hotel staff but also the entire population of Eastbourne. A queue formed around several blocks to register. Naturally I was one of them. However, after several hours standing in that queue and with my shift due to start, I decided that my past experience in acting the roles of Angel, Christmas Cracker, Chimney Sweep and sundry Servants

and Soldiers in school Shakespearean productions, was destined to be the extent of my life as a thespian.

On my return I ran into Mr. Cairns, the deputy manager, who
had been sent on a mission to purchase a radiogram, a specific
request from Mr Steele. It was the one piece of furniture, that was
not currently available in any suite of the hotel, but the general
manager felt would be worth making available for all the future
stars who would no doubt throng to stay at the hotel now.

I was now handed this task and headed off down to the leading
radio and television retailer. It was the start of a lovely aspect of
my career: I was able to purchase luxury items, that I would have
never been able to afford, at someone else's expense. This was a
most enjoyable experience and one that was to become part of
my life for many years. I only really appreciated this when I came
to retire, and found that all such luxuries were most definitely
then out of my budget as I faced a far more humble lifestyle.

Back at the hotel Mr Cairns, myself and the hotel electrician,
carefully manhandled the rather large radiogram to the suite of
Mr Tommy Steele. After a knock on the door we were about to
enter the suite when the door opened itself, and a diminutive
young man appeared at the door, with scruffy tousled blond hair
and a big smile. "That's great gents, just like Christmas! Where
can we plug it in?"

Thus spake England's Elvis – with a broad Cockney accent!

The next touch with stardom was to set a career benchmark.
The film legend Charlie Chaplin and his family, arrived one
summer in the mid sixties.[58]

When the news leaked on the hotel's grapevine there was a lot
of excitement, even amongst those who had been rubbing shoulders with the rich and famous for many years of their working
lives in hotels. Somehow he was different: he had been around
for all our lives. Even the younger staff around my generation

regarded him with awe, as if he had invented Hollywood. Which of course he had.

I was working in reception but when asked by Morris if I could help out, I agreed without hesitation, even if it meant extra hours and no pay, as it would give me the best of both worlds. One: to see Charlie as he checked in and Two: to possibly meet him in his suite.

The day of his arrival came and I was on the desk, but I was a little disappointed as when the family arrived there was initially no sign of Mr Chaplin. A very charming woman arrived, his wife Oona and the children, all smart and well behaved, and the girls *very* sophisticated. I particularly remember Victoria; we all looked at her admiringly until my fellow receptionist whispered, "Eyes off, she's too young."

I looked again and could not believe this young woman was only fourteen. She went on in a few years to be the subject of much international gossip, when she eloped with a young man Jean-Baptiste Thierree, and became involved with one of the first contemporary circuses, *Le Cirque Bonjour.* The younger children were all very sweet and - just like any kid anywhere in the world - were over the moon when given the opportunity to ride the horse belonging to our eccentric resident Mr Myers.[50]

Charlie Chaplin eventually arrived and on several occasions I was to wheel his breakfast trolley into his suite and set it up ready for him to enter the room once Oona had checked it was as he liked it. On his departure I was left an envelope with some cash and a simple headed note paper with a Swiss address, signed Charles Chaplin, which I still have today.

My next brush with fame came not with a Hollywood pedigree, but with much better benefits on the ground. It arrived in the guise of a famous radio DJ called Pete Murray. We had all listened to him on Radio Luxembourg, the only radio station in

Europe that played the latest 45 singles nonstop, and enjoyed its own commercial radio monopoly of English-language programming in the UK until March 1964. Radio Caroline then started daytime commercial radio transmissions to southern England from a ship anchored four miles off the coast, outside the three mile limit of British Territorial Waters. We had often listened to the Top Twenty on Radio Luxembourg on Sunday nights, under the blankets at school after lights out, on our large battery operated Bush portable radios. At the time, Pete Murray was a household name. [59]

I got to meet this icon of pop radio in my role as a room service waiter. He was just staying for a few days. I served his breakfast and found him an easy and chatty guest. Having listened to him on radio so often, and with my huge interest in pop music, I felt like I knew him. The fact that he was older and a hotel guest didn't come into it, which would usually be a barrier to me talking to him.

Whilst chatting, he asked where one could go to the *trendy* places around Eastbourne. I suggested a few bars; we always liked The Dolphin, in South Street. We often gathered in the back room to listen to folk music when our anti-Vietnam War mood took us, listening to Joan Baez sing *We Shall Overcome* and Buffy Sainte Marie sing *Until It's Time For You To Go*, but I realised this was probably not Pete Murray's taste. It also turned out very much to my surprise that he was a teetotaller as well as a vegetarian.

At the time, the disco scene had not really taken off. Well, not in Eastbourne anyway. There were coffee bars that had jukeboxes where young people gathered to listen and dance to the latest pop music. It was Finches in Grove Street that was the 'in place'. When I suggested this as a place to go, I was surprised when he turned to me as I laid out his breakfast and said

"OK, that sounds good, are you OK to come with me as I haven't a clue of my way around Eastbourne, I'm working today but tomorrow would be fine"

This was the most fantastic invitation. The hotel rule banning us from fraternising with guests was absent from my mind. Even if I had thought of it, I would certainly have ignored it. "Yes, sure but I doubt I can make it before 7.30pm." At least I remembered I had Mrs Benson to serve.

"That's fine. I don't suppose you could find me a date, could you?"

This stopped me in my tracks. Bloody hell, where would I find a girl at this notice and what should I say? "Er, I will try." Rather hesitantly.

"Come on. I'm sure a lad with your charm can do it."

Now the challenge had been laid down. And so it was that the next 24 hours of my life was to be spent in search of date for a famous DJ.

When I got off duty after lunch I confided in a fellow trainee who agreed to help if I could introduce him to Pete Murray. The deal being struck, we headed off to the Sussex Hotel to lay down our plans. We sat down for tea and cakes (the bars closed at 2.30pm), and ran through a list of possible girls who may fit the bill. Each one was crossed off as we looked at them. At that moment a young waitress came up. "OK what can I get you?" she said with a lovely smile. She was the spitting image of Sandie Shaw, the singer known as the 'barefoot pop princess' with a chart song *Always Something There To Remind Me*. Pulling my thoughts together, "Two teas and scones, please". Not the hippest of orders, but that was about all I could think of at that moment. "She would be perfect." We both agreed. But who was to ask her?

"You ask her," I said.

"No you. I'm bloody well not going to be a pimp."

I had not even thought of it like that, but my credibility was on the line. "OK, I will, but what the hell do I say?"

"You'll think of something, and you better think now as here comes our tea."

As she approached she gave me a big smile. She placed the teapot down, along with the milk, only the scones and jam to go, better start chatting. "How long have you been working here, I haven't seen you before?" Oh God what a shocking opening line… But then she seemed unfazed and ready to chat.

"Only about a week; where are you two from?" Ah at least she seemed chatty. The place wasn't that busy so she seemed happy to keep talking.

"We're trainee managers at The Grand Hotel". She looked interested.

"Oh is that the posh place on the seafront? Do you have lots of famous people stay there?"

This was as fantastic as if it had been scripted. "Yes, quite often." I then added, to impress: "People like Charlie Chaplin". This certainly had an effect.

"Wow, did you meet him?"

As if it was a daily occurrence. "Yes actually I did," laying it on a little thick about my close relationship with the legend, but she was impressed.

"Do you have anyone famous at the hotel now?"

This was all falling into place perfectly. "Well we have Pete Murray in at the moment, a really nice guy." As if we were old mates.

Then like a lamb to the slaughter, she asked, "Could you get his autograph for me?"

Slow down was the look I got from my colleague across the table.

"Er I'm not sure, I could try..." and then "I am out with him tomorrow night, maybe I can do better, would you like to meet him?"

At that she looked at me. Oh bloody hell, she thinks I am just shooting a line. "You are kidding me right?"

Now just when I thought it was in the bag she started to back off. "No I'm genuine, honest."

She looked at me. "I don't believe you."

I looked for help from my friend who joined the conversation, "He is being totally honest, believe me."

I then thought, let's try reverse psychology. "OK forget it, don't worry about it, if you're not interested that is fine."

"But I am, I just don't want to be left looking like an idiot..." She now seemed hooked.

"The invitation is there, I am sure he would be delighted to meet you, but it is up to you."

She looked at me again. "OK, but if you're playing a joke on me I'll kill you."

I looked her straight in the eye. "I promise you I'm not, you have my word." This done we then agreed on a time and place to pick her up. I could not believe how easy it was to ask a girl out. What is it about the star factor?

That evening I was picked up by Pete Murray at the rear of The Grand. He drove a Daimler with the number plate 'PM 208', which I thought was clever after the Luxembourg radio station 'Radio 208'. The next thing I discovered was that he also did not smoke. It was especially surprising for a celebrity in the rock and roll business, as at the time the press was full of the misdeeds of pop stars and drink and drugs. I wondered how life could be fun without drink and cigs, and asked him just that. He gave me a very understanding and logical reason that impressed me as to how nice the guy was. As we came to the place to pick up my 'Miss Sandie Shaw' my heart pounded as suddenly I thought that she may have changed her mind, and what an idiot I would look. Just as I was thinking of what I could say, she stepped out of the doorway, and I have to say looked stunning.

"Is that her?" asked Pete Murray. "She's gorgeous, and you are right she does look like Sandie Shaw".

We got out of the car and with some level of awkwardness I introduced 'Sandie'. He, with great gentlemanly charm, greeted her as an old friend, shook hands and opened the car door. As we drove to the coffee bar he chatted as if we were all friends heading out for the evening. It was all rather surreal I recall thinking. When we arrived, I suddenly felt an amazing burst of excitement as I noticed heads turn and whispers ran through the room as everyone noticed my celebrity friend beside me. We headed for the basement where the music played, to a little cashier desk where we usually paid our entry fee. As we walked in, the owner of the place with whom I was on nodding terms suddenly approached. "Hello, how are you, great to see you again."

I was overwhelmed as never before had I received such a greeting. "Hi George," I responded as if this was normal. As I reached for my money, George stepped up, and I realised he wanted an introduction. "This is George who owns the place - this is Pete Murray and 'Sandie.'

Pete Murray then played a card that made me feel ten feet tall. "Hello, nice to meet you, you obviously know my good friend Paddy who told me this was the only place to come in Eastbourne for a good evening."

This was probably the first time George had heard my name. "Oh that is nice of him, Paddy is a regular and we always try to look after him, come on down and enjoy yourself, the evening is on me." After we were seated he took an order of Cokes and coffees and then asked me for a quick word. "Paddy, I didn't realise you were so well connected, if you can try to bring other celebrities here you do not ever have to pay again. Come anytime you like… Pete Murray… fantastic… it will be all over Eastbourne tomorrow, thanks mate."

After a great evening of people coming up and asking for autographs or asking me if I can introduce them, I had never basked in the light of such celebrity status in my life. So this was what it was like to be famous. I even had the pick of the girls that evening and I admit that I didn't care that it was only due to the company I was keeping. Rock on! *Sandie*, I gather, also had a great night, or so it was suggested by the chambermaid who cleaned the room the following day.

The ultimate accolade came in his next radio broadcast which he suggested I should listen to. He dedicated a record to me: "…and now here is one for my good friend 'the uncrowned king of Eastbourne' Paddy Griffin." I will always be indebted, as such fame that followed set me up with more girlfriends from the neighbouring School of Domestic Science than I ever dreamed of. Such is the power of celebrity, then as now.

We had a madly enthusiastic bridge player who stayed at The Grand to attend one of the largest bridge congresses the hotel hosted. Following his appearance in the epic movies, *Lawrence of Arabia*, *Dr Zhivago*, and *Funny Girl* opposite Barbra Streisand, Omar Sharif was regarded as the heartthrob of the sixties.[60]

On his arrival at the hotel I was on duty and checked him in. He was accompanied by a rather fearsome secretary, not at all as I would have imagined, no entourage or sycophantic hangers on as one might have expected from a man of his newly acquired stardom. He was just an individual attending a bridge match, a game that he loved with a passion. He was absolutely charming, relaxed and chatty. At the risk of sounding a little star struck, I could not help but noticing he had the most amazing eyes I had ever seen, dark, deep, mysterious and rather made one feel weak at the knees. And that was just me; God knows how his female fans would feel. I would soon find out.

He was there for a week and during this time a number of people came to visit him, one of whom was another screen idol of his time, Dirk Bogarde. The girls on the desk were in raptures; if there was a war hero in a British film it was played by him. Good looks, a little shorter than I expected, but suave and full of English charm. Those doting young women didn't realise that they hadn't a chance; we only found out later he was gay. [61]

It wasn't long before the word was out on Omar Sharif, and groups of girls started to gather around the hotel, especially from the School of Domestic Science for Ladies opposite. One of these girls, Mandy, who I rather fancied but had not had much success with, suddenly called to me as I was leaving work one day. "Have you met him? What's he like? Is he as good looking in real life?" The questions were endless as she walked beside me back to St Vincents and my residence. "Please can you get me his autograph… pleeeease" she begged.

If this was the way to get her to show an interest in *me*, why not, I thought. "OK, I will see what I can do but I can't promise anything".

"Please just try; let me know tomorrow. Do you want to meet up, maybe we can have a drink?"

Back on duty, the bridge congress was in full swing. I was surprised to discover that there are few pastimes that seem to have such a committed following as bridge, and those who participate do so with an irrational zeal. As the players walked past the reception desk towards the areas of play, there would be lowered voices as competing pairs discussed strategy, and often on return lowered voices in heated exchanges, "Why didn't you come diamonds for God's sake." How a card game could evoke such passions baffled us.

It was after observing such an exchange that suddenly there in front of me was the man himself. "Mr Sharif, how may I help you?"

"I wonder if you could change this for me?" as he handed me a five pound note.

"Of course."

I handed him five crisp one pound notes, and as he seemed very relaxed and happy having I assumed won his game, I suddenly blurted out, "Forgive me asking but my girlfriend is such a fan of yours, as am I of course," I quickly added not to sound as if I didn't care, "and wondered if I might get your autograph?" Then realising this was a no, no, "I am sorry I shouldn't bother you..."

"My dear chap I should be delighted, but not now as I have to attend a press meeting."

As he started to walk away I thought that was the end of that when he stopped, turned and said with a big smile, "Pop up to my suite tomorrow, at this time, and do bring your friend."

I stood agog and he was on his way. Did he really say to go to his suite? And I could bring Mandy? Wow this would blow her mind; let alone the brownie points I would earn. Later however, reality set in. Not only could I lose my job for doing this but how on earth could I get Mandy in and out without anyone seeing? It would be the afternoon and not too many managers were ever around, and there would be all the guests, having finished their afternoon session, heading to their rooms, so maybe we wouldn't be noticed. Was it worth the risk? For Mandy? Hell yes.

I called the college's residential students phone line and asked for Mandy. After a few minutes a voice was on the line. "Sorry Mandy isn't around, she may still be in classes."

"OK can you tell her Paddy called and I have managed to get her what she wanted and can she meet me tomorrow at 4.30pm at the back of The Grand?"

"Ooohh sounds very mysterious. OK I will tell her, 'bye."

The following afternoon I was waiting outside the Compton Street entrance of the hotel, wondering if Mandy had got the message to meet me. "Hello I'm here," said a chirpy voice from behind. Mandy looked stunning in her black and white PVC mini skirt and black boots that were all the fashion. "Did you get his autograph, the girls are going to be sooo jealous".

I looked at her for a moment. "Well not exactly." I could see the disappointment in her eyes.

"I thought you said you had got it." She looked as if she was about to burst into tears.

"No I haven't got it."

"How could you …" she said accusingly.

"Hang on, no I haven't got it… YET."

She paused in her sulky pout. "What do you mean?"

"Well, how would you like to meet him and ask him yourself?"

She grabbed my hands. "Are you joking? Please don't joke." She let out a squeal of excitement and started to jump up and down. For God's sake what's wrong with the girl?

"Calm down. You have to do exactly as I say or we could be in trouble."

"Anything, anything!" she cried.

"I could get sacked if we are caught. Now follow me into the hotel and we will use the staff lift up to the second floor and then along the corridor to his suite. And try not to look too excited, or sexy."

After a few more instructions to which she nodded her head in submissive agreement and a promise of good behaviour, we set off on our mission.

What the hell am I doing, I thought to myself. Yes she is gorgeous but is this really worth it? We reached the lift, and pressing the button for the second floor I prayed that it would not stop on the way up. My prayers were answered as with a shudder the lift stopped at our floor. I pulled back the doors and my luck was holding as there was no one in the service pantry. I cautiously opened the door onto the corridor, which seemed empty with all the guests having retired to their rooms to prepare for the gala dinner that was planned for tonight. I beckoned Mandy to follow. As we quickly walked down the corridor towards the presidential suite, I held my breath, expecting a bedroom door to open or the ping of a lift to announce the arrival of a head waiter or manager. We arrived at the suite door, my heart pounding, and Mandy almost beside herself with excitement. "Bloody Hell, calm down," I almost barked at her, already regretting what I had done, as now I felt I was no longer in control of the situation. I hesitated, then with a deep breath knocked on the door.

The door partly opened, and both our faces dropped, far from the broad welcoming smile of Omar Sharif, was the very severe and serious stare of his bespectacled secretary. Quickly looking at us as at two maniacs who had broken through the security, she seemed prepared with the brush off before I even opened my mouth. "Er.. I am sorry to bother you but Mr Sharif asked us to come at this time as he agreed to give us an autograph."

My God how pathetic that sounded. What was I doing? I felt so vulnerable to discovery and although I had been lucky so far, I was about to apologise and beat a rapid retreat. Thankfully the door opened further and standing there was the wide white smile with the trademark gap that just seemed to add to the warmth.

"Ah yes my young friend from yesterday, that's OK," he said, turning to the puzzled secretary. "I did ask them to come up," and, turning to us, "Come in, would you like some tea?" Christ no, I was about to scream. That's all I needed was a member of staff coming in and serving us tea.

"Thank you, that is so nice of you, but I don't think we should."

Meanwhile Mandy just stood there like a deer in the headlights. "This must be your lovely friend," his dark brown eyes focusing on Mandy.

"Oh yes, this is Mandy."

He took her hand and gently shook it. Mandy just stood transfixed saying nothing but just gazing back into his eyes. What's wrong with the bloody girl? This is ridiculous. Embarrassing! "It was kind of you to agree to give us your autograph," just as a reminder as to why we were there.

"Oh yes let me do that for you." He turned to his secretary who was ready with two publicity photographs, took them and wrote on one then the other turning to me. "Who should I make it out to?"

"Er.. Paddy Griffin," I stuttered. "Oh, and Mandy".

He handed them to us both and I couldn't help but notice he had written more on Mandy's photo than mine. "Are you sure you won't have some tea?" he asked again.

"No thank you, I really shouldn't be here and we should go, but thank you again."

He shook my hand as I was about to turn for the door. He then turned to Mandy and took her hand. I looked at her, having said nothing in the time we had been in his suite and I was willing her, for God's sake say something. She looked into his eyes continuing to hold his hand, not wanting to let go and rather meekly said, "Thank you so much. I am such a fan".

Still holding her hand, longer, I was starting to feel, than was necessary, and in a low and accented voice he said to her, "No, *thank you*. I would not be who or where I am today if it wasn't for fans like you." At this point her legs seemed to just fold up and she collapsed in a heap on the floor. The silly girl had fainted.

"For God's sake get up," I exhorted her as if that was all that was needed. "I am sorry." I repeated this several times.

The secretary, now in command, shook Mandy and Mr Sharif handed her a glass of water. I realised that this was not a new situation for either. I just wanted to get out. Stupid, bloody stupid was all that was going through my mind. By now Mandy was coming around and suddenly seemed as embarrassed as I was and joined me in a chorus of apologies. "That's OK," he repeated, somewhat amused as to the reaction his charm had caused.

We rapidly beat a retreat, escaping undiscovered. I was wondering if it had been worth it all and Mandy was clutching her prized signed photograph of Omar Sharif. I never did discover what note he had written to her but I know that she was the envy of the entire student population of the college.

After that incident I felt it better to stay well away from young and impressionable women and to rely on impressing girlfriends simply by association and not actually run a risk that might lead to my downfall.

We had a number of other celebrities stay at The Grand but there was one woman who did stand out above others. I was on reception when a very elegant woman came to the desk to sign in. I greeted her with the usual courtesies and as the routine dictated I placed in front of her, a registration card for her to complete. I was about to ask her name when I noticed she was filling in the card with her pen, in bright violet ink. 'Violet Carson' it read, I looked again and realised that this well dressed cultured and charming woman was indeed the person who she claimed. I just had difficulty placing her in her famous TV role of Ena Sharples from Coronation Street as she looked so different. [62]

Although wine was starting to become part of my alcoholic menu, as trainees our dire financial situation dictated the limits of our choice, with the mainstay being simply beer. There were two options, mild or bitter. The more exotic lagers and other varieties had not yet appeared behind most bars. I recall a most popular drink that was an effective boost to getting pissed faster on a limited budget was a Beer and Queer; try asking for that in a bar today and see what turns up in front of you. Back in the day this was a delicious concoction of a half of bitter in a pint glass topped up with a Barleywine or Bass No1 Ale which were about 12% proof, to enhance the alcohol content.

Songs were a large part of the generational change during my teens. We listened to music non-stop; we danced to it, it lifted us up, and it softened the blow as emotional break ups brought us down again. Most of all music created The Mood to help with our seductions, or so we believed. In the fifties most popular music came from America, but very soon the British rock 'n roll invasion put the popularity of US music on the back burner for a while.

Women and all that related to them were without doubt my driving force of the era. It wasn't simply the fact as a generation we were afflicted with *satyriasis* (look it up; I had to). I'm sure what our parents got up to during the war was just as intense, but it was sanctified under the banner of 'it was the war and live for the day'. Now we were bringing sex into the open, so to speak, with a push for a more liberated society. In this regard, the Pill changed our whole perspective toward sex; with the fear of pregnancy almost totally removed and any fears of disease unknown, moral views on the subject took second place. Our overwhelming desire for knowledge of these new-found pleasures became paramount. The young women and men who formed our social network of trainees and students had by and large been cloistered in same-sex private boarding schools since they were eight or nine years old. Now we were hormonally charged and looking at life in a very different way from people of a decade earlier. My friends and I embraced the new liberation with willing passion and great expectations.

The words of my old boss still ring in my ears: *"Eastbourne is the biggest vice pit outside Rome,"*

This was far from my initial impression of the town, on seeing the very elderly walking, wheeling and shuffling along on their various supportive devices on Eastbourne's promenade. That innocuous situation only existed until the school term commenced.

Because of its genteel reputation, Eastbourne had become the home of numerous finishing schools and colleges, very English institutions that were falling into rapid decline in the 60s. These finishing schools were established for young women of wealthy families who desired that a young woman be schooled in the correct etiquette, social graces and virtues as their mothers had been in a bygone era. These skills would enable them to assist their future husbands in their climb up the social and corporate ladder. Studying at university was a dim possibility, limited to the very bright or the very wealthy as the more egalitarian 'red brick unis' did not yet exist.

The young women were happy to go along with their parents' wishes and attend the finishing schools. But as this was the 60s, rather than seeing this as an avenue to the roles of domesticity that had been so happily embraced by their mothers, the girls saw it as a way to fill the gap between the strict confines of boarding school and the excitement of the real outside world. The schools endowed them a level of freedom as yet unknown. Of these schools none was more famous, or more relevant, than the school located across the road: the 'Eastbourne School of Domestic Science' better known to all simply as 'Rannie's' where young women, recently released from the cloistered life of Britain's finest ladies' educational establishments, would prepare for coming out into a brave new world.

To quote from a story by Lesley Gerard in *The Independent* newspaper some 30 years later in 1996:

The people of Eastbourne have always known Eastbourne College of Food and Fashion as Rannie's. It was the affectionate nickname of the formidable domestic science teacher, Elise Orange Randall, who founded the school in 1907. At that point, she had £5 in the bank and one student. But her crusade to teach young ladies to be good wives, to manage households with servants, still endures. Lessons included ironing, bed-making, cleaning silver and woodwork, and special tuition in dusting chairs ...

This sprawling, whitewashed house was in a prime location opposite The Grand Hotel.

The freedom that these young women sought in the 60s included consorting with the young male trainees of The Grand Hotel. Next door, most conveniently, was located the staff residence, St Vincent's, for the hotel's trainees. As the patron or defender of vintners, this was a more than an appropriate name for the home of the testosterone driven young hoteliers. The residence became the base, for meeting and partying, the scene of the genesis of many a first love and romantic liaison.

We had many female friends as well as 'girlfriends'. One special friend of mine was great fun and certainly embraced freedom with alacrity. Curiously, yet again my friend was Irish, Annie O'Neill, the daughter of the then Prime Minister of Northern Ireland, Captain Terence O'Neill. She was a friend who could always be counted on to bring a smile to my face and cheer me up at moments of depression, usually brought about over one of my many break ups with one of the many girls of my dreams. She was particularly good at bursting into my room at seven in the morning after such an event. With a bunch of shamrock in one hand and a bottle of Guinness in the other, we'd start the day of March 17th, St Patrick's Day, in an appropriate manner.

We relied on our female companionship from the college. Although the young women had a measure of freedom, the faculty had a duty of care for those in their charge, and there were strict house rules, which included high standards of decorum and behaviour, only mixing with the 'right sort' of boy, and curtailed social hours, which were never late enough for us.

Having been out one evening with a young woman of my dreams, I returned her obediently on time, but felt an overwhelming desire to steal one last kiss goodnight. Being resourceful and aware of her dorm window, in true Romeo style, I started to climb up a drainpipe that happily ran close to her window.

I successfully reached the top of the pipe and gently tapped on the window. The first girl who noticed me considered me to be an ill-intentioned intruder and started to scream, a scenario I had not counted on. Others soon gathered round, joining in the screaming which only stopped when my young woman opened the window and identified me as her boyfriend, at which moment all the girls immediately started to appreciate the nature of the visit, as I had surmounted such a dangerous challenge in the name of romance.

Bathing in this adoration did not last long, as from somewhere below me I heard a mature female voice shouting out "Young man. Young man! What on earth do you think you are doing? Come down this instant."

Very sheepishly and with not a little fear and trepidation for what I might soon face, not just at the bottom of the pipes but in my journey down, as I now became aware of movement in the old Victorian downpipes that I had not noticed in my enthusiasm to scale them. Relieved to reach the bottom, my slow climb down was not wasted as I concocted a plausible reason as to why I should have climbed the pipe up to the female dormitory, other than the obvious reason that apparently I was a peeping Tom.

Fortunately the house mistress knew me, and was not much of a battleaxe. "Oh it's you; I am surprised, I thought you were such a nice young man, what on earth do you think you were doing and what will I do with you?" I looked as apologetic as I could and tried to pour on the charm.

"Please forgive me, I am so sorry for giving you reason to question the trust you have in me, but it really is not as it seems, as you know I am a friend of one of your young ladies and we had been out tonight. When we left, I realized I had her purse I had picked up from the table when we left the restaurant. Thinking she would be upset at the thought she may have lost it and understanding I was not allowed to call at this time, I decided I would try to return it to her rather than have the night to fret over its whereabouts."

"Is that true? I will be speaking to the young lady in question."

My heart missed a beat, but looking up I saw that the girls were still leaning out of the window and just hoped that I had said it loud enough for them to hear.

"You may have been trying to be gallant, but it was very foolish and dangerous and could have upset and even endangered the girls emotions. I am sorry but there will be consequences, although I will not be reporting it to the police or your employers."

"Thank you, I am so sorry and will of course respect whatever action you may take, but it was meant with the best intent, but I agree very foolish."

She gave me a very stern look, as only a house mistress can. "I will bear that in mind, but now go back home and please do not contact the young lady until a decision has been made as to what we are to do." Looking as contrite as I could, I bowed my head and departed. Once I was at a safe distance I turned to see the house mistress returning and the young women still at the window waving and blowing kisses.

The following day I learned of my fate, which initially I felt was worse than death. I had been blacklisted for the rest of the term and none of the young women were allowed to contact or associate with me. I was devastated. What would I do? As it turned out, to carry such a sentence had the opposite effect. The strong minded and determined young women did not take kindly to being told whom they may choose to meet. I was now seen as a bit of a romantic rake, and became one of the most sought-after trainees on the dating circuit. My romantic life had always been a case of feast or famine and right now my life was a feast of monumental proportions. At last I had earned the title of Uncrowned King of Eastbourne, so kindly bestowed on me by DJ Pete Murray on Radio Luxembourg.

It was about this time that it seemed to me that having a good time and just enjoying the 'Grand' life might not be all it was cracked up to be. The dropout rate was high amongst trainee managers, who were the lowest paid of hotel employees. We were expected to put in up to seventy hours in a five and a half day week. A day off was seen as a luxury. If we complained we were regarded as disloyal, an indication that we were not prepared to put in the effort and didn't have the stamina to reach the goal of becoming a general manager one day.

One such trainee who threw in the towel was Collins. He was a huge fan of the movies, and found the hotel work hours did not suit either the matinee or evening performances at the local cinema. He found the answer by joining the Rank Organisation as a trainee cinema manager. A few months later he made a return visit to his old stomping ground in Eastbourne. We shared a beer and he told me of his exploits. These included seeing all the latest movies for free, which we lesser mortals had to pay two shillings and sixpence to watch. And it didn't end there. In the 1960s many of the larger cinemas were also used to host the pop bands of the era. So Collins had just seen The Searchers and The Dave Clark Five perform, again for free. To cap off my envy, he was earning fourteen pounds a week. Fourteen bloody pounds just for watching pop groups and movies. Hell – I was on only *four* pounds a week, and getting crap from cantankerous old women to boot.

"Why not come down when you next get a day off and I'll get you in to see a movie for free? In fact, next week we're showing a new big movie called *The Sound of Music*, it's on for two weeks. Why not try and make it, you can stay with me?"

This was an invitation I really wanted to take up, so a week later I was on the train bound for Portsmouth where he was working at the local Rank Cinema. We met up that evening and headed for a local nightspot and after a few beers headed back to his room at a local boarding house. "Keep quiet as the landlady doesn't allow guests." Now he tells me. As he let himself in, I held back until he waved his hand that it was safe to enter. "Mind the third stair, it creaks."

Being a little inebriated my counting skills were not what they should be and, as I progressed up the stairs, rather than avoiding stair three my foot came down with full force as I tried to balance myself. *Creeaaaak.* It sounded as loud as a crack of thunder. We froze, waiting for the light that was sure to stream out from the landlady's door. There was a sound of a cough and shuffling from behind her door, but it did not open.

Whether it was the stress of the moment, or the quantity of Strong's Pale Ale we had consumed, I am not certain but at that moment Collins let out a rear 'creak' of his own. We looked at each other and both burst out in rather silly giggles that even the fear of discovery could not stop. All that was left was for us to make a dash for the relative safety of his room.

The morning came too soon, and with a mouth like the bottom of a bird's cage, I tried to recall where I was and how I came to be in this predicament. It occurred to me that it might have been easy to get past the landlady in the middle of night, so I had to go through a game of cat and mouse to get out in broad daylight.

The following day I watched the matinee performance of *The Sound of Music* as promised. The best seats in the house and free to boot. I loved the movie and after the show Collins fared me well as I headed for the station to catch the last train back to Eastbourne. My journey back was filled with thoughts of Collins's luck - not only at watching movies for free, but also meeting the pop stars of the day, and at the same time earning three times what I was earning. The seeds of doubt started to stir in my mind as to whether I really wanted a career in hotel management.

A few days later I called Collins to find out more and who to write to for a job. I wrote the letter and a couple of weeks went by before a letter arrived, in an envelope marked "The Rank Organisation", inviting me for an interview the following week at an office in Reigate. I got some time off and planned it to coincide with a trip home to see my parents, and - if all went well - break the news to them of my brilliant career move.

The day came. Rail ticket in hand, I headed off to Reigate. The interview went well, although I was uncertain of the impact I had made with my answer to their question as to why I wanted a career with The Rank Organisation. I recounted my experience of listening to a school lecture by the man, who featured in the film introduction as the famous Charles Atlas figure, banging the large gong at the start of all their movies, which had become the company's logo. The man himself was rather an ordinary little man, and his gong was only about two feet in diameter, rather different to the magnificent proportions displayed on film. He was a percussionist in some orchestra or other, who had this claim to fame and gave school lectures on the subject of percussion instruments in general. What sparked my imagination was that, in the movies, not all was as it appeared.

Following the interview, it all seemed very promising and I headed home to Warwickshire to tell my parents of my decision. Over dinner I explained how I felt a change in career was an exciting move, as I was *sure* they would agree. To my surprise, the support I expected from my mother was not forthcoming; she thought it would be disastrous. My father on the other hand seemed more phlegmatic. I found this very unusual for the man who had guided me through life with strong directions as to what was best for me.

Mother retired to bed with the headache that I had given her. Dad sat down in front of the fire and asked me to join him. "Would you like a beer?" I was immediately caught off guard. For one, he hardly ever drank, and certainly didn't encourage me to do so. Seeing this as some sort of father-and-son-lecture, I steeled myself to listen to the error of my ways. We chatted and he asked me why I was keen on doing this. He very gently offered his thoughts. We discussed the cinema business, its future, my prospects both short and long term. He asked me what I liked about the industry and what I disliked about hotels, which, after all, was a career in which I had already spent nearly four years, and was near completing. A shame to throw that away. He seemed to have a very rational argument that allayed many of my concerns. At the end, in the early hours, he said something I had never heard him say before.

"Look Paddy, it is your life and it is your career, I cannot tell you what is best for you. I am glad that we could talk together about it, but in the end only you can make the decision. It's late, so let's go to bed and you sleep on it and whatever you decide, I will support you."

My father had never before spoken like this. He now accepted I was a man who was in control of his own destiny. He had not instructed me, told me or directed what would be best for me. He had for the first time handed me the freedom to decide what I wanted to do. It was a defining moment in my relationship with my father.

That night I thought of all he had said. Of course he was right. Of course I would be crazy to give up four years of training, to go into a declining industry that had limited career prospects. He was right, but at least he had given me the final say as to what I would do. That night I realised what a great father I had; memories came back of all the things he had said in the past, and how right he had been. I was lucky to have had a father like him.

The next day he drove me to the station to catch my train back to Eastbourne and back to my hotel career. He gently asked if I had had any further thoughts on our chat and my decision. I think at that moment, even if I had wanted to change my career, I would have followed his advice and not done so. I was so overjoyed at this new relationship I had found myself in with my father that I would have done anything to please him. I told him that I was going to continue with my hotel training and felt it would in time offer greater prospects of a successful future. He replied simply, saying "OK, if that is what you have decided then I am pleased for you. When you reach the station maybe you could call your mother and tell her, it will put her mind at rest." This was the most important conversation I ever had with my father and it was one for which I was eternally grateful.

With renewed energy I now directed myself as to how to improve my career prospects. As I have readily confessed, both then and throughout my life, I have had little interest in the academic side of things and this certainly applied to my hotel career.

My brother Bob, was much cleverer than I, an A student, a brilliant sportsman and a thespian to boot - albeit always playing the 'femme fatale' at his all-boys boarding school - probably an indication he was better looking as well. He had gone on to attend Westminster, the premiere college for hotel management at the time. This was a benchmark I knew I could never achieve, yet it did not particularly worry me. I was pleased that he had given my mother some reason for pride in him, when she was faced with the stiff competition of her four siblings and their apparently gifted and talented offspring.

This was never more evident than when my grandmother came to visit. She had been a gifted operatic singer, touring with The D'Oyly Carte Opera Company in Gilbert and Sullivan light operas. As such, there were expectations that a piano be kept in the house and that all the grandchildren would be proficient players of that piano. My mother, in the eyes of Granny Langley, had failed to achieve either. The fact that my eldest brother Chris was skilled on the trombone and the guitar, whilst I could bash out something vaguely musical on a washboard and "double bass" - which in reality was a broom handle, waxed string and an upturned tea chest - appeared to count for nought. The family skiffle band didn't cut it for Granny Langley. [63]

With all this in mind, I never had held great expectations for my future success either socially, sportingly, academically or career wise. Therefore, the realisation that maybe I would like to achieve something in this 'chosen trade' I had now embarked upon, came to me rather as I imagine the blinding light came to Paul on the road to Damascus.

My epiphany, as good fortune would have it, was when a vacancy appeared in the Front Office. One of the young women in reception left abruptly, which naturally gave rise to a number of rumours, including the suggestion that she was pregnant. To add some spice, this may have been the result of a less-than-discreet relationship with a married member of management, whose wife had become aware of her husband's dalliance and promptly gave him an ultimatum. Although this was the 1960s and a spirit of free love and the sexual revolution were taking a generation by storm, none of this had as yet reached the genteel halls of respectability at an establishment like The Grand Hotel.

The errant member of management seeking to replace the young woman with a minimum of fuss looked to the ranks of the trainee managers, who were easily moved from one department to another, under the guise of 'progression in their training'. Few questions were ever raised, least of all by the trainee, all of whom were desperate to get out of uniform and into the smart pinstriped management suits worn in front of house office positions.

So good luck befell me, as I was next in line for a move; I was most easily spared from my current activities. When I was asked to go to the office I realised with excitement that my life was about to change.

1966 was turning out to be a great year. With my new position, I now required a set of pinstriped trousers and a black jacket and waistcoat that formed the morning suit, my new uniform. Obtaining this required a day trip to London and to Moss Brothers of Oxford Street, the gentlemen's outfitters. Their fame was widespread for fitting out men for their day at the altar. For those unable or unwilling to buy such garments, a hire service was available. After a number of such hirings, the slightly worn but yet serviceable garments were sold to young men in private service or the hotel business.

These pre-worn suits retailed inexpensively, which was fortunate as being a trainee one's salary did not allow for much. Prior to my purchase, I had been given a little advice as to how best to proceed to ensure the best deal. This valuable information involved something that was new to me and which filled me with trepidation, so, yet again, my comfort zone was to be expanded.

Upon entering the store I was met by a gentleman who, on recognising my John Collier suit, greeted me with a less than enthusiastic welcome, having already assumed I was not there to purchase a top of the range suit. Before I could speak a word, he directed me to the basement where I would find what I was looking for. At the foot of the stairs I was met by the congenial twin of Mr Humphries from *Are You Being Served.*

"How may I help you sir?"

"I am looking for a morning suit, one of the second hand ones?"
"We rather prefer the term 'pre-loved suits'; so much nicer; come this way." I was taken to a long rack generally divided into sizes. "My you *are* tall and *very* long arms, now lets see what we have. What sort of price had you in mind?"

He explained that the suits varied in price according to wear and tear, although the quality was the same. As I tried on one after another within my limited budget, I noticed that indeed some were most certainly much more 'loved' than others. It was now that I put my tactical advice into play. Reaching for a suit that I could see was almost new and which cost a lot more than the one selected that was within my price range, I laid it on the table. "What about this one?" Placing two pound notes in the breast pocket beside the label.

Mr Humphries eyed me with a look that made my palms sweat. "Which hotel did you say you are from?"

"The Grand Hotel in Eastbourne."

"Ah yes, we have fitted a number of young men with morning suits. Now, what is the name of your Deputy Manager?"

Speaking the name was like the passing of a secret code. A relaxed smile returned to Mr Humphries' face. "Now let me see..."

He deftly pulled the label from the top pocket along with the pound notes that vanished into his own top pocket. "Oh, there seems to be a slight mark here and the seam appears to have a stitch or two missing."

I peered at the spot he pointed to, saw nothing, but nodded in agreement all the same.

"Yes, I think we could do this within your budget."

With the transaction done I left the store with an almost brand-new morning suit, looking over my shoulder rather guiltily. Once confident that no policeman was about to arrest me, I headed for Oxford tube station, to Victoria and on to the five-twenty to Eastbourne.

The following morning I donned my smart new morning suit. With one look in the mirror at a very dapper young man, I was ready to take on the world. My collar was starched, my grey silk tie, a gift from my father, was tied in a half Windsor (a full windsor being too large for a starched collar), and, to complete the ensemble, I had a waistcoat. The guilt of my dealings of the previous day was long forgotten. I was at last starting to feel like a manager; it was as if dressing up created a change in me that I had not hitherto experienced. It gave me confidence that this was the career for me.

All this new enthusiasm was also helped along by an event that year that brought massive optimism that all was well in the world. On 30th July 1966, England beat West Germany 4-2 after extra time to win The World Cup, the ultimate achievement in the world of football. As with any world stopping event, whether Kennedy's assassination or man landing on the Moon, everyone remembers where they were. I watched it at a friend's home in Polgate, on the outskirts of Eastbourne, as he had a large colour TV, a rarity at the time. I, to the horror of many, have never followed football but this event was one that the whole of England watched. The players were not the only heroes of the event. In the build-up to the tournament, the Jules Rimet Trophy had been stolen from an exhibition. After a nationwide hunt it was discovered wrapped in newspaper by a dog called Pickles, who sniffed it out from under some bushes in London and shared the glory on the day.

The first World Cup was played in July 1930, when Uruguay defeated Argentina, coincidentally by the same score, 4 to 2. It took England thirty-six years to win and since that wonderful sunny day in 1966, we've been waiting for it to happen again. I'm resigned to consider it a 'once in a lifetime experience'.

My first weeks in hotel reception were uneventful. There were systems to learn and machines to operate. This was very much before the computer age. We relied upon a Sweda Register, a mechanical machine that whirred and clanked so loudly whenever a button was pressed that in today's office I am sure ear defenders would be mandatory to operate such a machine. One had to enter each and every sales docket into the machine by guest room number, department key, and the amount, which would then print this information onto a self-duplicating card, which in turn was placed in the slot in the machine. All this relied upon the operator not making a single error when reading handwritten dockets that arrived from the bar, restaurant, telephones or anywhere the customer had booked a service to his room account. Not an easy task for one like me, especially as many staff came from different parts of Europe where numbers were often written in different styles like the French seven or German one. All of this merely added to the impatience of those female front office staff who, at best, tolerated public school fops like me who'd been dumped on them to train, and who slowed them down in their normal efficient routines.

Why was it that women were so much more adept at punching things into the machines than I ever was?

Most of the time the reception girls got us out from under their feet by sending us to collect the 'checks' from the different departments for posting to the guests' bills. Apart from the restaurant and bars there was also the telephones. The switchboard was located in little more than a box room under the stairs, opposite Mr Pickles' barber shop. This was the domain of two women, Jean and Maureen. They were GPO trained and spoke with perfect clipped English pronunciation when speaking on the telephone to the guests.[64]

The telephone switchboards were manually operated, and switchboard operators connected calls by inserting a pair of phone plugs into the appropriate jacks. When a guest called from a room the operator would plug in the jack above which a small light lit up. The guest would ask for the number, with the town first, such as Mayfair 123, the operator would then call the GPO operator and give the number, requesting an 'AD & C' or Advise Duration & Charge. A few minutes later the GPO operator rang back and the hotel operator would connect and announce the call, often listening in if there was any good gossip to hear. When I did my training it was not as easy as it seemed; one had to note which room had requested which number as failure to do so would cause untold problems, as happened when I connected the wife of a guest to the wrong room and another woman answered thus necessitating a great deal of explanation and apologies to the berated husband whose wife assumed he had a woman in his room. I only did it once after which I was returned to reception.

Jean, one of the operators, was a very large woman with a lovely voice that could melt butter. So much so it was not unusual for gentlemen callers to regularly seek to obtain her number with regard to a possible off duty liaison, but Jean maintained the mystery and never allowed such things to happen

As I write, I realise that the one thing that has changed the world most since the 1960s is communication. I could never have imagined life as it is today, and neither can my children comprehend my life then, with a switchboard system and a Telex machine, soon to enter service in hotels. Facsimile machines were twenty years away. Mobile phones were things of science fiction. At the time only top end hotels had telephones in bedrooms, or for that matter televisions, and these were promoted as luxury facilities. Not even every home had them, relying on a friendly neighbour if the need arose. When living in Thailand years later, I found a switchboard identical to the one I had trained on, displayed in a luxury hotel in Hua Hin, in my favourite restaurant, aptly called The Museum. I went there with my son and was attempting to explain to him how it worked, when I heard a laugh and an American voice behind me said "Now that's a real museum piece!" I can only assume he was referring to the switchboard.

With the exception of the Front Office Manager, all the hotel office staff were female. Mary was a well-built young woman with a lovely smile and pleasant countenance. Angela was a redhead with a love of folk music and an ability to do a good rendering of Joan Baez's *We Shall Overcome*. Anita was very much the *femme fatale* of the day, with mascara'd lashes and eyeliner that reminded one of a panda. Lorely, or Lori as we knew her then, was a very glamorous young woman, but for me, very intimidating and way out of my league. She had no patience with trainees and even less for me, especially when I made mistakes and was unable to balance the machines at the end of the evening shift. This would then result in a lengthy process of checking every entry that had been made and often took several hours. This did not endear me to Lorely who - invariably - would have a date awaiting her.

There is a postscript to the lovely Lorely and me. Shortly after I left The Grand, it was taken over by De Vere Hotels, and the managing director was Mr Reg Constable, her father. Over the next twenty years he was my boss and mentor, and Mrs Brenda

Constable was to become a maternal figure to me, the young developing manager. On a visit back from Australia many years later, I was to have lunch with an old friend and colleague my deputy from The Cavendish who went on to become the General Manager of The Grand, Peter Hawley, together with Reg and Brenda. Much to my surprise, Brenda asked me why had I not married Lorely, as she seemed to imply we were such a great match. I didn't like to tell her that Lorely had never given me a second look. Lorely and I were not to see each other again until, together with her husband Barrie, they visited me in Sydney, forty years later.[65, 66]

The front office comprised three distinct areas. At the Reception, staff would check the guests in and handle all guest reservations on a complexed Whitney rack system, with the General Manager signing letters of confirmation to guests. Cashiers handled all the financial transactions. The Control Department was located above Reception and Cashiers. Accounting staff beavered away checking everything that cashiers had done and revelling in the mistakes they found. This created a rather strained relationship between 'upstairs' and 'downstairs'. As a trainee, I was expected to work in all three departments. One learned early on *always* to be diplomatic and never burn any bridges between the three. However this was easier said than done.

It seems incomprehensible now, but all the hotel staff looked at ways of 'improving' upon their meagre incomes of the time. The term 'perks' was applied to anything that supplemented one's income, even if by today's standards it would be blatantly criminal. Bar staff had their ways, as I discovered when working in the American Bar, but at the time their perks somehow seemed morally acceptable. In the front office we were not dealing in drinks or cigarettes but in pounds, shillings and pence, which my father had instilled in me meant no shades of grey, it was simply black and white.

Sunday lunch in the restaurant was always busy with a lot of casual 'walk ins' as they were known. This was pre-credit card, with everyone paying cash or cheque. As the dockets for the meals came through from the restaurant, the table number was recorded and the price of the dish entered in the columns, being totalled at the end of the meal. The *maitre d'* would appear at the desk. "Table 21 bill please". It would be handwritten and presented to the guest. End of transaction.

What was *really* happening was that the Sunday lunch accounts book was all done initially in pencil. Whoever was party to the perk would then simply erase one or two entries and pocket the cash. At the end of the shift it was re-entered in ink, and if anyone were to ask why then it was simply blamed on the head waiter's inability to clearly write the check which then needed amending when the customer queried the bill. This perk came to an abrupt end with what might have resulted in a royal diplomatic incident.

One Sunday in 1967 the King Bhumibol Adulyadej and The Queen of Thailand came to the hotel with their daughter and son to celebrate the son's fourteenth birthday. The Crown Prince was at school in nearby King's Mead School at Seaford. At the time, this was not seen as a major event as Thailand was still a place few had heard of other than in the Rodgers and Hammerstein musical *The King and I*. This King was far from the vision of Yul Brynner, albeit the Queen certainly did turn heads. Having said this, the visit was big enough to bring the General Manager in on a Sunday, with his daughter who was ushered forward to present a bouquet of flowers to the Queen.

Their Royal presence for lunch in the restaurant created little attention and almost went unnoticed, other than the fact that there were a number of foreigners dining, something of an unusual occurrence in Eastbourne.

It was a day or so later that the local press got wind of the fact that the Thai Royals had been at The Grand and, it being a slow news week, asked for some comment from management on the occasion. One question was "what had they been eating?". This resulted in a request for the red accounts book which would have the meal recorded within. Unfortunately for that Sunday, the cashier on duty did not anticipate there would be any questions and had carefully removed one entry that had netted them a nice little amount for a night out. When the question was raised as to which entry was that of the Royal Party, a similar entry was found and described to the press.

The press statement contained a selection of dishes that were in fact consumed by a local doctor and his family, celebrating his wife's birthday. This was questioned by the waiter who had served the Royals, however he was not vocal enough to bring it to anyone's attention. The outcome of this was to create such a fear of discovery amongst all concerned that they immediately returned to the path of righteousness. From then on all items were entered in the Sunday lunch red accounts book correctly and in ink. From my perspective, this was a pleasing result; due to my impending move to the Control Department upstairs, I would have been faced with the moral dilemma of whether to expose the wrongdoings of the staff in Cashiers. This would have most definitely ruined any future relationships I might have wished to develop with the girls of that department.

At the time, I would never have come close to imagining that fifty years later I would be retired and living in Thailand, where the same King upon his death was revered with God-like status, and the young fourteen year old son who we had served lunch then ascended the throne of Thailand.

I had now reached the closing stages of my training in management. The front office was as far as the training took a young man. I had honed my skills in most departments of the hotel with very little formal instruction but a lot of real life experience. I hoped at the time that this would be enough to understand the workings of a luxury hotel.

I look back now and think that in a changing world it was a sound basis on which to build a career and one I had enjoyed. It was all about the people one served who came from so many walks of life: the privileged, the educated and the wealthy as well as those from the other end of the scale who have almost nothing, with little education and a past life of hardship just trying to get by. I would not have crossed paths with the latter type of people without the hotel, but these were the people from whom I really learned a great deal.

The other technical and industry knowledge I would need to develop over the years was yet to come: deeper understanding of fine wines and food, specialised understanding of concepts like 'marketing' which was pretty well unknown at the time. Ahead of me yet were terms like 'Human Resources', the massive growth in legislative regulations and 'political correctness'. Most of all, what lay ahead was what really changed the hotel industry and indeed the whole world: the computer age. And the accountants. The key skills were to be able to adjust, develop and adapt.

Chapter 13

#comingofage #summeroflove# #doubledutch

It was 1967. Four years previously I had very nervously walked through the back doors of The Grand Hotel. Where had the time gone? Now, resplendent in my morning suit, working in the Front Office, exerting what small authority and status I could with the guests, I realised that there were no more departments in the hotel that would be of use to me.

There were two sources of motivation for me: the thrill of becoming someone of more importance, someone in charge, and the improved opportunity as to my earning capacity. Even though my current five pounds ten shillings a week was a substantial increase on the original salary, it was just pocket money as food and room were included. It was sufficient to keep me in cigarettes and beer, albeit half pints of mild and bitter. I felt as a university student today must feel on nearing completion of their studies. The work was hard with long hours, but, unlike a university student, the cerebral aspects were never really called into play, with the exception of the need of the occasional burst of creativity and adrenaline to get out of a difficult situation with a manager or guest. My tactics were always to overcome the situation with some humour or, when this failed, abject apologies that would have made even Basil Fawlty flinch.

"Where to from here?" started to play on my mind. In hotels at that time, it had been the tradition for a young man completing his training in luxury hotels of an international standard to do what was in hotel parlance referred to as his 'stage'; an unpaid internship to work briefly somewhere in Europe, which really meant France. The main purpose was to open a young man's eyes to the ways of those foreigners across the Channel, whose service and culinary skills were regarded as far superior to any that England could offer. The other purpose was that to complete a young hotelier's education, he should of course speak another language apart from his mother tongue. The latter filled me with fear as it would require much academic effort; not my strong point, but without the language how could I survive in a country like France? It was not known for its goodwill and warmth to its Anglo neighbours. With De Gaulle in power and harbouring a grudge against Churchill since the war, France was certainly not extending a welcoming and understanding hand to any Englishman who now chose to take up residence there. I was more than worried that without any French language skills at all, this could be my Waterloo.

Something else had filled me with terror of a placement in France. My eldest brother, whom I looked up to, had for a short while flirted with the idea of hotel management but thankfully he changed his mind for a far more lucrative and successful career in film and television for which he gained some fame, and I could bathe in his limelight from time to time. However, during his mild flirtation, he had himself spent a 'stage' at a small *pension* in the south of France. His tales of early mornings, late nights, and scrubbing floors translated to me as slave labour with a very unhappy French overseer.

With this playing heavily on my mind, I sought out the advice and counsel of the Deputy Manager, Mr Michael Cairns. I had worked under him in my initial training at the Manor House Hotel prior to his appointment as second in command at The Grand. He was a man one could not help but admire, although, unlike many of his public school trainees, he spoke with a definite Mancunian accent. He would quip that "my school was so *public* everyone went to it" and was very straight talking and sports mad, cricket being his game of choice, although squash also featured. Cricket as I have said before was *not* a great game for me after my school day experiences, but squash seemed to be better and faster, with the basics easier to master. Surely all one did was to run around, bashing a little ball between two lines on the walls? It was also a game that one could fit into a spare hour of a day and did not encroach on pub opening times. I discovered that Mr Cairns regularly played the game at the local sports club, and, thinking this might aid me in getting a little closer to his social plane, the man who would indeed bring to bear some influence on my future, I carefully manoeuvred to be at the squash court when he had booked a game. It was very fortuitous that his partner had failed to show, and he asked me what I was doing. I said that squash was a game I had always wanted to learn but with the work hours, I had not been able to do. As a northerner with a reputation for thrift, rather than seeing his two shilling booking go to waste, he kindly invited me to join him for a basic lesson in the game. It was far harder than I had imagined, but at least being light on my feet with a long arm stretch I was able to return a few of his masterly shots. Although this did not make us friends, it did gain from him a little personal recognition of my existence.

The morning I had decided to make my approach for advice for the future, I found myself again in the right place at the right time. As I stood outside his open office door I could not help but overhear his entreaty to his secretary to reconsider her earlier agreement to baby-sit his two children, a commitment she could no longer honour. For Mr Cairns this was a major blow as it was late in the day and he and his wife had a very important event to attend that evening. I was about to turn around and quietly disappear as this was not the time to speak to him, when he noticed me in the doorway.

"What do you want Griffin?" I could hear the edge of frustration in his voice.

"No problem sir, I can come back…"

At that moment a flash of pure genius crossed my mind. He was bordering on panic at his dilemma, his wife had already called to say she had left the hairdresser and not to be late, he could see no way out of what was about to turn into a disaster. At the time I did not appreciate it but know now that what happened next changed my life.

"Forgive me sir, I couldn't help but overhear you are facing a baby-sitting problem? I fully understand if you prefer to make other arrangements, but I have nothing on tonight and certainly little cash to enjoy the evening if I had, so if you would like me to baby-sit I should be more than happy to do so. It would be nice to have an evening watching TV."

The reply was immediate, "That would be fantastic, I would really appreciate it, you are a lifesaver, I owe you one." Wow. An even better reaction than I could have wished for. "You had better get back to your room, change and meet me back here in an hour. It may be late but I will get you a taxi back, are you OK with that?" Am I OK? The idea of ingratiating myself and he owing me was a brilliant outcome.

We drove to his home, I chatted lightly about what's next for me, but not in a direct way as to push my luck. He in any event was more focused on his important evening ahead. His wife was very thankful and I met the children, was given a briefing, the phone contact, where the food was and how the TV worked. As I settled in Mr and Mrs Cairns prepared to depart, again thanking me for stepping in, telling me to help myself to food and make myself comfortable. Just as he was leaving, he pointed to some international hotel magazines sitting on the coffee table.

"If you get bored with TV, have a read of those magazines, some interesting articles on the future of hotels. There's a great article about the American chain Hilton coming into Europe, the first to do so. They are in London, Berlin, Brussels and Amsterdam. Those are the hotels of the future that you should go to, bugger the little provisional French places. You won't learn much from them, the world is moving on."

With that his wife dragged him out the door, and with a smile and a nod they were gone.

TV that evening *was* boring, the kids were quiet and asleep. Comfortably ensconced on the sofa, armed with a ham sandwich and a glass of orange juice (I didn't want to risk losing favour by hitting his drinks cabinet), I picked up the magazines and started flicking through them.

I soon found the article on the Hilton drive into Europe. How refreshingly modern and exciting the hotels looked, they almost jumped off the page. The Amsterdam Hilton, as it was called (as yet the city name came first before the hotel brand). Located in the south of the city, on the elegant avenue of Apollolaan on the bank of the canal, it was designed by a Dutch architect of great reputation, Hugh Aart Maaskant. The man charged with the task of establishing the Hilton name in Amsterdam and other European cities was an American, Mr Ralf Starkey. With typical American confidence and enthusiasm he spoke of the new world of hotels and the future. I was sold by the second paragraph. It was exciting, it was new and it was blowing away the cobwebs of age old traditions of the grand hotels of Europe whose service and operating methods had not changed in a century.

This was what I wanted for a future, not just the new style and the American pizzazz, but Amsterdam. Not some little town in the south of France. And didn't most Dutchmen speak English? So elated was I with my new focus for the future, I didn't even notice it was past midnight before Mr Cairns returned. They thanked me again with mellow gratitude after a successful night out, for saving the day. I quickly mentioned my enthusiasm for the article. "Take it with you but let me have it back when you are finished. I have paid the taxi, and here is ten bob for you."

It was an enormous percentage of my weekly salary for a relaxing evening in front of the TV. As a penniless trainee I do not know why, but before I could rethink I simply said "No, that is fine, the kids were great and no problem and I enjoyed the night in".

"No take it, you have no idea how you saved the day".

"That's fine," I repeated. At that point the northern thrift kicked in and the ten bob note returned to his pocket. Never ever decline a gift from a Mancunian.

Over the next few weeks I spoke more to Mr Cairns about the future of Hilton and he suggested a letter to Mr Starkey. "After all, what harm can it do, he can only ignore you, or, if you are lucky, at least get a letter from Hilton and your name on their files. You are good at writing letters, impress him with your enthusiasm. I can lend you a book on US Hotel Operations."

The book 'Modern Accounting - As laid down by The Hotel and Motel Association of America', was not as I had wanted; accounting was far from a subject I was interested in (for God's sake - after three attempts I still could not pass my Maths General Certificate at school). But I persevered even though it was not a great read. There was lots about some system called 28 day accounting, whereby months were divided into 28 day periods, rather than the traditional calendar months of various lengths, a system that seemed to have some logic behind it where at least like was compared with like. This newly gleaned knowledge made me think that rather than the usual application for some internship in food and beverage operations, and all the hours that accompanied such a position, I would apply for an office type of job, in a control or accounts department.

So putting pen to paper I composed my letter to Mr Ralph Starkey. I emphasised my motivation for learning new things, my ability to work hard, how impressed I was with his views on the future development of the hotel industry, I added my English public school background, my family immersion in banking (I mean my father and grandfather had been with Lloyds so something must have rubbed off), and finally wrote about my initiative in studying 'Modern Accounting - As laid down by The Hotel and Motel Association of America.'

After several attempts, and numerous questions to friends on spelling and grammar, I ventured to share my letter with Mr Cairns. He read it and smiled, made some rather caustic remarks on family background and his standard public school joke, and handed it back, "Fine. Why not? It will only cost you a stamp."

So together with my hand crafted CV and with the boss's input to my letter, I sealed the envelope and headed to the post office at the rear of the hotel to buy the special overseas stamp that would send my letter winging its way abroad to the other man who might shape my future. [67]

I waited. Days turned into weeks. I kept asking if I had any mail. Mr Cairns occasionally enquired if I had heard anything and when I told him no, he smiled and said, "Well there is always France."

Then a letter arrived. A cream envelope with a most impressive modernist crest in the corner, which looked like two drunken men leaning against an upright post with three large diagonal crosses on it. Almost too nervous to open, I tried to make sense of the logo. It was a vertical version of the flag of the city of Amsterdam, three white St Andrew's crosses on a black background with an angled 'H' that was more an 'A' either side of the flag: Hilton Hotel. This problem solved I turned the envelope over; on the back, 'Apollolaan, Amsterdam - Z., Holland'.

I steeled myself to open the envelope. Would it be a *thank you for your interest but we are unable to offer you employment?* Might I get lucky and be asked for more information by way of a standard application form that Americans were so fond of? An offer of an interview was something that was beyond any expectations I could have had. Gently I started to open it, not wanting to destroy the smooth lines of the designer envelope. I carefully withdrew the embossed letter headed single page of notepaper and started to read.

Dear Mr Griffin.

Mr Ralph Starkey has passed on to me, your letter of inquiry for a position with The Amsterdam Hilton.

Thank you so much for the interest you have expressed in joining our team and I acknowledge your background and enthusiasm. I note your interest in our accounting methods and the efforts you have made to learn them.

We will be requiring a suitable person to fill a position within our 'Bon Control' department in the course of the next few months and should such a position be of interest to you, we should be pleased to forward more details to you.

Please reply to my office at your earliest convenience.

B.H.G.Nijenhuis
Personnel Manager.

I turned the letter over; nothing more. Checked the envelope again, nothing else in there.

I read it again. And again. Not sure I really understood. His English was perfect. Could he, being Dutch, have meant something different as to how I interpreted his letter? It seemed clear and straight forward - I was being offered a job. No more information sought, no interview, just say yes and more details will be sent. No date but an indication, no salary offer, but who cares? I ran to Mr Cairns' office. I was scared the print would disappear like invisible ink before I could have someone witness and confirm the contents of the letter.

"Mr Cairns." I could hardly contain my excitement. "I've heard from Hilton!"

"Let me see it then." He looked, read and read again. Looking up he gave a little smile. "Well there you are; nothing ventured..." As if an afterthought, "Good luck."

The meeting was over.

"Oh Griffin, make sure you let me know when you plan to leave so I can get someone to replace you".

My acceptance letter was in the post within hours.

The news of my good fortune soon spread, especially amongst my fellow trainees. By and large all were congratulatory. There were a few *you jammy bastard* or *how the hell did you manage to swing that?* In any event they all seemed pleased with my good fortune, as indeed was I. As it sank in, I realised that I would now be sitting in an office, hopefully working reasonable hours and in an exciting city like Amsterdam where at least I had half a chance of finding people speaking English.

I had managed to escape the horrors that had, up until now, given me nightmares at what might follow my Grand training: scrubbing floors, working day and night in some French provincial hotel, being the *bouc emissaire* (whipping boy) for patrons who had never forgiven the English for thrashing Napoleon at Waterloo.

The other major event of that year was about to take place, this being the year of our Lord 1967. I was about to reach my coming of age, obtain the keys to the door and even have the right to vote. Two years later the voting age was reduced to eighteen.

On informing my parents by phone, they expressed their delight, and managed to cover up their surprise. It appeared that at last I might be getting my act together. Due to the enormity of these upcoming events, surely I might be allowed some time off now to return home to see them, when both achievements might be accorded the appropriate celebrations with the family?

It was January and Eastbourne had fallen under the spell of winter, cold, grey and wet. One could have fired a cannon down The Grand Parade with little fear of hitting anyone and so it was not a problem when I approached Mr Cairns to seek a week or so holiday, particularly as I had not taken one in a couple of years. As a trainee manager, holidays were not expected to be taken, and were as unheard of as a weekend off. Split shifts and unpaid overtime was the trainee's lot. To my surprise I was granted ten days.

My birthday was on the 3rd of February, and was almost upon us. A date was set to travel north to Leamington Spa. Big brother Chris and Jill, his wife, who happened to be very pregnant with their as yet unknown first son, heir to the Griffin dynasty, would also travel up for the celebrations.

It was agreed that we would drive up together on the Friday, which happened to be the 3rd, and hold a celebration at my parents' home on Saturday. Being at rather short notice it was decided to keep the event as a family affair, with just a few close friends and relatives and of course my current girlfriend, the tall and statuesque Jenny with whom I had become rather more involved with than was normally the case.

David, a fellow trainee, was the only one with a car, thanks to his parents who were distraught at never having him visit them in Richmond, and bought him the little 1955 Austin A30. He kindly offered to give us a lift to my brother's home in Kingston on Thames, which happened to be on his way, providing I chipped in for petrol. Being midwinter I was more than happy to do so.

Friday arrived and, in the early morning chill on a typically windy Eastbourne morning, the three of us, with bags squeezed into the confined space of the Austin set off on our journey. It was one of those little cars that looked more like the car driven by Noddy and Big Ears than a vehicle that could transport four people. Mind you we had in the past managed to make it to parties in London with six on board, willing its little 803cc engine to climb some of the gradients on the A23.

Although February was relatively mild thankfully, as the Austin's heater did not provide much comfort. As we neared London the dark grey skies opened up and it bucketed down, putting maximum stress on the short wipers that desperately tried to move the water cascading down the windscreen. Eventually, in the early afternoon, we arrived at my brother's. With little time to spare, we transferred to his car so that we could arrive before nightfall. The transfer was easier said than done as we realised Chris had changed the car and now sported what was regarded then as a rather nifty Triumph Herald, the problem being that this two door product of Coventry's Triumph Motor Company was hardly, if any, bigger than the Austin, but now had to accommodate four adults, one of whom was very pregnant, and of course our luggage.

Eventually we crushed in and were on our way, with Chris at the wheel, Jill in the front and Jenny and I, knees up to our chins with a case each on our laps, in the small rear seats. The journey up to Leamington Spa was not comfortable and the rain just got worse, with the windows constantly fogging up. We arrived in the dark to warm greetings and sympathies from our mother. "Come in dears, you must all be exhausted, go into the sitting room and Jill you must relax and make yourself comfortable on the sofa in front of the fire and we will have some tea".

I have never understood why tea was the beverage and panacea for all occasions in our household and the choice of beverage to welcome a guest to our home. I would have rather have had a beer. After the obligatory cup of tea, we went to our rooms to wash up and get ready for dinner. As I and Jenny headed up the stairs to my old room, mother called out, "I have put Jenny in the green room, I am sure she will be comfortable." My parents had yet to accept the standards of the easygoing sixties and at this stage I was not particularly in the mood to either shock, rebel or explain our relationship even if I was about to 'come of age'.

That evening we settled in to catch up on news and plans for the following evening's celebrations. There were about twenty people coming, although my favourite aunty Joyce - who was always the most generous of aunts - was not sure as she and Douglas, the respected doctor in the family, would need to stay at home to receive their daughter and her husband, also a doctor, who were bringing their new son for a visit. They would try to make it along later.

The next day was busy sorting out the format for the evening, who would say what. At least it was to be informal with no black tie nonsense, just some nice food, lots of alcohol, and thank God there were spirits as well as the selection of sherries. My parents were not big drinkers, unlike many of the relatives. God bless the relatives.

At about seven family and friends started to arrive and the celebrations got underway. Chris as always was the life and soul of the party and all were full of good humour and congratulatory comments for both my birthday and the fact that I was heading overseas to Amsterdam - quite an adventure. Lots of advice and the odd nudge and a wink were received about some of the stories my cousins had heard of this rather wild city, now gaining a little bit of a reputation for the 'Flower Power' culture of free love and drugs. This news rather cheered me on, but thankfully it had as yet not reached Royal Leamington Spa and certainly not my parents in their salubrious home in the tree lined Northumberland Road (a road that had so much influence with the council that they erected a sign stating 'No Heavy Traffic Allowed' so as not to disturb the tranquillity of the neighbourhood.)

As the evening became a little more riotous, we could not help but notice that Jill was starting to look exceedingly distressed. She wasn't due for another week or so and she and Chris had planned to return to London where she had a room reserved at her maternity hospital. Suddenly in the middle of the Beach Boys' *Good Vibrations*, having had special dispensation given to play pop rather than my father's *Salad Days* LP, Jill decided that it was unlikely she would be making the trip back to London that evening.

Chris adopted the 'oh shit what the hell do we do now' approach. Father, calm as always, in a considered but firm voice said "Call Douglas" (the doctor uncle). Chris immediately grabbed the phone and called Douglas. By now silence had fallen on the room and all listened intently to see how the drama might unfold. Jill looked a little concerned and definitely aware that something was about to happen. Mother was holding her hand and a few women were also giving advice, but no one asked me to put the kettle on and get towels as I always thought was the order of the day. Jill, who was always considerate and the kindest of people, managed a little smile in my direction as if to say *'sorry to take the limelight'*, which had not entered my head. Now I realised that my grand event was about to be upstaged by something rather special. "No of course we can't get back to London," Chris said. "OK we'll be over within 30 minutes."

Fortunately, Uncle Douglas lived only a short distance away in what we all regarded as a mansion of a house in Tachbrook, the one in which I had spent so much of my youth with my cousin Tim. Father agreed to drive, having a larger car, and went out to make it ready. He always hated sudden journeys, as he was convinced that not allowing the engine to warm up meant driving with the choke out and this might damage the engine. Someone threw some items in a bag and Chris with husbandly concern edged Jill into as comfortable position as she could manage on the back seat with a few pillows, and off they sped into the night.

We returned back to the warmth of the house. Somehow the alcohol had worn off and the atmosphere mellowed. The conversation had rather changed, with the focus no longer on me.

"Thank goodness Douglas was there..."

"Isn't David the son-in-law a doctor as well - at least Jill will be in good hands..."

"Two doctors..."

"Does anyone know if she is expecting a boy or a girl..."

"It must have been the long journey up here, he really shouldn't have come up just for a party..."

Oh great. Now I was to blame for all this. The evening did go on, but my moment of glory was lost. I recall a couple of speeches which had the inevitable concluding words "Well, this will be a night you will remember. What a gift from your big brother - a nephew." Yes indeed it was.

The weekend wasn't over. As if to rub salt into the wound, my mother and father insisted on us all meeting at the Manor House Hotel for Sunday lunch, the same hotel that I had initially trained in before moving to The Grand. Cigars, champagne and numerous toasts followed to the newborn child, Peter, the first grandson, who had been delivered at 4.00am on Sunday. At first just accepting, but then actually getting caught up in the excitement of the moment, I started enjoying the idea - it was something I could dine out on for years to come. I still remind Pete when his birthday comes round, even though he has now turned fifty.

That afternoon I put Jenny on the train so that she could return to Eastbourne and I remained to catch up with relatives and start to make sense of all that had happened in the past couple of weeks. I returned to The Grand the following week, and as I pulled into Eastbourne railway station I thought of just how much I had changed since my arrival a few years earlier. I also pondered how I had never really got to know the general staff of the hotel; although I often worked alongside them, we were very much segregated because social mixing between management and the rank and file staff was frowned upon.

It seemed The Grand was the last bastion of an antiquated class system that was being washed away in the post-war period of Britain, what was being called 'the Swinging Sixties'. By today's standards, it is hard to imagine The Grand ever existed. It was kept alive by the ever aging and diminishing number of guests who sought it out, and as long as there were the 'old retainers' such as Morris, Charlton, Stapley and Marion walking the corridors and lounges of the hotel, it would remain alive. I feel in some ways privileged to have experienced it, to have met these unique people who had known nothing else other than private service, and had been dedicated to those they served. Not for money, and with no care for the hours they worked, but simply the pride in serving and caring unquestioningly for their guests and masters.

It might be hard to understand how such old-fashioned ideals would assist in setting a young man on track for modern hotel management, but it gave me a mindset that was to shape my entire life. I had learned empathy for those I had worked with, people from a different background and far less fortunate. I had learned about other cultures and other countries. I learned how the 'other half', the 'privileged', lived, acted and behaved, which did not always impress me. I had learned how others saw me as exceedingly privileged, and could appreciate their opinion.

Nowadays when I watch a period drama on TV or at the movies, such as *Gosford Park* or *Downton Abbey*, I can see in Maggie Smith's portrayal of the Countess the image of the hotel guests I had served, who were still accompanied by their lady's maid, chauffeur and valet. Having read Kazuo Ishiguro's *The Remains of the Day*, and watched the film with Anthony Hopkins playing the butler James Stevens, I see an amazing likeness, in looks, character, mannerisms and bearing to The Grand Hotel's butler, Charlton, whose ghost is probably walking the halls to this day.

I was soon to receive the confirmation letter I had been eagerly awaiting, with the date that had been set for me to commence my new life and career at The Hilton Hotel in Amsterdam. Monday 1st May 1967.

March and April drifted by and eventually on Sunday 23rd of April, I packed my suitcase, bid farewell to my friends to whom I had become so close over the past few years. I had a last look at my room in St Vincent's house. It had been my home since arriving in Eastbourne and I thanked the Gods that walls could not talk. Jenny was waiting for me at the foot of the stairs, along with my friend who was to drive me to the station. I had imbibed a little too much and a little too often with this guy, but he was a very lovable character and the first Aussie I had met. He was true to the image of an ex-Bondi lifesaver, blond and rugged, who had come to England as part of his walkabout, as he called it. At the station and with firm handshakes we bid our goodbyes. I charged him with the job of looking after Jenny and making sure she was OK, as I would return some day and hopefully resume where we had left off. Jenny hugged me and seemed reluctant to let go. I felt that she had so much to say, but she held back tears and just looked at me. A final hug, and I boarded the train with that heavy clunk that accompanies the closing of a carriage door. There was an incoherent announcement that I did not understand, a whistle blew and we lurched forward. I leaned out of the window, muttering something or other as the train gathered speed. My God - the moment was playing in my imagination - was that really Rachmaninoff's Piano Concerto I was hearing? Was that Celia Johnson on the platform? Was I becoming Trevor Howard in *Brief Encounter*?

Pull yourself together Griffin. You are off to Amsterdam, at this time the wildest and most sinful city in Europe. Get with the programme. Farewell Eastbourne, *Sun Trap of the South* and God's waiting room, farewell The Grand Hotel. Hello Hilton, the modern future of the hotel industry and hello Amsterdam, city of lights, Flower Power and the Summer of Love.

Chapter 14

#Amsterdam67 #frites'n'mayonnaise #americansabroad

I had less than a week at home in Leamington Spa before my departure for Holland. It seemed that I had hardly unpacked my suitcase after my years in Eastbourne, and I was packing it again for another unknown and exciting venture. This time however I felt more prepared. I was older, and I had seen and experienced much more of life. Even if it was only Eastbourne.

My father had arranged a ticket for me and, as was his way, went through all the stages of the journey with me in great detail. My father was into detail, and wanted to ensure that I understood. He seemed to enjoy this, and I listened intently, not wishing to sound ungrateful or remind him that I was now an adult and could look after myself. I nodded in understanding each location point where a change of transport was required. He said he would come with me on Sunday to London to see me off. He felt it better that mother said her farewells at home for fear she might get a little emotional - and that would be most inappropriate, as well as embarrassing. I appreciated his thinking.

He explained that I was to take the train from London's Liverpool Street Station, where we would say our goodbyes, and travel to the Port of Harwich where I would board a ferry that would cross the North Sea and eventually dock at the port of The Hook in Holland, very early on Monday morning. From there

I would get a train directly to Amsterdam where I would alight the train at Centraal Station. I would easily find a taxi that could take me to The Hilton hotel in Apollolaan. He added that the city had an excellent public transport system with trams should I wish to be economic with my limited funds. In my mind I had already plumped for the taxi.

My father knew the local bank manager and had kindly ordered an amount of travellers cheques and some local currency of guilders. At the time the exchange rate was about ten guilders to the pound which pleased me as made for easy conversion. I also sold ten pounds of premium bonds, the gift of preference from maiden aunts on Christmas and birthdays.

As I started the final pack I sat on the bed and counted the money. 30 pounds. More than I ever held in my hand before. "Now take care of that and don't spend it on cigarettes and beer; that needs to see you through until you get your first pay, and as you are salaried, that means in one month," my father reminded me. The idea of having to budget for a month was a thought that had not entered my head. I was a hand to mouth type - money burned a hole in my pocket. This could be tough. "It is about time you learned to budget." The banker was coming out again. I was waiting for the *Neither a lender nor a borrower be* speech. Father loved to quote Shakespeare. Thankfully on this occasion he did not.

Sunday eventually arrived, my mother fussed around. "Now you have got enough shirts? And underpants? Did you pack a vest? The weather in Holland can be very changeable and being so flat I am sure it will be windy. Maybe you should take your scarf?"

"Mother for God's sake - I am fine and have all the clothes I will need. Anyway it's summer, so it will be fine".

As she stood at the door, looking rather anxious, I tried to reassure her that Holland was a very civilised place - they even have a Queen as we do. Nothing to worry about. In any event, it was not that far away and I would write... often. A promise I confess I was never good at keeping. Turning over in her mind what other disasters or dangers I might face, she found one. "Oh Paddy, for goodness sake, do not accept a drink or cigarette from any stranger, it might be drugged. I have heard about these things happening."

The adult version of 'sweets from strangers'. Rather prescient, as we shall see.

I was desperate to get on my way, as was my father, who was driving to Leamington station where we had a train to catch. I looked back and saw mother still standing at the gates of the drive as we turned the corner and disappeared out of sight. At that moment I knew she was heading to the kitchen to put on the kettle for a cup of tea.

The trip to London was uneventful, rather quiet, with our small talk combining with the rattling of the train. On arriving in Euston, we took the Northern Line tube to Kings Cross and the Circle Line tube to Liverpool Street, to meet my connection to Harwich.

We found a train compartment marked 'Third Class'. Britain is famous for its class system and nowhere was the division between the well-to-do and the less well-off more visible than on the railways, even though it had been dropped ten years before as part of the post-war emancipation of the classes. It spoke more of the age and state of British Rail carriages. Putting my case on the rack above, I returned to the platform to await the train's departure and to say goodbye to my father. We had always found these moments a little difficult, never being quite sure what to say. My father was not a demonstrative man, due to a very strict Victorian upbringing. He loved me without question, but I can never recall him giving me a hug. Shows of emotion were just alien to him. We always shook hands.

Things started to look as if they were about to happen with the train, so I went into the carriage and, for the second time that month, lowered the sash window to say a final goodbye. Suddenly father grabbed my hand and shook it and started to speak as the train was about to pull out. I was expecting "have a safe journey" or "take care" or even "we will miss you", but I heard instead "Paddy, never forget you are an Englishman in a foreign country, and you represent us; how you behave will reflect on England, so don't let us down." And that was it. He stood there for a moment and then turned and headed off. I realised that this was purely and simply my father's code. It was in his upbringing: stiff upper lip, never let the side down and always remember that you are British. With this ringing in my ears, I sat back watching the backs of the soot stained terraced houses go by as we headed out of London, gaining speed on the route to Harwich.

I arrived at the port in the early evening with plenty of time to spare, as the night ferry didn't depart until much later. I'd still have more than enough time to get to Amsterdam at a reasonable hour after docking at the other end of the journey. After a few formalities I boarded. The *Queen Elizabeth* it was not. More like the Dover to Calais Ferry, although a little larger. I was thankful for this, as I had heard that crossing the North Sea may not be for the faint hearted. With this in mind I made a note of life rafts, life jackets and any other floating item that I might grab onto in the event of an emergency. And why not? Look what happened to the *Titanic*.

I headed for the bar. I later discovered that it was possible to book one of the limited number of berths, but the ticket my father had purchased for me did not include such luxuries. I like to think that he thought I was adventurous, young enough and tough enough not to need such pampering - after all I had survived an English boarding school. In reality, I fear he was just being frugal.

As I entered the bar, being one of the first to board, I thought I would get the best pick - a comfy sofa so I would be able to get some sleep on the nine hour crossing. Imagine my disappointment to see that the bar furnishings consisted solely of wooden tables and chairs, upholstered with a thinly padded green vinyl seat. What did catch my eye though confirmed my earlier wisdom of checking out the lifeboats. All the chairs and the tables and indeed any movable object were connected to the floor with a hefty piece of metal chain. I now truly believed the tales of how rough the North Sea crossing could be.

With this playing on my mind, I thought it prudent to start imbibing a few beers before we left the safety of port to give me some Dutch courage for the journey ahead. It then occurred to me that, where I was heading, that was probably rather an inappropriate expression, disparaging, as it was a reference to the habits of England's Dutch allies in a long-past war against the French. At least I would enjoy downing it and hoped I would not regret it as we hit the open seas, when I might find myself racing to the head, which I believe is the nautical term. Note for next job: check out the loos.

With a pint of bitter I looked for a table and chair that would be home for the crossing: what should it be, the deck exit or loo? I opted for the exit, settled in and stored my suitcase under the table, managing to attach it to the chain. The last thing I wanted to see was it sliding at speed to the other side of the bar, skittling passengers as it knocked their legs from underneath them when we hit the first wave.

I got little sleep, occasionally nodding off, only to suddenly wake and check we were still afloat. At about two in the morning I needed to stretch my legs so I ventured very cautiously onto the deck. I was pleasantly surprised that it was a very lovely night; the sky was clear and the sea with a bit of a swell wasn't anywhere as bad as I had feared. After a couple of laps I returned to my vinyl chair and suitcase. In those innocent days, there was no concern with leaving luggage unaccompanied.

We entered The Hook at six in the morning. It was a clear day and looked as if the sun might even shine on my arrival, although, as I was to learn in Holland, the sun can shine at ten and you can have torrential rain at eleven. The Dutch would always rib me when this happened. "Typically English weather eh." I used to smile. English weather was bad but it didn't change with such rapidity; in England when it rained, it rained all day. I passed through immigration with a cursory glance at my British passport, which said inside 'Allow the bearer to pass freely without let nor hinder.' I always loved that. Not that I ever understood what 'let' meant, but it seemed to work with the Dutch immigration officer.

As I left in search of the railway station I noticed that The Hook was now Hoek van Holland.

I followed the signs to the railway station and found the ticket office and purchased my ticket for the two-hour train ride to Amsterdam. The seats were still upholstered in green vinyl, but so much more comfortable than the one I had passed the night on. The other thing I noticed was just how clean everything was. So unlike British Rail. Didn't we invent the train?

My 7.00am train bound for Amsterdam Centraal went via The Hague and Leiden, where Rembrandt was born and educated. We passed through Haarlem. Was this the place that the Americans named their suburb in New York? I'm fairly sure I would choose the Dutch version over its American namesake any day. On arriving in Amsterdam I picked up my suitcase and went in search of a taxi. There were plenty about, so took the first I found, proudly holding my little piece of paper on which I had copied a few Dutch sentences from a phrasebook, "Goede dag - Kun je me naar het Hilton in Apollolaan brengen?"

This was meant to mean 'Can you take me to the Hilton in Apollolaan, please.' However when the driver turned and looked at me with no small amusement I suddenly wasn't so sure. I tried "Spreekt u Engels?"

The smile remained. "OK, where do you want to go?" he said in perfect English

"You speak English?"

"Ja, of course and I think better than you speak Nederlands," he laughed.

In all the time I was living in Holland I learned very little Dutch. It wasn't that I was lazy, or didn't want to. Every time I tried they would simply speak to me in English. Partly because they just didn't want the hassle of trying to understand an Englishman's awful Dutch accent, but more often than not to simply show that they were multilingual, often flicking from English to German to French, subject to the make-up of the group. I have to admit I did admire them and was rather envious of their ability to communicate so easily. I eventually asked a Dutch friend as to why they were so multilingual.

"Patrick, Holland is a very small country; if we don't learn the languages, who would talk to us?"

Obvious. It did make me realise just how insular Britain was, with our assumption that English was all we needed to get by in the world.

The taxi ride took about thirty minutes. As we drove down one street or 'straat', it struck me how the Dutch have a double 'a' in words, which then turned into 'e' and 'o'. They just love their vowels.

This time the driver did not drop me at the back entrance but drove straight up the slope to the *porte-cochère* and The Hilton main entrance. A doorman immediately stepped forward and opened the door. "Goede dag", he said with a genuine welcoming smile, considering my rather dishevelled appearance after my long journey and sleepless night, together with being rather too youthful to be a guest. How different to the aloof, judgmental assessment of an English five star hotel doorman. I wisely didn't attempt any Dutch but simply said that I was here to work and had to report to Mr. Nijenhuis, the Personnel Manager (hoping I had pronounced the name correctly). Again, a reply in perfect English, and also with a degree of understanding and warmth. "Then welcome to the staff. Where will you be working?"

I said I was in accounts and in the 'Bon Control' department - which meant little to me at that point. He gave me directions to the staff entrance at the side of the hotel and I went off in search of it. I started to get a little nervous - working in accounts? What was I thinking? I had failed my Maths 'O' Level on three occasions. I had read a couple of chapters of *The Uniform System of Accounting*. I did, however, have three back-up plans in the event that I made mistakes. First, *I am sorry, I don't speak Dutch and misunderstood*. This was proving to be the worst excuse as everyone spoke English. Second, *I am sorry I am just not used to this adding machine*. I now thought that sounded feeble. How different can the machines be? My third 'get out of jail' card was the best one: *I am sorry how stupid of me - I was still working in English pounds, shillings and pence*. I regained a little of my confidence.

I came to a steep set of steps that led down to a door, but then I noticed an unlight neon light above a larger doorway, which I worked out read something like 'Fietsotech and Bar'. This must be the hotel's disco, so I went further in search of the staff entrance. As I walked around feeling rather lost I noticed at ground level a set of windows that showed a basement full of people busily working at desks. I must have looked lost and rather forlorn at the window. Someone looked up, smiled and mouthed something, and I remained looking puzzled. He then started to gesture, pointing back the way I had come. By this time a number of other office staff started to notice me and join in the gesturing. I headed back, realising that the door adjacent to the disco was in fact the staff entrance and I descended the steps and cautiously opened the door, only to find it opened up onto a large fluorescent lit area with a turnstyle and security man checking all who entered and departed. I explained who I was here to see and he politely directed me to an office to the right clearly marked 'B.H.G. Nijenhuis, Personnel Manager'. Upon entering, I was greeted with the warm and friendly smile of a young woman that I assumed was his secretary.

"Hello", she greeted me. "I am Anna. Ja, ja, we have been expecting you - how was your journey?"
"Good, but long." I explained a little.

"You must be very tired - Mr Nijenhuis is out at the moment but let's see if we can sort you out." Her English was impeccable. This will be easier than I expected, I thought.

She gave me some papers to fill in and explained for health insurance I would need a medical, but they will arrange all that.

"We have made arrangements for you to rent a room, not too far from here, either a short tram ride or a little walk. It is with a lady called Mevrouw de Vries, she has a house in Frans van Mierisstraat. I am sure you will be comfortable. If you like art, it isn't too far from the Rijksmuseum".

I must have created a good impression - did I look like a person who was into art and museums?

"While we wait for Mr Nijenhuis, let me give you a quick tour." With which she was up and out of the office. "Along here are the changing rooms and showers, opposite is the staff restaurant where you can have your meals at a nominal charge and the food is quite good, I don't think they do steak and kidney pie though," she joked.

I hadn't realised I would actually have to pay for my meals; I was really going to have to watch my money. The one thing that I just couldn't get over was just how spotlessly clean everything was. Then again, the Hilton was a brand new building as opposed to The Grand, which was, after all, built in the 1870s and had seen some tough times. [68]

I am not sure that I was taking everything in as I was starting to feel very tired. As we returned to the office, Anna pointed out the office on the other side. "That's the accounts office. We have time so let me take you in, and introduce you."

Although she was being very kind, this was the last thing I wanted. Meeting the new boss after a long journey, still wearing the clothes I had set off in from Leamington Spa the day before. I had always thought you only get one chance at creating a good first impression. As we opened the door on the large room full of people at desks they all looked up. I noticed the windows that only minutes before I was looking through, rather lost and to the amusement of those now looking at me. "Oh shit," I thought. "That's all I need - not only looking like something the cat dragged in, but also the prat who couldn't find the staff entrance". I had a very brief introduction to my immediate boss in bon control, who was Egyptian and introduced himself as Tamir. He seemed pleasant enough.

I was whisked off again. "I am sorry," Anna said. "I didn't think, after your long journey, you would like to freshen up maybe take a shower? You can get a towel from the laundry I showed you". Oh my God, do I smell? Has she detected that special smell that clings to you after boats, trains and railway stations? I said it was OK, but once finished it would be nice to go to my room and get a little sleep. Anna was very understanding and seemed guilty at rushing into sorting out paperwork and introductions. Mr Nijenhuis had still not returned, so she very kindly said, "Look, you go to your room, I will call Mevrouw de Vries and let her know you are on the way. I will explain to Mr Nijenhuis, and you can see him tomorrow. If you can be here by 8.30am we can finish things up then and I will hand you over to Tamir and he will look after you."

She then started to give me directions to what was to be my new home in Amsterdam. I could hardly believe it. I was here. The other thing I could hardly believe was the names in the directions she was giving me.

"Once you leave here you turn left on Apollolaan towards Breughelstraat. Take J. M. Coenenstraat to Bartholomeus Ruloffsstraat, continue on Bartholomeus Ruloffsstraat. Take Jacob Obrechtstraat and Nicolaas Maesstraat to Frans van Mierisstraat, it's number 14."

What? "Coenstraat, Ruloffsstraat, Obrech..." Something or other that sounded like an object was caught in the back of her throat, and she was trying to clear it out. I had heard this a lot in the past few hours. She noticed my stunned expression. "I will write it down for you."

As I walked off, I thought over everything so far. It struck me just how different it all was to what I was used to - the friendliness, the welcome, the introduction to my new job. I wasn't even a manager, just an ordinary employee. I thought if this is the way American companies treat their staff, then England is due for a wake-up call. Maybe they were just being nice to a foreigner (although they weren't reputed to be so warm and relaxed). In any event, I was starting to feel more relaxed and my fears of a foreign land and a vengeful French *patron* disappeared.

I was starting to notice things as I headed up the *straats*. Many were cobbled, which I noticed was admirably clever as I passed a workman fixing something underground. No jack-hammers digging up tarmac: just lift a few cobbles, dig your hole and put the cobbles back. Another cobble-related observation was that none of the young women I passed had on a pair of stiletto heel shoes, as was the fashion in England. The heels would simply slip and break - far too dangerous, as confirmed to me by a woman another time. Something else I spotted: many houses flew flags. Not just the national red, white and blue flag but lots of bright orange ones. As patriotic as we English might be, you won't see many houses there with a Union Jack hoisted.

Frans van Mierisstraat was a small cobbled street with very thin tall buildings in the Dutch style. Limited space so you squeeze in what you can. The houses were four or five storeys high, and they didn't look like apartments but individual dwellings. I arrived at number 14, marked by a nice Delft blue plaque, went up a few very steep steps and looked for a doorbell. No bell but I spotted a large brass knob and hesitantly pulled it. I heard no sound, nor heard anyone coming to the door. A mechanical noise and a click sounded, but the door did not open. I heard the noise and click again and this time I pushed the door and it opened. There was no one to be seen, just a very steep set of ascending stairs. I entered and heard a woman's voice shout from somewhere above "Ben jij de Engelsman, kom de trap op" or words to that effect.

I climbed the Everest-like stairs, noticing the clever mechanical device that had opened the door. Who would wish to run up and down all these stairs simply to answer a knock at the door only to find a Jehovah's Witness? By the time I reached the top I was out of breath. The woman awaiting me was small, thin and looked quite old. How on earth does she manage all these stairs?

"Mevrouw de Vries?" I had been repeating the name in my mind, hoping I pronounced it correctly.

"Ja, Ja", she said, a little impatiently, obviously annoyed at the repeated pulling of her door lever. "I speak a little English, but not so good".

"I am so sorry I do not speak Dutch but your English is excellent." I was trying the charm offensive, but obviously failing.

"Come this way."

As much an order as a request. We walked along a corridor and as we did so she pointed to a door "Badkamer" which I assumed was the bathroom, up another flight of stairs and to the end of the corridor. She opened the door onto a rather small room, with a single bed, a small cupboard and a chair and table. "Your room." She then stated the rules. "I give you a key, please do not lose. Please don't bring guest in or make much noise."

I wondered where would another person fit?

"The hotel will pay me and you pay the hotel. When you leave please tell me a month before when the rent is paid."

Looks as if I am here like it or not. Once all the rules were explained, "I will go now".

That was that. She was more like the Dutch people I had expected, a little cool and not full of humour. Once the door closed, I took a better look around, which only took a few seconds. I went to the window and was pleasantly surprised. Being high up on the view of the street below looked nice, and very Dutch.

I would now take a shower, get sorted and have some rest before I ventured out to explore my neighbourhood surround- ings. I took my towel and wash gear, I wasn't sure what to wear to go to the bathroom on the floor below, so I took off the non-es- sential clothes and headed down in my shirt and trousers. As I opened the door of the bathroom I was horrified to find no bath or shower, just a lavatory and a hand basin. Surely there must be another room. I went outside but there were only doors that looked as if they entered another bedroom. For fear of walking in on someone else, I retreated back into the 'bathroom' where I stripped off and washed as best I could, and then went up to my room to ponder my plight.

I managed to sleep for a couple of hours but was awakened by hunger. I decided to explore my local area and see what I might find in terms of food. After walking the streets for a while I eventually came across a shop with snacks behind small win- dows. I discovered that these were filled from the rear, and to purchase an item you placed a coin in a slot and the window popped open. Very clever! I had never seen anything like this in England. The only person I saw in the shop was a young man whose job was to fry the chips.

Being very conscious now of the need to be frugal with my limited funds this was ideal. Good sustaining chips, and an array of other food. I ordered my chips or 'frits, and before I could make a decision, the young man had tipped them into a paper cone and proceeded to pump over them a good dollop of what I could make out was mayonnaise. I had never had this before, preferring tomato ketchup or vinegar, but as I had no choice in the matter I said nothing. Being so hungry they could have put anything on it and I would have eaten it. Next came my selection from behind the little windows - I selected what I thought was a sausage roll, put my coins in the slot and the window opened. It turned out to be some sort of spring roll. I scoffed it all down and was surprised to discover that mayonnaise with chips was rather nice - to this day it is my choice of sauce.

The 'Automat' as they were called were as common as burger outlets nowadays. They became my main source of dining when not eating at the hotel. Now feeling a little better I headed back home to prepare for the following day and - I hoped - have a good night's sleep.

I set my trusty alarm for 7.00am. I wanted to get to the hotel early and take advantage of the showers that were offered: the first shower I would have had in over two days. Mind you, not that anyone would have noticed. It was not unusual for Englishmen at that time to be content with a bath once a week, whether they needed it or not.

On arrival at the hotel next morning, I showed my security pass and headed for housekeeping to get a towel. After a little discussion, and establishing the rules of being given a towel, I headed for the staff locker room. It was well lit, large and spotlessly clean. English hotels really had something to learn.

The shower was wonderful. The water shot out with so much force it was like a massage. Back home, in any domestic shower hovering above the bath, one had to run around to just get wet. I was now ready to face the day.

Promptly at 8.30am, I knocked on the door of the Personnel Office. Anna was already busy with papers, and through an open office door behind her I saw a man at a desk. Mr Nijenhuis. On seeing me he stood up and came out from behind the desk. With hand outstretched he said simply "Nijenhuis".

It caught me a little off guard, so I quickly replied in the same formal manner: "Griffin". He ushered me to a chair and after a few pleasantries ran through the general detail of my employment and the Hilton Hotel philosophy. He spoke of the hotel's mission statement (whatever that was), and stated that the Hilton *raison d'être* was to *'cater for the American abroad.'* He then handed me two books and said that I should - as soon as possible - make myself familiar with them, particularly before I was introduced to the General Manager, Mr Ralph Starkey (the man to whom I had originally written) within my first month.

The first book was one about the Hilton, its founder and history; the second was an employment manual, with all the hotel's information, the do's and don'ts and general information to enable an employee to settle in. Hilton was so well organised; we had protocols for everything. This level of staff consideration was totally alien to me. Even the friendly welcome had never been experienced, ever, in England. In that era, one arrived at work, were pointed to the department, and just expected to get on with it. *Personnel management* simply fell under the control of an assistant manager who just hired and fired; concepts such as 'induction training', 'staff development' or 'staff welfare' did not exist. This difference left an indelible impression on me, and helped to formulate much of my thinking in my future career in regards to dealing respectfully with staff.

My meeting came to an end and Anna was on hand to take me through to the accounts area where I was to start my job in 'bon control'. I was introduced to the head of the department, and then handed over to Tamir, whom I had met the previous day. He then introduced me to my two work colleagues: Johan, a Dutchman and Filip, a Belgian. I took immediately to Johan, who on first impression was a warm and friendly guy. Filip on the other hand, was less so. I was shown to my desk: a hand cranked adding machine, some files, a box of pens, a large stapler.

Johan Beijerman was to play a major part in my life over the period I spent in Holland, and spent the first day explaining what I was expected to do. It was all rather simple really, what with the established protocols. Much to my relief I realised I might get away with my *slight* exaggeration of my knowledge on 'uniform accounting'.

I soon picked up the routine. My purpose for existence was to collect the *bons*, the checks, from the various restaurants, calculate the 12.5% gratuity that was added to each bill, and credit it to the waiter whose name or number was on the check. Waiting staff were paid a ridiculous pittance - something like a guilder - and more or less their entire wage came from the gratuities. There was always a queue of waiters outside the office to check that we had allocated their gratuities correctly. The upside for the hotel was that the waiter would try to direct the customer to order the most expensive dishes and upsell as much as they could. It was one of the greatest motivators I ever came across in the industry, but it did rather depend on having extremely low wages. There seemed to be very little else involved in my job, but I could live with it. We had a half hour break for lunch and Johan took me along to the staff restaurant. For one guilder you had a choice of soup, hot meal or various salads and desserts. It was all rather good, however buying food at the hotel or in an Automat still added up each day.

The afternoon went much the same as the morning. When it came time to pack up for the day, Johan explained the 'clean desk' policy: we were required to clear the top of the desk of any paperwork and equipment. It was 5.00pm and that was the end of the day; I could not remember when I had ever finished work at 5.00pm. This was going to be a doddle - note to self to write and thank Mr Cairns for pointing me in the right direction.

As we were leaving, Johan said, "We often go for an after-work beer at the American Hotel in Leidseplein, if you feel like joining us?" Being the new boy, it was not a hard decision. Johan had a small motor bike, and gave me a lift sitting pillion. I now discovered the negative aspect of cobbles; they do not offer the greatest road grip, especially for a two-wheeled vehicle. I often felt the back slip away as we took a corner, so I was delighted to see the large sign of The American Hotel. I was exhilarated that we had survived the journey. [69]

The bar at the American Hotel was unlike any I had ever seen before. The bar was enormous; high vaulted ceilings, large arches with white tiles and black tiles like piano keyboards, ceiling hung with large decorative glass lights, walls hung with black and white lithographs of old Amsterdam. It was beautifully art deco, and it was all original. A trio of musicians add to my sensory overload: a violinist, a bassist, and a man with a large moustache playing an accordion and perambulating between the tables. [70]

We found ourselves a table and a few others joined us. They introduced themselves in the usual manner - surname only - and only later moving to a less formal first name basis. I discovered we had quite an international team: several Dutch, a German, a French guy, an Egyptian, Filip the Belgian, and me, an Englishman, making eight. The great thing about this was that the

Dutch loved to speak English. No one spoke Dutch, so English won through as the common language of choice. Another fear laid to rest.

We pulled a couple of tables together and settled in. A waiter in a long white apron almost touching the ground appeared at our side, pulled out a check pad with a flourish from his belt at the back of his trousers, looked disapprovingly at the fact we had moved his perfectly aligned tables, and said *"Goedenavond heren"* but, seeing we were speaking English, immediately swapped into "What drinks would you like to order?"

Tamir answered, "Acht Amstel-bieren alsjeblieft," as if to prove one of the foreigners spoke the local language.

"Dank je." As if to make the point, and departed towards the large marble topped bar that was the focal point of the room.

He returned with a large round tray held above his head, and with the same flourish with which he had produced the check pad, brought the tray down with a perfectly arched movement, his arm maintaining the centrifugal forces of nature, so that full brimming glasses of beer were delivered down to waist level without so much as a drop being spilled. The beer was not my usual room temperature mild and bitter, but an ice cold rather gassy lager from the local brewer Amstel. It was delicious nonetheless. When in Rome - or in this case, Amsterdam - drink what the locals drink. The Amstel Brewery and I became very well known to each other.

We all chatted and got on well, and then even better as the beers kept arriving and everyone relaxed. I was the youngest in the group: the eldest was a local Dutchman who was gay and lived with his partner of many years in a loft warehouse conversion in the main canal area. What amazed me was the fact that he was openly gay, but not wildly effeminate. In England, it was still illegal and had even almost led to the downfall of a government. I needed to think about this. The Frenchman. Well, he was French. The German guy came from Heidelberg, and although he was very pleasant, one could not help but feel there was a little tension from the Dutch, who less than twenty years earlier had suffered terribly under the Nazi occupation. Some of the group were just old enough to remember, and, as yet, had not been able to forgive. The Egyptian guy came from Cairo and was still a little sensitive in being the only non-European in the group. He was in Cairo at the time of the Suez Crisis, in which the English and French were involved, but all seemed to be forgiven and forgotten. Finally, there was the Belgian guy, who I was a little wary of. He showed that he, without doubt, had strong opinions on a range of issues and liked to express them.

Belgium is a tiny country with a history of occupation. The country became independent from the Netherlands in 1830, but was occupied by Germany during World Wars I and II, it has three official languages, Dutch or Flemish in the north, French in the south and a tiny part in the East speaks German. One fact that I greatly appreciated was that it holds the title for the greatest number of individual beer brands and as such it has been known as The Disneyland of Beer.

With so many things that our Belgian friend could be so proud of, I was uncertain as to why he wanted to turn his back on his mother country and place his allegiance with France. He held France in the most passionate regard. As I got to know him better, my wary opinion of him did not change. His admiration for Charles de Gaulle bordered on fanatical. "I love the man, he knows how to lead, fuck the Americans and kick them out, he says fuck to Britain joining the Common Market, he also demands the independence of Quebec from Britain", when in fact he famously stated "Vive le Québec libre!" in July that year.

I couldn't help but think of my dear mother, who had never been a supporter of an English union with Europe, or the plans for a tunnel under the Channel, saying "That little stretch of water has saved us more than once from invasion", and that de Gaulle's adamant *Non* on the Common Market was because "The poor man was so very badly treated by England during the war for what others in his country had done in capitulating to the Germans". Britain did eventually join ten years later to Britain's jubilation - a somewhat different story as I write this in the shadow of Brexit. *Plus ça change.*

The evening at the American Bar came to a close at around 9.00pm, and the check was called for. I was a little nervous at this point in case it was announced that the 'new boy' by tradition was to pay for the first evening of drinks... did I have enough money? The elder Dutchman took the check, studied it, did a mental calculation, and announced that it was so many guilders each with some for the tip. With this, we dug into our pockets and money started to pile up on the plate. Considering the volume we had consumed, and the fine establishment in which we had consumed it, I thought it quite reasonable. The money was counted and checked and, once given the nod by our respected elders, the waiter came and collected it. "Thank you gentlemen", and, with a nod and due deference to Tamir, "Dank je".

Johan offered to give me a lift back on his motorbike.

Thinking of the outward journey, I said "Thanks Johan, kind of you, but I could do with the walk, it isn't that late and some fresh air will help me sleep better". With this, he kickstarted the bike and disappeared into the traffic. Those who remained finishing their conversations with each other said farewell to me. "See you in the morning, it's been nice to meet you and I hope you settle in OK". There was no such farewell from Filip my Belgian friend, who maintained his staunch allegiance to the French.

I was starting to feel that Hilton was not only going to be great for my career, but that Amsterdam was going to be fun. With that pleasant combination of fears laid to rest and euphoria, assisted by the fine Amstel brewery, I set out in the direction of home. After a few passes it suddenly occurred to me I wasn't sure where home actually was. Half an hour and many detours later I arrived at number 14, Frans van Mierisstraat. I carefully opened the door and crept, very very quietly up the steep staircase to my room... *and so to bed*.

From my second day, life fell into an enjoyable routine.

Up at 7.30am.
Walk to the Hilton.
Take a shower.
Into the office.
Sort desk.
Walk to Cashiers Desk in the front lobby.
Collect the checks from last night's business that had been posted to the guests' account by the night auditor.

These were the checks from The Diamond Restaurant, the Hilton's top restaurant, The New Amsterdam Grill, the Bar, Room Service and the *Fietsotech*, the hotel's disco. I would also collect these at various intervals during the day. I always enjoyed going up to the lobby to see what was going on, and observe the hordes of Americans who had obviously answered the clarion call of the Hilton: to "be catered for when abroad".

On occasion, you could overhear a conversation and pick up on the accent as to where in the USA they came from. The owner of one of these, that I admit I found a little like nails on a chalkboard, was a woman from New York. In a high pitched nasal tone she was getting more excited by the minute as she demanded the change from the US dollars, with which she had just paid her account, *in* US dollars rather than the guilders being offered.

"What am I supposed to do with this toy money? I want real money!" she demanded.

The cashier maintained her cool; after the onslaught she tried to explain, "Madame, this is the currency of Holland; there is no other."

The cashier faced a further barrage. "Well, it's silly money, and I want good American Dollars!"

You could hear the capital letters. After the arguments had run their course, the husband, who had remained rather meekly in the background, tugged his wife's sleeve and interjected. "Come on, Martha, it's only a few dollars and the tour guide is waiting for us."

Most of the Americans visiting Europe in the sixties were new to travel outside the USA. They believed in safety in numbers, and always travelled in a group tour, accompanied by a guide who walked everywhere in front of them with a brightly coloured umbrella or flag or pennant so the 'tourists' would not get lost. These tours usually took in several cities in two weeks, spending two nights in any one location at most. This tended to confuse some, who may have never been further from their home State, let alone been carted around exotic Europe. On one of my trips to the lobby I heard a rather colourfully dressed American man, in bright red golfing trousers, enquiring of a fellow traveller "Hey George, are we in Amsterdam or Brussels?"

"I think it's Amsterdam, but check the schedule, I think Brussels is tomorrow, but I *do* know we are in Berlin on Saturday."

Each time I returned to the office I would report the latest details overheard in the lobby; most of the team smiled, some just simply shook their heads.

Once back at my desk, I would start sorting the checks and allocating the gratuities. This was not as simple as you might think, first I had to get to know who the waiters were and then read the handwritten figures. This was rather hard, as in Europe the number 1 is written like a 7. Then I discovered that in Europe they cross their sevens. This formation of the numbers flowed through to other figures as well, and certainly took some getting used to. I had managed to escape the problems of the verbal language but not the idiosyncrasies of the handwriting. I had a few grumpy waiters who wanted to double check that the new guy had not underpaid them with *ten* guilders rather than *seventy*. Word soon got around and it was a little while before I was able to re-establish confidence amongst the waiting staff.

There was one unexpected benefit that came out of my errors, and that was getting the attention of the Coffee Shop staff, who tended to be female. In particular, one very attractive young woman immediately became the focus of my attention. She spoke perfect English, and I was later to discover, when I actually managed to get her out on a date, that she had a Ford Mustang. She was definitely my type of woman.

Johan and I became good friends over the next few weeks and often went out for beers together. I became used to zipping around the city on the back of his bike. The more hair-raising moments occurred when crossing the many tram lines that were laid in the road around the city. They were quite wide and the tyres on the bike were quite narrow, so it needed a great deal of skill on Johan's behalf to manoeuvre across them. My skill involved maintaining balance as a pillion. We soon got a system going; he would shout over his shoulder "Tram!" and I would be ready for the quick lean to the left and quick lean to the right to keep balance.

I became a regular at the Automat on my days off, although the menu selection was a little restricted: there are only so many fries one can eat even with the newly discovered accompaniments of mayonnaise. By chance I picked up some pamphlets from the concierge desk when doing my daily rounds: 'things to do in Amsterdam'. One in particular caught my eye: 'Tours of the Amstel Brewery'. Right up my street.

On my next day off, I headed straight for the brewery, which was within walking distance of my digs. The tours went every two hours and they were free. It was 11.00am when I arrived at their door and I waited inside where a few had already gathered. I passed a few minutes looking at the old photos around the reception area as more visitors turned up. A young man came out and greeted us, welcoming us to The Amstel Brewery. He asked a few of us where we came from. There was a mix of Europeans, mainly German, a couple of Americans and an Australian, all male. The guide decided to speak English (he also naturally spoke French and German) and all seemed content.

We started our tour. "The brewery was founded on June 11, 1870 in Amsterdam and named after the Amstel River, the waters of which also served for refrigeration. By 1872, Amstel was annually producing 10,000 hectolitres. For the purpose of storing the beer, winter ice from canals was kept in special double-walled cellars." As we went from one area to another, we were taken through the process of ingredients, kettles, timing, production quantities, *ad infinitum*. Eventually we ended up in a large wooden panelled room, with a long table and benches. Best of all, there were glasses on the table. We were invited to sit.

"Does anyone have any further questions?"

Of course there were questions from the Americans. After that, "Well gentlemen, may I invite you to enjoy what you have seen produced today at The Amstel Brewery, for the next half an hour, with our compliments. It has been a pleasure to show you around Amsterdam's oldest and finest brewery. Please enjoy."

Cue the two women with large trays laden with jugs of Amstel Beer. These were placed on the table, with baskets of cut Dutch Cheeses and sliced baguettes. My lunch! I wasn't disappointed - there was no limit as to how much you drank or ate but you had to depart after half an hour. Consuming as much free beer as I could, and in between gulps scoffing free cheese and bread, I was a very happy man. The beer had been downed on an empty stomach and greatly assisted my feeling of well being. Seeing there was some cheese leftovers, I could certainly not permit it to go to waste. I quickly thrust what I could into a paper napkin and into my pockets, hopefully unobserved. The lovely Amstel people bade us farewell and saw us on our way, "Do come back and visit us when next in Amsterdam".

I didn't know if they really meant what they said, but I took them at their word. Each week, on my day off. There were several guides who rotated shifts, so they weren't immediately aware of my regular routine. Eventually they started to recognise me but, far from throwing me out, they were rather amused and ignored the fact that I was just along for the free beer and cheese. I have no idea why they turned a blind eye, but I was very glad they did. My complimentary lunch on my day off was my favourite thing.

As work had become very routine, my days off became the centre of my life. They were usually on weekends - again something to which I was totally unaccustomed. It was a challenge to fill them without spending a lot of money. Sometimes I was joined by Johan, and we went off somewhere, but he had a girlfriend, or visited his parents who lived two hours south of Amsterdam in 's-Hertogenbosch. Thankfully it was just known as den Bosch. On the occasions I wasn't with Johan, I sought out my own entertainment to fill my days off.

I found a little shop that sold second hand books very cheap, and a lot of them in English. So with my spare change I bought books and started to read. Due to the limited choice in English, most of what I bought were romantic novels, abandoned no doubt by women tourists. The first book I bought was *Love is Eternal,* about the love between Mary Todd and Abraham Lincoln. Apparently Abraham engraved his name on Mary's wedding ring, with the title of the book. Well at least it ends in a good assassination, I thought when I bought it. As it turned out, I actually rather enjoyed it. Yes it was hugely romantic, but it was was historical and I loved that period of American history and the Civil War. With the sun in the sky and a newly acquired book under my arm, I'd set out for *Vondelpark,* one of the largest and most famous parks in Holland. It was west of the *Leidseplein* and the *Museumplein* which I knew well, and had become my local haunt.

In the sixties this park was the main gathering area for hippies or Flower People as they were now being called. This also became a favourite spot for me as it was full of 'happenings'. Groups would sit listening intently to someone strumming out a Joan Baez anti-Vietnam War song on a guitar. Everyone was so colourful, there was lots of laughter, and peace and love signs everywhere. I assume the smiles were brought about by the 'roll their own' cigarettes they were smoking. When walking past, it was impossible to miss the 'herbal' smell of smoke that hung in a haze above these groups. No one seemed to care or worry. I later discovered that there were shops and cafes that openly sold pot and marijuana cookies, but I was never tempted in. [72]

The shady park was wonderful, as I could enjoy my book and also drink in the sights and sounds around me. On days when the weather was not as good, I'd go to the cinema. Once I found a theatre showing a new movie, a 'spaghetti western'. This concept was new to me, but it introduced me to Clint Eastwood and *A Few Dollars More*. I bought my ticket, in an allocated seat (unheard of in England). I climbed the stairs to 'the Gods'; the stairs went on and on. On arriving at the doors to the auditorium, a young woman, torch in hand, was ready to escort me to my seat.

The screen inside seemed to be very close, and then I noticed that the rows of seats were almost vertical, with at least a two metre drop to the next row below. The leg room was tight, especially for someone as tall as I was. The young woman pointed to my seat with her torch, and hovered there. Naturally my first reaction was to assume she wanted me to reach my seat OK and not trip over into the row below, but I suddenly realised she was waiting for her customary tip. I fumbled for coins, and dropped God knows how much into her gloved palm. With this she left me to reach my seat alone or trip over the edge and hurtle to my death below, whichever the case may be.

I did eventually reach my seat and got as comfortable as humanly possible by leaning forward and resting my arms and head on the barrier in front of me. This not only gave me a good view of the screen but also the patrons below, who resembled a bird colony attached precariously to the side of a vertical cliff. The movie started, thankfully in English with Dutch subtitles. Clint slaughtered the bad men in the black hats with his Colt 45 that never ran out of bullets, accompanied by jarring dramatic music chords and a wailing harmonica. Throughout the movie I could not help but notice the couple below me, upon whose heads I looked down, had spent most of the movie in a passionate embrace, hardly coming up for air. Obviously they weren't into spaghetti westerns. It was a good movie and I liked this actor and his gravelly voice. As the lights came up and people stood to leave, I was taken aback to discover that the couple who spent so much time embracing were in fact both men!

A short time later there was a hue and cry in the press about two men actually getting married to each other. As time went on I started to realise that, next to San Francisco, Amsterdam was one of the gay capitals of the world. What with the hippies and the drugs as well I was finding Amsterdam to be an eye opening, rather shocking city of revelation to a twenty one year old boy who had spent half his life in a boarding school and the past few years in 'God's waiting room', Eastbourne. I was starting to wonder what this city held in store for me, and very soon I found out.

Life was a whirlwind of weekend activities and fun, interrupted only by five days of attending the Hilton for my work routine. My European stage was doing little for my technical education in hotel management, but most certainly developed my life skills in leaps and bounds.

Johan decided it would be good to take in some fresh sea air that blew in from the North Sea. The plan was to head out on his motorbike to a town called Scheveningen, a seaside resort with a long, sandy beach, an esplanade, a pier, and a lighthouse, about an hour or so to the west of Amsterdam. With a good jacket and a thermos of coffee, we set off. The country was flat, with a strong head wind and some rather ominous dark clouds. Luckily, as usual, they blew over very quickly. We arrived at lunch time and sat by the beach and had our coffee and a chunk of cheese and fresh bread that we bought in a local 'bakker'.

I was fascinated to find many remnants of the war, with old German defences still standing, pock-marked by bullets and shrapnel. The fact that they were hard to demolish and remove must be a testament to good German engineering, although by now, twenty or so years after the war's end, it probably was not the sort of monument for which they wished to be remembered.

Johan explained to me the significance of the town's name. Many Dutch had been part of a resistance movement and the Germans often tried to infiltrate the cells of the brave Dutchmen who faced immediate execution if found to be part of the organisation. One way the Dutch would test if a German was posing as a Dutchman would be to ask him or her to name the resort in which we now were. The Dutch language has its own special raspy, throaty accent, and in the pronunciation of *Scheveningen* there was a unique Dutch pronunciation that a German, however good their Dutch was, could not replicate.

This talk of war brought up many questions I wanted to know about life in occupied Holland. I was always fascinated by this piece of the world's history, as many of my age were. I had known my aunt, whom we visited in France, was in the French Resistance and to me she was a childhood hero. I was full of admiration for Johan when he explained his father, a doctor, had also been in the resistance, in a cell in his hometown of den Bosch. I hadn't appreciated that Johan was quite a bit older than I, but his stature and boyish looks made him look much younger than his years. He had memories of the war.

His father had been warned that there were Germans disguised as British flyers who were attempting to escape. A man came to their door purporting to be an English flyer, recently shot down when returning from a bombing raid on Germany. Johan's father was conscious of the danger and turned him away. Hours later a stray bomber ditched his unused payload of bombs on the unfortunate town of den Bosch. Being a doctor, Johan's father rushed to assist. On arriving at the site of a collapsed house, among those scrabbling with bare hands to find the occupants buried under the rubble, was the so called English flyer in the RAF uniform, trying to help alongside the local Dutchman, with little concern for his own discovery.

This heroism, or stupidity, impressed Johan's father, as by that stage in the war, if airmen were shot down on a bombing run over Germany and caught, they were not treated well. He realised only an Englishman could behave in such a rash and selfless fashion of 'doing the humane thing', as he could not imagine the Germans of his experience doing so. He immediately threw his coat over the flyer's uniform and as fast as he could took him away from the area that would, without doubt, soon be swarming with German troops. Once home, their airman was given food and hidden in a small attic in the roof. It is hard to imagine just how brave these people were; had he been discovered Johan's father would have faced summary execution and the rest of his family, including Johan, would have been sent off to a concentration camp. The consequences and penalties were terrifyingly brutal.

Each night the Englishman came down from his hiding place in the attic to share with the family what little food there might be as by that time in the war the Dutch were almost on starvation rations. Johan remembers he helped teach him some English words and before he went to bed the airman produced a small block of chocolate that they were issued with as emergency rations. Johan admitted that he had never seen chocolate, let alone tasted it. With great care the airman had taken out a pocket knife and cut a small piece under the watchful gaze of Johan and gave him a small piece. This act was so significant to the young Johan and such an unbelievable luxury, that he never forgot it. As a result, Johan's positive view of the English was locked in from that moment on. The words of my father, echoed: *'behave,*

as you and your country would be judged by your actions.'
Prophetic indeed.

I could not help but feel that the airman's actions twenty-odd years before were part of the reason Johan had been such a good friend to me, helping and supporting me with such kindness in Amsterdam. I enquired what had happened to the airman; after about a week of chocolate at bedtime, Johan one morning found him to be gone. He was passed on down a chain of resistance workers who arranged the escape and return to England of downed airmen; to little Johan he had just run out of chocolate and had gone back to England to get more, but Johan never saw him again. I returned to Amsterdam a little wiser about the war years in Holland, and full of admiration for Johan's family. I was also covered with sunburn, from lying on the beach.

As I walked to the Hilton the following day, 5th June 1967 an international incident occurred; apart from the little matter of changing history, more importantly it had an indirect impact on *my* situation. The headlines screamed out from every newspaper: *'JEWS, ARABS WAR!'* The initial reports said that a coalition of Arab countries had invaded Israel, although this proved questionable as Israel had launched what it claimed, were a series of pre-emptive airstrikes against Egyptian airfields.

The war was a very brief affair as far as wars go, known as the Six-Day War. Israel, with a well-led, professional and motivated army, soon gained the upper hand and not only repelled the Arab Coalition but took large swathes of land hitherto outside their control. It has ever since been the cause of angst between Arabs and Israelis, in particular the Palestinians.

Anna, the secretary from Personnel, who it turned out happened to be Jewish, had got it into her head that I was also Jewish; perhaps it was my nose.

Anna, had access to a radio in her office, and followed every minute of this very fast-evolving war. As I sat at my desk, in what had started as just another day at work, I found that the events in Israel were becoming a major subject of interest. Tamir, my Egyptian boss, was particularly concerned, as suddenly he felt he might be seen as an aggressor among his office colleagues, particularly in a country with a large Jewish population. For me, although I was not oblivious of world events, I was twenty-one and my interests were local and egocentric. My interest in the Middle East was a ruse to be part of the conversation rather than any real concern as to the outcome.

This all changed mid-morning on that Monday. At the door of our accounts office I saw an excited Anna looking around and then making a beeline for me. We had never spoken apart from polite hellos and how are yous. Now however she was heading straight for my desk. What have I done? What does she want? She didn't look angry, though, rather more concerned, but yet excited.

"Patrick, have you heard the news, the Arabs have invaded Israel. It looks as if they have taken on more than they had intended," she said with agitation. By this time the rest of the office were looking up to see why I was getting all the attention from the Personnel Manager's secretary. "It looks as if the army has held them - this is amazing."

Tamir was looking extremely uncomfortable as the only representative of the invading forces of Egypt. The rest of the office seemed neutral with a smidgen of sympathy for Israel - having been invaded after all. No one said anything. That then left only me, and now, thanks to Anna who only minutes before had simply been a secretary, I was now in the Jewish camp and ally to the one person who most obviously was committed to the

Israeli cause. You could feel the team distancing themselves, understanding that the boss was Egyptian and now the new boy was his opponent in the war.

Johan leaned over, and in a lowered voice, "I didn't know you were Jewish."

"I'm not."

"Well Anna obviously thinks you are".

"This is all I need - now Tamir will be pissed off with me".

Johan looked in Tamir's direction. "Well, just tell him, rather than letting an atmosphere build up. God knows where it will all end."

I waited for our coffee break, when I knew Tamir went to the staff restaurant, and followed him out, hoping that Anna would not come out and think I was consorting with the enemy. At first the hostility was palpable, but as I explained that I was not Jewish and had no opinion on what was happening, he relaxed. For good measure, I added "I do hope you haven't any family serving or caught up in this." He seemed grateful that at least someone had given his situation some thought.

In the afternoon, Anna came in again with a news update. "The news is saying there is a massive tank battle going on," mentioning some names of which I had never heard, but was assumed to know. As quickly as she appeared, she disappeared again.

Over the next few days, Anna's visits became more frequent as the tide had certainly turned in Israel's favour, which in itself was quite an achievement considering the disparity in numbers of the two opposing armies. I could not help but feel some empathy for Tamir's position and hearing, from his perspective, such an onslaught of bad news and humiliation for his nation.

The final visit from Anna came on the 11th June when it was announced that a ceasefire had been signed between Israel and Egypt. The outcome of the war was that the area under Israeli control tripled, with fewer than 1,000 Israelis killed compared to over 20,000 from the Arab forces. The displacement of civilian populations resulting from the war would have long-term consequences, as 300,000 Palestinians fled the West Bank and about 100,000 Syrians left the Golan to become refugees. Across the Arab world, Jewish minority communities were expelled, with refugees going to Israel or Europe.

I am pleased to say that in our little world, within the week following the 11th June, things soon settled back to normal amongst the team. We continued with our little group gatherings at The American Hotel almost as if nothing had happened. As for me, it seemed I had a new friend in high places: Anna, private secretary to The Personnel Manager.

One afternoon, the F&B Manager (that's *Food and Beverage* to you) came into the office, asking if anyone had 'waiting' experience. I told him I had trained as a waiter in England. "How would you like to earn some money for working a banquet tonight?" I could always do with extra cash so I readily agreed.

"OK, come to the banquet department at 5.30pm when you finish here and we will sort out a uniform and let you know what we expect from you."

At 5.30pm I was there and instructed to go to the laundry, draw down a uniform and meet back in the ballroom in half an hour. I was issued with a pair of high waisted trousers (not as easy to fit with my longer than average legs), a bow tie and a red 'monkey' jacket, again fitted with some difficulty, due to extremely long arms but rather a less-than-Tarzan-size chest. Transformed, I went in search of 'The Ballroom.'

I pulled open a massive floor to ceiling door that opened up to an enormous open space banqueting area, with fifty or so tables, each seating ten guests, around a dance floor. There was an enormous banner at one end over a stage that would eventually accommodate the band. The banner read *The Hilton welcomes the 71st World Philatelic Convention...* I didn't realise so many people were interested in stamp collecting. I gave away my collection when I left school.

A microphone whistled and a voice came through in Dutch - not good for me - but then I heard, "I will repeat this in English afterwards... Phew. When the English version echoed out, he explained that staff would be allocated a table of ten and this would be our responsibility for the evening. New staff would be paired with a more experienced waiter. He explained who the guests were, the numbers attending, and the order of the evening's events. The highlight was to be the presentation of the dessert by all waiters, with a grand Hilton fanfare. This all sounded very American to me. Finally, he went through the four-course menu. Soup, fish, a main and then THE dessert, and coffee.

We stood in line to be designated our table and, in my case, my paired experienced waiter. My waiter was a small (compared to me) Portuguese man, who was not at all happy to be paired with an Englishman. After this we were taken through to the kitchen and the pass that separated the kitchen staff from us mere mortals, where we would collect the plates and dishes. It was going to be silver service, which worried me a little as it had been a long time since I had learned this artform, and even then I had not been proficient. Always the optimist, I thought 'how hard can it be?'

There was a commotion in the kitchen when the German head chef screamed at a commis and then hit him around the ear, sending him to the floor. I was astounded, but the experienced waiters didn't bat an eyelid and were thankful they had a long stainless steel counter between the kitchen and the waiters. The chef, seeing us there, then came over to vent his anger further and shouted to all present, presumably in German, that he expected us to get the food out fast and all together, he and his team hadn't worked all day to have his food served cold, and not to screw up the service… *et cetera et cetera.*

I started to get nervous. My paired Portuguese partner didn't seem interested, so I started to pray. The guests filed in, a group of Americans filled my allocated table; at least I could converse with them if needed. We got the nod to retire to the kitchen and collect the first course. The first hurdle, and one at which it looked as if I would fall, was THE SOUP. We collected the plates, easy enough. Place them in front of the guests. OK. It was here that I started to worry; I could see no waiter's station, a table from which you serve, rest and place things.

Ah - we had to serve the soup directly from the tureen - which we held in our arms - into the soup bowl on the table below in front of the guest. Waiters marched out to the kitchen. On a long counter were the large silver tureens, filled with soup, the silver serving ladles, sitting on large silver salvers. These were heavy to balance with two hands yet we were expected to carry with one hand and serve with the other. The problem was compounded by the fact that if you didn't keep it absolutely level, it slipped on the salver. At every moment I ran the risk of a tureen of hot soup shooting to the edge of the salver and either tipping to the floor or – even worse – all over a guest. I was stressed and just about managed the first couple of guests, when my Portuguese partner looked at me in glaring horror. "Just stop before you drop it… I will finish my table and come and help you."

His projection of absolute disgust was palpable. I hovered for what seemed like an age, but in reality a couple of minutes, he took the salver and completed my table. As we lugged the empty salvers out, he made a few choice remarks in Portuguese that thankfully I didn't understand. Then in English: "I think we need to work out how we do this - before you cause a disaster."

We were in full agreement that I would serve as his commis and do the carrying and he would serve the two tables. Although feeling very embarrassed, I kept up the apologies which I fear fell on deaf ears. The next courses worked well under our new arrangement and I don't believe I caused any issues or was noticed by the supervisors patrolling the room like Stasi agents.

Dessert was something I had never seen before. We all waited outside. I was selected to be a torch bearer, the torch resembling one carried by Olympians which looked to be quite fun. "Can you *Cha Cha?*"

What? My hesitant confusion was naturally taken as a *yes*. I was handed my *Olympic* torch, and a bunch of instructions.

"OK, when I tell you, the Gueridon trolley (*Google it dear readers.*) will be wheeled out. I want six of you on each side. When I give the signal we will light your torches. The lights will go down so don't fall over as we don't want to burn the place down. You will enter the room when there is the fanfare of trumpets. When this stops and the music starts, you will *cha cha* down the center of the room, around the dance floor and stop in front of the stage. Does everyone understand? You are on stage and you are performers, so stay in step and let's do this with style, movement and some *PIZZAZZ!*"

The lights went down, the torches were lit, the fanfare was sounded and the trolley started to move. I looked at the trolley. An ice cream bombe, with some simple spun sugar on top, a bowl of black cherries in Kirsch, alight with small dancing blue flames; behind this, a display of sugar *pastillage* as a Dutch stamp. Good God, is that it? We had served an identical dessert at The Grand with sombre regularity and without ceremony at all, and fittingly the guests greeted it in the same manner. It was the English way.

In we went, fanfare sounding, Latino music blaring, I in my best *Cha Cha* mode around the ballroom. Fred Astaire I was not. To my utter surprise, we were greeted with a standing ovation, cheers and applause. We were obviously presenting some totally wild, *avant-garde* and unique culinary creation. I realised – and this was the most significant knowledge I was to glean from my 'European stage' – Americans know how to put on a show, how to wow an audience, and how to present the mundane and the ordinary as something very special - how to add *PIZZAZZ*.

I was paid for the evening, but somehow felt I would never be asked again. Luckily my sentiment matched theirs, for that matter, as I never wanted to do it again.

Chapter 15

#adearjohn #closeencounters #sneakymove

It was now a few months since I had (trustingly) left my girl-friend in the hands of my best friend, the good looking Aussie lifeguard. Letters had started well, but it was now at least two weeks since I had heard from her. Suddenly this mattered. I was alone in Amsterdam. I tried to call a few times but got no answer. What could be wrong? It is extraordinary what goes through a young man's mind when he is convinced he is in love.

I become so concerned I decided there was only one thing I could do. Go back and see her. I put my plan together: a ticket on the 'Moonlight Flight' out of Schiphol Airport on Friday night, leaving at 10.30pm on BEA's new Trident Jet. As best I recall it was expensive for me at £14 ($25) return, coming back on Sunday. My small bag packed, I headed to the airport, with no other thought than to get to England. I was through customs and out of Gatwick Airport at around midnight. Only now I realised that I faced either a very long walk or had to somehow find a ride to Eastbourne. I decided to first get to Brighton, which was on the main road out of Gatwick.

I started to walk and kept my thumb out every time I heard a passing car. I'd been walking for about fifteen minutes when I heard a truck coming. Thumb out, air brakes applied, a friendly trucky's head saying "Where are you going?"

"Eastbourne?"

"I can take you as far as Brighton if you like."

"Fantastic."

He didn't tell me what he was hauling from Manchester to Brighton. I explained that I was living in Amsterdam and just home for the weekend to see the girlfriend. We chatted about Amsterdam, and he was interested to know if the tales of sex and drugs were true. Even with this spicy conversation, I was starting to doze off, and he let me sleep.

The next thing I remember was being shaken awake. "We're here mate, this is as far as I go." I thanked him and climbed out of the cab. "Good luck with the girlfriend." he smiled with a wink, as he disappeared into the dark. I was on the roundabout near the Royal Albion Hotel. I started to walk in the direction of Eastbourne on the A259 coast road. After about two miles I looked up, it was a clear well lit night and saw dawn was drawing closer; I could see the dark silhouette of the grand building of the world famous girls' school Roedean on the hill above the road, looking rather foreboding in the dawn light bringing images of Daphne du Maurier's *Rebbeca* and Manderley. The alumni of this school, a female version of Eton, often became household names. I remember Nancy Spain, the journalist and TV personality known for her lesbian views, thought as very outrageous for the times. There were also a number of actresses over the coming years. I was a fan of the unlikely named Honeysuckle Weeks, when she played the part of the driver in *Foyle's War*.

The Roedean motto was *Honour the worthy*, although I was never quite sure how this aligned with the very risque rugby song we used to sing in our schoolboy days.

We are from Roedean, good girls are we,
We take great pride in our vir-gin-ity,

We take precautions,
And avoid abortions,
For we are from Roedean School.
Up school, Up school, Up school!

It grew considerably worse as the song went on, the Eton Boating Song it was not, but even they had a rugby version.

I was singing this ditty to keep me going, as I was extremely tired. I had just finished the second chorus when a Humber pulled over in response to my thumb.

"Where are you heading?"

"Eastbourne?"

"I can take you as far as Seaford if you like?" He didn't need to ask a second time as I was already in the car. "What are you doing hitching at this time in the morning? Miss your last bus back?"

I told him my story so far. "Well looks as if you have certainly had a long trip." He also left me to nod off. In about twenty minutes I disembarked in Seaford. It was now coming up to about 5.30am, so I started to do a military fast march, estimating I could do the last ten miles in about three hours. About halfway into my route march I really started to think I was raving mad to have even started out on this trip. I was here now and just had to keep going. More cars were on the road now, as the new day broke. My thumb was out at the sound of any engine, but I wasn't expecting to suddenly see beside me the car emblazoned with POLICE.

"Where are you going, lad?" the uniformed man called to me. I explained my trip as briefly as I could. "You look knackered, mate. Hop in the back and we'll drop you off at The Grand."

"Thank you, thank you very much, I have to say the idea of walking another step was becoming a nightmare. You're absolute gentlemen."

Comfortably settled, I headed for Eastbourne. They dropped me off outside The Grand on the Parade at about 6.00am, too early to go knocking on doors. I headed for the beach, found myself a deck chair and made myself comfortable. I lay back and in seconds I was asleep.

I was awoken by a dog barking and someone shouting a command. It was nearly 8.00am and I knew Jenny, my girlfriend, would be heading for work. I waited near the hotel back entrance that I knew so well. Jeremy, an old friend, arrived on his way to work.

"Bloody hell Griffin what are you doing here?" he spluttered.

I briefly explained, feeling more stupid as I progressed through my story. He looked rather uncomfortable, and then he was so sympathetic to me, I knew there was something wrong. You'd think I could have worked it out during, if not even before, my journey here.

"Look Paddy, I think you had better see her and let her explain; but you look like shit. When did you last sleep, where are you planning to stay?"

I explained I hadn't got that far yet.

"Look I'm on duty until 4.00pm, use my room in St Vincents if you have nowhere else, and we can sort things out when I get off duty." With which he handed me his keys.
"Good luck, but don't expect too much. See you later."

A minute later I saw her coming towards me. At first, she didn't realise it was me, then she hesitated and was about to cross the road when she obviously thought twice. She came towards me with a look of *how the hell do I handle this*? I said a rather pathetic "Hello."

There was no fireworks just "Hello, what on earth are you doing back here?" A question to which I would have thought the answer was bloody obvious.

"Well to start with, I wanted to see you, and as I haven't heard from you in a while, I was worried."

She thought for a moment. "Look, I have to just go in to work and tell them I'm here. Have you had breakfast? Go to the Crompton Tea Room and have breakfast, and I will come straight back. We need to talk, OK?" It all sounded very ominous, like a 'Dear John' letter, but I had few other options. I was never one to go crazy and I was too tired to argue.

"OK, see you there in a few minutes."

She walked off.

I ordered my English breakfast. How wonderful to have English sausages, the one thing I had missed most in Holland. As my plate was almost clear, she arrived and sat at the table. As we waited for our coffees to arrive, there was some awkward small talk. How was I finding Amsterdam and the job? Had I found some new friends? How is *your* job going? How is my Aussie mate going? At this, she shifted in her seat uncomfortably. Ah ha - so that was it.

The coffee arrived, and she started with, "Look Paddy, you shouldn't have come back, the fact that you had not heard from me must have told you something…"

I just mumbled something. She continued, "It isn't possible to have a relationship between two people in different countries. The first few weeks I was so upset and missed you so much - it was hell. He was so kind looking after me, it just seemed to happen."

I thought, *he was always a charmer*. How stupid was I? *Can you take care of her, you blonde, good looking, tanned, Aussie, life-saving bastard*. What did I expect? Still, I rather pathetically said "But I trusted him, he was my best mate...".

She looked a little tearful at that moment, but what she said next nearly had me fall off my seat. "Paddy, I love him and we're engaged. I am so sorry, I really didn't want to hurt you."

That was about it. I think I said another inane comment like, "Are you sure?" but I realized there was nothing more I could say or do. The lack of sleep, the unwanted exercise and the emotion of the moment all swept over me. "Look, maybe we can chat later, but right now I must get some sleep. I'm flying back tomorrow night so I might try to catch up with some of the lads tonight."

Obviously relieved that I had not thrown a tantrum, and that I had taken the news rather placidly, I think she was happy to agree to anything. "OK, when you feel up to it, maybe after I finish we can have a chat. Where are you staying?" I told her I was in Jeremy's room.

"OK, I have to go. I am sorry." and with that she left.

I ran a bath at the house, as I felt I was covered in grime. After a soak and a shave, I felt wonderful. I just about made it back to the bed, keeled over and descended into unconsciousness. I woke at about 3.00pm to a tapping on the door. I wondered why I was back in St Vincents, and then the events of the past 24 hours flooded back. The knock on the door came again. "Paddy, are you there?"

The voice was vaguely familiar but I couldn't place it. "Paddy, it's Jenny, the other Jenny, I work at the same place..." I opened the door to a petite blonde woman, whom I now recognised having met her once before.

"What are you doing here?"

"Look I don't want to interfere, but Jenny asked me to come and chat with you. She feels really bad and honestly didn't want to hurt you, but now you are here she feels even worse, and just can't face you."

I was feeling much better after some sleep. "It's OK - I suppose I knew it deep down before I even left Amsterdam, but wasn't ready to accept it." We chatted for a while and then she suggested we go for a cup of tea. Good old England: TEA is the salve for all ailments. It was, however, a nice gesture, so I accepted.

We chatted a lot and got on very well; I liked her - was it a rebound reaction or was I callous and just moving on? She mentioned that there was a party on that night and was I interested in going? Of course I was. I didn't want to waste an airfare and a weekend. We agreed to meet in the Saloon Bar of The Grand at 8.00pm. I wondered if she was genuinely interested or simply *following orders* to keep me out of the way. Anyway, by now, I didn't care. My first task was to find out where I was going to sleep that night. I went back and found Jeremy.

"No problem, you can crash here as I am staying with the girl-friend tonight over in Bexhill. Anyway, if you are going to a party tonight you might get lucky."

I started to sort out what I had to wear; I didn't have a lot of choice but I needed to look smart. I also needed to check how much English cash I had, to save some for the train to Gatwick tomorrow and - much more importantly - to cover my drinks tonight.

I tried to get a little shut-eye and ponder the unexpected date I had for tonight. By 7.30pm I was feeling alive again - ah the sweet flush of youth - and headed for the Saloon Bar. I was no longer concerned, by now I am sure all would have been aware of the situation, and I wasn't sure of the right reaction that the cuckold should have. To my surprise, there were many old friends gathered there, Mac was behind the bar and it turned into a welcome committee – I was the Prodigal Son and I had returned. Drinks were offered all round: no need to worry about cash then. Everyone was keen to ask me all about Amsterdam – Sin City. On this topic I was happy to expound, and also embellish.

Under all this jollity was still a great wave of sympathy for me. The general opinion was "how could they have done that to you, I mean your best mate, what a shit." I rather bathed in all the sympathy. I was back to my preferred position: the centre of attention. No broken heart, and at worst a little bruised pride.

At 8.00pm *new* Jenny had not appeared. I was suddenly feeling a little vulnerable again, but she appeared, and looked lovely. Heads turned as she came in my direction and, once they realised she was heading in my direction, I got looks and comments. "Bloody hell Griffin, you don't waste much time." Some of the sympathy seemed to have evaporated.

With the mellowing effect of a few drinks, Jenny suggested we move to the party. It wasn't far to walk. I found there were a few people I knew, and again the conversation revolved around Amsterdam. This city held obviously a huge fascination, mainly due to the focus on sex, drugs and the Flower Power Hippies and 'the summer of love'. I discovered I was regarded as an adventurer and fun seeker as there were few local people of my age who had spent much time overseas – let alone LIVED in Amsterdam. Add to this my moonlight flight for the weekend jaunt and I was a local *cause célèbre*. The party was fun. My relationship was warming up. Eventually after midnight, I was invited back for coffee, as I had hoped.

The following day, I was full of chat about keeping in touch and writing. I was a little surprised, then, when she replied to my proposals quite coolly. "Paddy, it has been a great weekend, but you are going back to Amsterdam and I am staying here. I think we should just leave it there. If and when you come back, I would love to hear from you and then we can see how it goes from there."

How pragmatic, I thought. Obviously she had no intention of embarking on a teary farewell and then going home to sit alone, waiting for my letters and my return one day. I am not totally sure if I was disappointed that I hadn't swept her off her feet. Of course she was right; what a very modern woman. It made me realise that *I* must be the one to pursue her affections.

Jenny did come to the station, and we did say an affectionate goodbye. Once again a train pulled out of Eastbourne station and I was heading back to Amsterdam on the 'moonlight flight'. I invested in a taxi from Schiphol airport and finally got into bed at about 2.00am. I set the alarm for 7.00am and just hoped I would hear it and have the energy to get to work. With all the events of late, I really felt life was just one big adventure. My pre-Amsterdam life was all very dull and ordinary in comparison with post-Amsterdam.

One piece of my education, however, was one I might have preferred to avoid. My belief in my streetwise worldliness was brought down to earth by learning the hard way that I was still a callow naïve youth in the big wide world.

Friday of the following week, I was happily enjoying a beer in what had now become my local, *The Britannique*, just off Leidseplein Square. A bar fitted out as if it were a little England; what was not to like? It gave me a little touch of my home country in moments of homesickness, of which, at twenty one and missing my girlfriend/s, there were a few. I was on my barstool, and a smart-looking man in a suit sat a few places down from me. He surveyed the bar and then turned to me and asked in English, "What beer would you recommend?"

"I just tend to drink the local ale, Amstel or Heineken, it's cheaper than some of the specials, and to my taste, it's fine."

With this advice he ordered a Heineken. "For that good advice, allow me to buy you a refill."

Not wishing to appear rude, I, not surprisingly, accepted. "Thank you, that's very kind of you."

The ice was broken and it was nice to have a fellow Englishman to chat to. Although he was older than I, probably in his forties, it didn't bother me as in the hotel business you tended to only chat with older people. "By the way my name is John." He lived in Brighton and knew Eastbourne well. He said he used to go to The Grand for business meetings and raised the possibility that we may have even met before. As the evening went by we covered many subjects. He was very interested in what I was doing in Amsterdam. "By now I imagine you know it quite well".

I wished to sound as if I was well versed in all aspects of the city, and I agreed that, by and large, I was. It was now close on 7.30pm.

"Have you eaten?" he asked.

"No, but to be honest I am not very hungry." This was not altogether true, but my funds were limited and he looked as if he was not the sort to eat in an Automat.

"Are you sure, I am going to eat something, as I only flew in this afternoon and haven't eaten since the snack on the plane."

Sensing that there might be another reason than not being hungry, he added, "I would be delighted if you allowed me to treat you - I hate eating alone."

Having already told him of my 'impoverished' trainee status, it was now becoming difficult to refuse. I agreed and we went to a little Indonesian restaurant near The American Hotel. The relaxed conversation continued, we discussed the Six-Day War, the Amstel brewery, the Clint Eastwood movie I had seen, the cinema where one almost hung from the wall, and what had surprised me in the seats below with the two male cinema-goers. We discussed the rather liberal and open attitude of the Dutch in regard to homosexuality. He commented, "It does seem the case that everyone is queer in Amsterdam".

"Well, there certainly appears to be a lot, there is even a very nice guy who I work with, who lives very happily with his partner in a loft in the canal area."

We finished our meal and left the restaurant. I started to walk past The American Hotel on my way home when John stopped. "This is where I'm staying, they have an amazing Art Deco bar. Come in and join me for a nightcap. You know how it is when you have already had a few drinks, somehow one more doesn't seem a problem."

That was all the persuading I required. After what turned out to be a couple of nightcaps, John started to ask about the nightlife. I told him of a couple of interesting bars, a nightclub and a disco. John then proposed "Look, we're getting on so well, let me get changed out of this suit, and you can show me what the Amsterdam nightlife is all about." Although unsure, it had been a good night and it was the weekend tomorrow. Why the hell not? "Let me get you another drink. Do you only drink beer?" John asked

"I do like a good malt whisky but it's very expensive, so I stick with beer."

"Well it looks as if it could be your lucky day. I've got a duty-free bottle of Jack Daniels. Come on up while I change and we can have a drink to set us up for some nightlife."

I didn't think anything of it as we headed up to his room. I can already see you smiling in amusement, dear reader. He had a single room, with a desk with his papers, his case on the armchair. So there being nowhere else to sit, I sat on the bed. I was waiting for my Jack Daniels, and John started to undress. Normally when undressing in proximity, men will remove trousers first and allow their shirt tails to provide a level of modesty. New trousers can then be donned under the shirt and then the shirt can be changed with decorum, but with John it was shirt off, trousers down. Standing in his Y-Fronts before me he asked, "Do you fancy that *quicky*?"

At last, the Jack Daniels. A nanosecond later: Jack Daniels was not being offered. *Oh shit… Oh no…*

John was a respectable businessman. He wasn't flamboyant in his hand gestures, he didn't speak 'gaily', or with an affected effeminate voice. I knew a lot of queer guys. They wore colourful clothes, and chiffon scarves. Not business suits. The evening flashed through my memory. He came from Brighton, known for its 'gentlemen's' clubs; *"everyone is queer in Amsterdam…"*; he bought me dinner; I had come up to his room. Oh bloody hell. If I had been feeling a little tipsy for the drinks I had had that night, now I was as sober as a judge.

By now he was standing point-blank in front of me, thankfully still clad in his Y-Fronts. *Oh Jesus.* He put his hand on my shoulder and said softly, "Come on, you won't find it so bad…"

Panic was setting in, but controlling my shaking, the combination of fear and embarrassment, I simply said, "No thanks I am not into that". I was calculating how many steps and how long it would take to reach the door. I decided it was too long, and I wasn't waiting for him to move any further. I jumped up, and that movement alone rather took John by surprise and he rocked back on his heels, clearing the way for my getaway.

I was at the door and out of there like a rabbit. I didn't wait for the lift, and took the stairs three at a time, and was out of the front door and literally running down the street towards the safety of home.

I eventually stopped. I tried to catch my breath. I was really shaking and my mind was racing. Why me? What did I say? What did I do? How could I have been so stupid? What I had just escaped?

A family walked by, and could see plainly I was distressed. I heard a friendly North Country accent saying "Are you alright lad?" The plump motherly-looking wife chipped in with "You look very worried, what's the matter?" The daughter and son looked on with curious concern. I started to blurt out the events of the evening, but before I got a few sentences out, the man held up his hand for me to stop. He turned to his wife and the girl. "Walk on Mabel and take Cynthia with you, we will be along in a minute".

It wasn't a request, it was an order. The wife knew his tone of voice, and they walked off.

"OK lad, now tell me and Harry here what happened."

I explained what had happened that evening, and eventually reached the bedroom scene. He listened intently and eventually exploded. "The dirty bastard. Don't you worry, Harry and I will sort him out. What was his room number?"

I realised they were going back to give him a beating. I didn't want any more problems that night. "No, please don't, I really just want to go home."

He understood, although I truly believe they would have been quite happy to have gone to John's room and thumped him. "OK, let's get you home. Where do you live?"

Mabel and Cynthia were allowed to join us now, and Mabel gave me a sympathetic smile. I think she had pieced it together.

Surrounded by my new found North Country family, I walked to my door. "Will you be alright, dear?" Mabel asked.

"Yes, I'll be fine and thank you all for being so kind, I feel rather stupid now…"

"Just get to your room, have a nice cup of tea (again those magical English words for all life's troubles) and get to bed. It will all be OK in the morning." Motherly advice.

The father simply said "Just don't be so trusting next time."

"Sleep well," said Mabel.

They stood at the front door until I was safely inside and only then turned and left, all looking at the father to fill them in on the full story. I climbed up to my room, fell on the bed and let the alcohol of the night kick in. I slept.

Back at the desk on Monday, I told Johan what had happened. He was genuinely shocked and very sympathetic, and couldn't help but ask, "Didn't you realise what he was? How could you be so crazy as to go to the guy's room?"

I honestly had no answer. Looking back down the years, it seems unbelievable I could have been so naïve. I didn't realise just what an impact that evening had had on me until a few days later. One of the lads asked if I wanted to go for a drink, and I looked at him and wondered, was it only for a drink? For the next month, apart from going out with Johan, much of my time I just stayed at home in my room and read my books.

As I sat in my room, I was gripped with the desire to find somewhere new to live, with my own bathroom. My friend in Personnel might be able to help, as the rooms were as scarce as hen's teeth in Amsterdam. Having to give a month's notice made it almost impossible to vacate one premises and then be able to find somewhere new. I didn't want to take advantage of my special friend in high places, but hey, wasn't friendship all about helping each other? And did it matter if I wasn't really Jewish, even though my grandmother's maiden name was Saul.

I went to see Anna and explained that I really wanted to move, as amongst other things, the lack of a bathroom was a real concern to me. She was very understanding and explained the notice period. She also understood the difficulties that caused in trying to find a new place. She thought for a moment. "We did have one employee who just left one night and returned to Germany. We explained to the landlord that there was just nothing the hotel could do." She gave me a knowing look. "Not that I would suggest that you should find somewhere, then just pack and disappear one evening. Maybe you just had to return to England?" Again she smiled. "Have you tried the university notice board, rooms are often posted up there?"

I smiled back and thanked her. "I *am* feeling very homesick, I think I may need to return home to England for a while…" I think she rather enjoyed the plotting. Anna winked and I went back to work.

I told Johan what Anna had said and he was only too happy to help. "Thursday is the day that anyone who wants to rent a room posts it on the university information notice boards. The university nearest to us is the Vrije Universiteit in De Boelelaan, only about 15 minutes away." He explained that there is always a rush by students to get the accommodation first, so we needed a plan.

"We can go to the university, walk in as students, and see what gets posted. If there is a room that looks good we will need to get there as fast as we can. What I suggest is we grab a couple of bikes, which at that time would be the best way to get through the traffic and just hope we get there first."

"But neither of us have bicycles?"

Johan just looked at me. "Look around you – this is Amsterdam. Everyone has a bike, all we need to do is borrow two for an hour." Did I hear correctly? We steal two bikes?

"Look, everybody does it. Just pick the closest couple of bikes and off we go. As long as we return them, it's OK. They probably won't even notice they have gone."

Optimistic that I would find a new room, I planned my escape from my "warder", Mevrouw de Vries and my bathroom less little cell in her attic. I hope I may be forgiven for feeling that this gave me some empathy for Anna Frank having visited her home. Each day, I took a few of my clothes with me to work and stored them in a locker at the hotel. There wasn't really that much, but it was the large suitcase that would be a problem. So when I next saw Mevrouw de Vries returning to the house, I went down the stairs as if to meet her by chance and in my best Marcel Marceau mimes tried to convey that "suitcase gebróken. Where can I get repaired?"

She understood what I was saying but could not explain to me where to have it fixed. I could smile and say "OK, nee problem", and now she knew I had to take my case out to get it fixed.

On Thursday afternoon Johan and I arrived in good time at the university. We parked the motorbike nearby, and took up our position in front of the noticeboard with a number of other students. At 4.00pm to the second, a man came out with a single sheet of paper, posted it up with thumb tacks, and left. As if it was the announcement of a major world event, the students rushed in a scrum around the paper. There were eight rooms up for grabs. We had agreed to just pick one and go for it. Johan, knowing Amsterdam, would decide which one and he picked a room in President Kennedylaan, We had already 'cased out' the bicycles we were going to 'use' and found two that did not look too expensive, nor too individual, and as if they had been there a while. The size we would just have to work around.

It was as if Shakespeare's Henry V had shouted *Cry havoc and let slip the dogs of war*. Everyone in the scrum turned as one, and ran. We just hoped that not too many would head in the direction of Kennedylaan, but in any event we aimed to get there first. We ran to the bikes. I panicked for a moment – I thought I saw an owner heading for 'my' bike... ah, he kept walking. We grabbed our bikes and started pedalling like mad, Johan in the lead. Weaving in and out of the traffic and trams, after about twenty minutes we arrived at the door of a modern terraced house in Kennedylaan, out of breath and exhausted. It looked like we had achieved our goal as none of the competitors in the race had arrived as yet. Johan did not hesitate, he went straight to the door and rang the bell. A man answered the door and welcomed us in. He spoke very little English, so Johan did the talking. I have no idea what Johan said, but the man ushered us upstairs to inspect the room. It was three floors up, at the top of the house. It was bigger than my current attic, with a nice window overlooking one of the main bridges across the Amstel River towards Brussels. Opposite was a public swimming pool called De Mirandabad and a park. I asked the big question: was there a bathroom? The man looked at me as if I were stupid. "Ja, ja, natuurlijk."

I almost hugged him, but I thought the natural Dutch reserve might not be able to cope with such a show of gratitude. Johan looked at me, as if to say, *well?* But he added, "The only negative is that you won't be able to walk to work, you will need to take a tram and that will add to the cost; it is a little way out of the city." I already knew the rent and I didn't think the travel cost and time would be a major issue. Johan pointed out that there was a tram stop at the bottom of the road that would take me to Apollolaan.

"Can you tell him I should very much like to take the room. How much do I need to pay him now? When can I move in?"

The translation satisfied the man; he smiled, and I shook his hand. I paid him a month's rent and the deal was done. It seemed I was just in time; no sooner had we agreed on everything, than the doorbell rang. On our departure we saw two disappointed Dutch students standing forlornly at the door.

All that was left for me now was hopefully to get away with the two crimes I was committing: the return of the bikes and absconding from my cell in Frans van Mierisstraat and its guard, Mevrouw de Vries. Over time, I had rather unkindly cast her in the role of Rosa Kleb, the Bond villainess.

The return of the bicycles went without a hitch; as Johan had indicated, no one had even noticed their absence. Now for the Great Escape. Johan returned to Frans van Mierisstraat with me and waited in the street. I lugged down the suitcase with my remaining items and handed it to Johan. If I was confronted, Johan was to say he was taking the case to be fixed. I returned to my room, where I planned to stay that night, to give me a full day in the event my warden started to check on me. It was a Friday, and Anna and the administrative staff would not be in the office over the weekend. I felt comfortable that nothing would 'hit the fan' until Monday at the earliest, at which time of course I would have 'returned to England.'

By the middle of the following week I felt safe. I was in my new home and loved it, I had the tram routes sorted, and, true to her word, Anna sorted the issues out with Mevrouw de Vries. I was replaced by another young employee, Dutch this time, which made 'Rosa Kleb' much happier than having another deceitful Englishman occupying her room. Routine was re-established, my homophobia was fading, and I was a much wiser and more experienced young man.

Chapter 16

#flowerpower #canals'n'cannabis #vietvetsAWOL

It was time for me to check out a few things for which Amsterdam had gained its rather dubious reputation.

Firstly, it had become famous for its nicotine-stained "brown cafés," which I learned were where you could go to buy and smoke marijuana. Hard drugs were strictly illegal, but marijuana was relatively new and could be bought and sold. I eventually discovered a place by accident while wandering around. I passed a window full 'hubble bubble pipes' and other drug taking paraphernalia: all indications that the coffee shop didn't sell much coffee. The other dead give-away was the name: *Mellow Yellow*, the name of a chart topping hit for Donovan in 1967. It was rumoured to be about smoking dried banana skins, which were meant to provide a hallucinogenic effect. This was of course a load of rubbish; I did not even like bananas to eat, let alone to smoke.[71]

I poked my head in the door, the waft of 'herbal' smoke pervaded the air; is this for real? At that moment, my mind filled with all the warnings I had received from family and friends about the dangers of drugs, From my Uncle Douglas the doctor, whom I thought would never even have heard of 'pot', to my film producing brother Chris, who probably knew more about it than he should. It ended up being Chris's faint words that stopped me going into the 'coffee shop'.

"Pad - don't get started on the stuff, it turns the brain to mush and it is the first step to things a lot worse." It was an unusually sober bit of advice from my big brother, but it had the right effect on me that day.

Having at least entered the doorway and thus having earned the right to tick it off my list, it was now time to seek out the other famed vice for which Amsterdam was known: the infamous canal district. I had an idea of where to find it. Canals were everywhere; which canal? Which district? I walked towards the main railway station, as I was told that, by tradition, that was where such things began. I never really understood why *railway stations*? Having reached Centraal Station, I looked for the nearest canals and started walking. I crossed the bridge that took me to Damrak, and then turned left. After a while I came across some bars alongside a canal, and naturally decided to have a beer.

I learned something in that bar. First, it was fascinating to watch the barman line up glasses under multiple taps, flick the levers and watch the beer froth up in the glasses beneath. Once the froth was overflowing, with one deft stroke, like a conductor wielding his baton, he swiped a long white spatula across the top of the glasses, taking off the excess froth, and with a continuous movement flicked on the taps for a quick top up.

As I sat at the bar sipping my beer, I lit up one of my cigarettes. Unfortunately I could not get the brand I now was partial to, *Guards*, partly because the English cigarette brand was hard to find and therefore expensive at more than two shillings a packet. I started to smoke the cheaper, local brand, *Caballeros*, not the best of cigarettes; if you tapped one on the bar counter, you would be left holding the paper between your fingers with a little pile of tobacco on the counter. They came in a brown pack with the image of a Mexican *sombrero* and a slogan that read *Smaak vor twee*: 'Taste for two'. This took on a new meaning when a man sitting on the stool next to mine simply took one of my cigarettes with a smile and a nod. "Bedankt".

As if to add insult to injury, he picked up my lighter to light it. After a while, he did it again. Not wishing to offend, I left it for a few minutes and then put the pack in my pocket. I told Johan about this, and he said that it wasn't unusual, just something people do in a bar.

It was now late afternoon on a Sunday. I decided to venture further to see what all the fuss was about with the canal district. After a short while I stopped on a bridge that crossed the canal, taking in the view on either side. At first glance I saw nothing; no women in low cut red dresses, no very short mini-skirts leaning against a lamp post. Well, after all, I thought to myself, it was a Sunday afternoon.

Out of the corner of my eye, I caught the movement of a curtain being pulled back, and spied a very voluptuous young woman making herself comfortable on a chair inside the window. I then noticed another; and another. Suddenly, they were everywhere. So this is what it was all about. I walked off the bridge and wandered along the canal as if I were totally unaware of the young women in the windows. It only needed a split-second glance and the young woman had already made eye contact and offered a very inviting smile. Feeling rather embarrassed, I picked up my pace until I reached the end of the street. However, as I needed to get a tram from the other end of the canal, I found myself doing a lap of honour, and felt this was much to the amusement of the women.

When I reached home, I reflected on my afternoon adventure. The closest I had seen anything like this was a simple card on a doorbell in a side street in London's Soho, that read *French Maid 1st Floor*. I never saw a French maid and had no desire to. Amsterdam was a very different proposition. It was fun, colourful and didn't feel seedy. It was equally a tourist attraction and a place where women engaged in the oldest profession in the world. Well, I convinced myself anyway. I had no desire to participate (never mind that I had no money for such adventures). It was all such a new experience for a twenty one year old from Eastbourne and Royal Leamington Spa. One could sit outside a bar and watch the traffic in London go by, or one could sit here and watch LIFE. I decided next week I would go back and watch a little more of LIFE.

I agreed to meet up with Johan early afternoon on the Saturday, and went around to his place, on Prinsengracht, by a canal. I arrived, rang the bell, and waited. No reply. After about half an hour I was getting a little concerned - had I mixed something up? Little did I know that it was going to be a long wait. I discovered later his girlfriend had had a major problem and Johan had to give her a lift somewhere. Unfortunately, in the pre-mobile era, there was no way to let me know. I waited, sitting on the side of the canal, watching the passing tourists in the open topped sightseeing boats, listening to the guides' monologues which they repeat hour after hour, day after day. I wondered if they even heard it themselves.

"Along the way we will see Anne Frank House, The Gouden Bocht, in English: "*Golden Bend*", the most prestigious part of the Herengracht in Amsterdam, the Reguliersgracht and the Skinny Bridge, also the Flea Market."

This is normally where they slot in a joke, here it comes. "Here in Amsterdam they say, if you have your bicycle stolen, and you run fast enough to the Flea Market, you might arrive in time to buy it back."

Pause for laughter. Depending on how many English-speaking tourists are on board, and if they are listening, you might hear a polite chuckle.

The boats passed by, sending a small wash lapping against the walls of the canal. I heard a voice in the distance calling, "Hello, hello." I shook off my reverie and realised a girl on a houseboat moored on the other side of the canal as calling "Hello" and waving me to come over. I checked that there was no one else around, so I assumed she was waving at me. I looked questioningly and pointed to myself. "Ja, kom hierheen."

I walked a few yards to the nearest bridge crossing the canal and walked down to her barge. There was a bit of a party happening with about ten young hippies on board. The girl who had called me over said "Op wie wacht je."

"I am sorry, I am English and..."

"Ahh English, OK I speak English. Who are you waiting for?" I explained my dilemma. "Why not join us? It looks as if he's not coming."

"Thank you - sitting on the side of the canal was getting a little uncomfortable." Boarding the barge, I could see this was obviously their home; what a great way of living.

"Here, would you like a drink?" with which she handed me, of all things, a sherry.

Not what I thought would have been their drink of choice. Being polite, I accepted. Maybe they thought, being English, that this is what I would enjoy. I had noted that in Amsterdam there were many bars that actually specialised in this type of fortified wine.

We sat down and started chatting. I was struck by just how friendly and welcoming they all were, not at all in the manner of the rather austere, rather humourless Dutch. They were also very knowledgeable of British politics; I could not name a single Dutch politician, and they were naming half the House of Commons. I felt rather ashamed at my own ignorance. I was becoming the centre of attention. "What do you think about Britain joining the Common Market? You know the Dutch have voted for you to join?"

I didn't know that of course, but felt that I should, and so expressed my thanks for them supporting our application. They wanted to know what I thought of Bobby Moore getting an OBE for captaining England in its World Cup victory in the previous year against the Germans. This result had pleased them all. They turned then to the news that Francis Chichester had completed the first single-handed voyage around the world in his yacht, *Gipsy Moth* in nine months and one day.

"You know, the Dutch are also great sailors; take Barend Fockesz, a 17th-century captain with the Dutch East India Company. He was renowned for the uncanny speed of his trips from Holland to Java. What about Abel Tasman who discovered Tasmania; Australia should really be ours."

I was not going to argue, and maybe it might have been better if they *had* settled Australia, thus preventing the development of a nation that would end up beating England at nearly every sport of which we thought we were masters. We then turned to Vietnam and why the Americans were there. The afternoon thus continued. I remember the music that was playing which made me a little homesick, the songs that take me back to that day on the canal in Amsterdam - *Respect, Summer in the City, Whiter Shade of Pale, Waterloo Sunset* by the Kinks and of course the anthem of the time, *San Francisco by* Scott McKenzie. They were all hits and became timeless in the summer of 1967.

At some point, someone suggested that I should join them at a party in a loft somewhere in the canal area. By this time, feeling a little mellow and most certainly one of the group, I agreed without hesitation. Where could I get some drink to take along? "Nee nee, breng gewoon een bloem mee... *sorry no drink just bring a flower.*"

Did he say "a flower?" "Yes, a flower." OK. A flower

As we walked towards the party, it was now dark and I was curious as to what sort of party it was going to be. I had seen all these Flower Power groups in Vondelpark; was it a pot smoking fest? Was everyone going to throw off their clothes and make love not war? As we passed a flower vendor, I bought a bunch of tulips. I felt rather strange walking along with the very colourful group of hippies all carrying very colourful flowers, some with just one bloom, others with a whole bunch. Being the guest, I thought I should at least make an effort and take a bunch.

We eventually arrived and climbed the usual almost vertical set of stairs to the loft. As we reached the summit, I heard Otis Redding crooning *Dock of the Bay*. One of my group banged on the door which was slowly opened by a face checking on who had knocked. The flowers seemed to be the entry ticket, and the door opened to allow us in. We entered a long room with bare wooden floors and not a lot of furniture; very minimalist, I thought. There must have been about forty people there and most were just sitting on the floor. There was some conversation, but there was a lot more gazing into space or just swaying with the music.

Could I get a beer? A pleasant young woman waved vaguely. I headed in that direction and eventually found a few bottles; hmm, unless they were expecting some biblical miracle, this was going to be a fairly dry event. The next thing I noticed was that practically no one had a beer in their hand.

I found a spot against the wall, next to a couple of American guys. No one attempted to introduce themselves, but one of the Americans leant over offering me a cigarette. Having my suspicions about its provenance, I declined and took out one of my own Caballeros. Rough as they were, I felt it might be a little safer. I started to drink my beer; being aware of the limited supply, I took small sips, to make it last. What I found amazing though was the effect it was having on me. It must have been some super-strength beer, as it was very quickly giving me a feeling of lightheaded euphoria.

Argh! It dawned on me. It wasn't the beer. Passive inhalation of the haze of marijuana smoke was inescapable in the tiny loft. Ah well best go with the flow. Thus I justified the very pleasant feeling of well-being that was overtaking me.

As I contemplated this, the American next to me asked in a southern drawl, "Where do you come from?"

"I am English, from Stratford on Avon, the birthplace of Shakespeare". He showed no sign of recognition. "Where are you from?"

"America."

Conversationally, I followed up. "Where in America?"

"Alabama, Tuscumbia." As utterly unfamiliar to me as had Stratford on Avon been to him. "It's the birthplace of Helen Keller."

OK. Point taken. I asked what they were doing in Amsterdam, and thus ensued a story. It was hard to know how old either of them were, as they both looked older than their years. Maybe it was all the pot, but there was something missing in their eyes. They lacked any of the light or life that one would expect in guys my age. The reason why became more evident as their story had unfolded. They had both fought in Vietnam, and on some R&R in Thailand had decided enough was enough. They went AWOL and ended up in Amsterdam. I have to admit that my stiff-upper-lip-Englishman-opinion of them was pretty low, as I believed in 'Queen and Country' and 'doing the right thing' if called upon to fight, just as my father had done when England stood alone for a year in 1940. I thought, those Americans never had that sort of back bone…

I knew very little about Vietnam at that time as the war was still in its early stages, but I could barely believe the tales they started to tell me. I thought they were justifying their desertion. They spoke in a denigrating way of gooks, slant eyes, zips, dinks. Anything but *Vietnamese*. It seemed the first rule was to dehumanise their enemy …with racism.

"Are you talking about the Viet Cong?"
"They are all the same, North or South".

I was trying to get my head around this. Weren't they there in support of the South?

"They are all a bunch of corrupt bastards. We shouldn't be involved. It's not our fight. Who cares if a few gooks want to kill each other"

Obviously these guys were not believers in Eisenhower's 'domino theory'. "But I thought you were winning out there?"

"Government bull shit. We ain't winnin' 'Nam; we don't even know who we are fighting. So we shoot 'em all. If we don't meet a body count, we get our asses kicked by command, so we just pile them up. We just find a village, if they look suspicious, we just waste 'em and burn their hootches."

Whilst unbelievable, I had a morbid fascination for their stories. I just could not bring myself to imagine this level of inhumanity taking place in the world of hippies and flower power. I could see that these guys were just kids who had never before been out of Alabama, let alone the USA. In a country that was hostile, hot, rainy and steamy, and a culture so alien, they might just as well be on Mars, they couldn't comprehend it and they didn't want to be there. Fighting in a jungle where they could hardly see the enemy, it was a case of survival. Any humanity that they had to start with was just sapped away in the heat and the violence. The Vietnamese people all became dehumanised, and their derogatory names were part of the alienation. Killing anyone, enemy, friend, man, woman or child was just an act that evoked no feeling or emotion. They just wanted to survive and get home alive.

In the ten years of the Vietnam War, or the 'American War' as the Vietnamese people call it, it is estimated that the death toll was in excess of 2.5 million, many of whom were women and children. According to some documentation after the war, the horrors are hard to comprehend.

Guenter Lewy estimates that around 220,000 civilians in South Vietnam were killed in US, Army of the Republic of Vietnam and other allied land operations.

Seven massacres officially confirmed by the American side, with the largest at My Lai and My Khe with 420 and 90 men, women and children murdered.

Two further massacres were reported by soldiers who had taken part in them, one north of Đức Phổ in Quảng Ngãi Province in the summer of 1968 (14 victims), another in Bình Định Province on 20 July 1969 (25 victims).

Tiger Force, a special operations force, murdered hundreds, possibly over a thousand, civilians.

In the course of large-scale operations an unknown number of non-combatants were killed either accidentally or deliberately

– with the Army Inspector General estimating that more than 5,000 died in the course of Operation Speedy Express.

According to the Information Bureau of the Provisional Revolutionary Government of South Vietnam (PRG), between April 1968 and the end of 1970 American ground troops killed about 6,500 civilians in the course of twenty-one operations either on their own or alongside their allies. Three of the massacres reported on the American side were not mentioned on the PRG list.

Years later I read a book called *Kill Anything That Moves* by Nick Turse. This was a comprehensive description of the war, written with mastery and dignity, including what American forces actually did in Vietnam. The book discloses almost unspeakable truths. A number of incidents occurred during the war in which civilians were deliberately targeted or killed. The best-known are the massacre at Hue and the My Lai massacre, for which James Calley was initially charged and spent time under house arrest but no one was ever really found guilty of these or any atrocities committed by American forces in Vietnam. I wish this book could be taught in American schools where much is covered over, but of course it will not be. I think people rather just hope that such things will go away, be better forgotten and will not happen again. I always think that if we don't learn from history then it will be repeated. And of course it has been many times since then.

I had had enough of my American friends and decided to work the room. By now most people were on a different planet and I felt I would soon be joining them. The air was thick with herbal aromas. I thought it might be time to get some fresh air and head home. Not being able to find any discernible host amongst the growing numbers to whom to say my farewell- I still believed in English politeness- I decided to just slip away.

Skillfully negotiating the hazardous descent down the stairs, I reached base camp without incident and headed down the canal towards my tram stop. This took me through the red light area, which at this time was a hive of activity. It was an interesting walk. I observed life and human nature and national characteristics.[73]

I found myself following a group of drunk American sailors, obviously out for a good time, but in so doing showed contempt for anything or anyone who did not come from the great US of A. After what I had heard this evening I had somewhat lost respect for my colonial cousins. Looking at these sailors, I was even less impressed.

"Hey honey, want a piece of this," shouted a sailor to a girl in a window, with a rude gesture. Another grabbed his mate by the arm, trying to steer him towards an attractive black girl sitting in another window. "Come on, I've never had a n****r..."

The three of them headed in her direction, and she made her feelings known with a one digit gesture, and a sharp pull on the curtains, signally well and truly closed for business. This led to another chorus of abuse from the sailors.

I moved on past them, noticing a German man confidently standing at the door with a young woman, looking as if he were having a conversation about the weather but naturally would have been discussing the price and the level of services on the menu.

As I continued my *educational* walk home, I found myself following a man who walked along the canal looking furtively in the direction of the boats on the canal, and then in the direction of the girls, and then back to the canal as if seeing nothing of what was on offer. In a final furtive lunge, with the lighting speed of a rugby player making a dive for the touch line, he disappeared into a doorway. The woman was a little taken aback by this sudden appearance of a man but welcomed him in. She was perspicacious enough to note his embarrassment and immediately drew her curtains. All things considered - he just *had* to be English.

Being in Amsterdam, I had hoped to have a galaxy of film stars checking into the Hilton, but, sadly, this was not to be. Most of the 'stars' we did have were really only known in their home countries.

Sammy Davis Jnr came to Amsterdam to appear in concert at the *Concertgebouw*, and stayed at the Hilton. He was not the nicest of men. He and his crew had a number of guests in their suites after the show. One of these guests was a lovely young woman who worked in our news-stand, and with whom I was rather smitten. She was to regret her star-struck ambitions; as Sammy and his team departed, a stack of Polaroid photos was handed to the porter, who thought this was in lieu of a tip. His mouth fell open as he discovered that the photos were of the star-struck young woman, in rather acrobatic positions with various members of the entourage. Racy even for Amsterdam standards of the day. The lovely young woman was not seen in the employ of Hilton from that day forth.

Another visiting star was Curd Jürgens, the Austrian-German actor whose resume included *Inn of the Sixth Happiness, And God Created Woman,* and later was to be a James Bond villain, Karl Stromberg in 1977, in *The Spy Who Loved Me* and just about every World War II German general in between. His past was interesting in that during the war he was critical of Adolf Hitler's National Socialist regime and in 1944 he was sent to an internment camp in Hungary as a 'political unreliable'. During the last days of World War II he tangled with the brother of high-ranking Gestapo official Ernst Kaltenbrunner, resulting in his being drafted into the army. He died from a heart attack in

1982. He was truly a charming man, who stayed for a few days, with the only challenge for the waiter serving breakfast being to avoid getting mauled by Curd's wife's pet cheetah, who travelled everywhere with her.

The Amsterdam Hilton really hit the world's headlines in March 1969, when John Lennon and Yoko Ono staged their famous week long 'sleep-in' in the cause of 'World Peace'. Sadly, that effort does not seem to have made any impact on the world to this day.

The story was well documented and remains popular to this day. It's probably the best bit of marketing the hotel has ever executed. From 1969 onwards, the hotel attracted more film and rock stars, and, following a renovation, the room was reassigned as number 702, and marketed as the *John and Yoko Honeymoon Suite*. Couples could be married in a civil ceremony, and many still make the pilgrimage to do so.

I had left by then, having returned to England, but it didn't do my resume any harm to feature 'Hilton, Amsterdam'. After the sleep-in, everyone knew of the Hilton, Amsterdam, and without fail regularly asked "Were you there?"

Chapter 17

#feelingdeflated #thermometers'n'bedpans #maldemer

Late one night after a sociable evening, I managed to catch the last tram back to my room in Kennedylaan. I lay on my bed, and I wanted that last cigarette of the night. There were none left in my pack. A tobacco addiction is a terrible thing; the more I thought about it the more I had to have a cigarette. I could take it no more; I arose set forth in search of a cigarette machine. I must have walked for at least thirty minutes and still not found one, eventually arriving back in a worse state than I had left.

I did something on which I look back with sheer disbelief. Finding an old packet of cigarette papers, I took one out and collected all my old cigarette butts from the ashtray, I retrieved the remaining tobacco shreds, and carefully rolled what I had into the cigarette paper, and sealed the sticky edge. Satisfied it would hold together, I lit it, took a deep draw, felt the nicotine and tar fill my lungs, and instantly had a coughing attack that made my lungs burn. I had slated the craving. I lay back and slept.

A few weeks later a cough I had just wouldn't go away. No amount of cough syrup or lozenges seemed to help. Going to work, I jumped off the tram and started to jog towards the hotel. I felt a sudden most searing pain in my chest. It stopped me in my tracks. I grabbed hold of a tree and leant against it, just wanting the pain to stop. I was finding it hard to breathe. What the hell just happened? Surely it couldn't be a heart attack? *I'm only twenty one for God's sake.* What was it? Eventually the pain eased, I was able to stand upright, and I took a few tentative steps. I could still walk, and if I took it slowly I was OK. I got moving and felt alright again, with only a strange uncomfortable feeling in my chest.

I got used to it over the next couple of days, and naturally did nothing about it, being young. After all, it didn't hurt, and the only thing I had to get used to was finding that if I did try to move too quickly, something in my chest flopped about a little, rather like a piece of wet fish. So for the next few days life went on. The following weekend, Johan invited me down to stay for the weekend at his home in 's-Hertogenbosch, or known as, den Bosch, a beautiful historical city. "We can go for a sail on the waterways, my father has a boat". It all sounded great. I packed my bag for the weekend and we headed off, little knowing this was the last time I would ever see my room in Kennedylaan.

We arrived at Johan's home, or two homes. Holland has a very strict policy on space and home ownership, due to the population and limited land space. There are the controls as to the size of home you could own. Johan's father was fortunate; being a doctor, he was allowed two apartments. One for a home, and the second for a surgery. Both were 'home'.

His father was an interesting man. Not only had he been a resistance fighter as per the tales Johan had told me, which in itself made him rather a hero in my eyes, but he had also received an award from the Queen for his works in bringing together the two Dutch faiths, Catholicism and Calvinism, in the medical world. I had not appreciated how these had divided Holland over the years.

Over dinner, much was discussed, and I was touched by the warmth of his family. During the evening Johan mentioned the problem I had with my chest. Naturally his father said, "We can look at that in the morning if you would like?"

"Thank you, that would be great, but I am sure it really is nothing". I was more interested in talking about the possibility of going sailing the next day.

After breakfast I thought my chest had been forgotten. However, Johan's father appeared. "When you have finished, would you like to come through to my surgery and we can have a look?" I got up and followed him next door. I sat down and he started listening to my chest.

> "Deep breath. And again." He checked one side and the other, first front and then back. After a few minutes he looked at me. "You definitely have something wrong. Your lungs are not breathing evenly. We need to take you to the hospital and do some further checks."

This shook me. "I'm sure it's nothing? I can check it out when I get back to Amsterdam?"

He was having none of it. "You must come with me to the hospital." He spoke to Johan, and off we went. Arriving at the *Protestants Ziekenhuis,* I just followed their orders. It was obvious that Johan's father was someone of note, as I was immediately taken to be x-rayed. There was much discussion amongst the staff. I was by now not a little concerned, as I had no idea what they were talking about. I was ushered to a seat, but when I rose to take a walk I was immediately instructed to sit down again. They didn't want me making any movements.

After twenty minutes, Johan and his father came over to explain their concerns. The first issue was that I might have tuberculosis, which would require immediate isolation and treatment, but they would need to do further tests to confirm this. I tried to explain that I had had my hotel medical only a few months ago and did not have TB then, but they still wanted to check. The second issue was that my left lung had collapsed, in itself serious enough, but life-threatening if the second lung followed suit. In any event I was not going anywhere, and a bed was being prepared for me in the hospital.

I was allocated a single room with a nice view. The good news was, as a Hilton employee, I had full medical cover. My real worry was about work, my room and all my bits and pieces. Johan once again came to my aid and told me not to worry; he would sort all these things out. I settled in bed and the nurses and doctors took control. Johan and his father said just relax, rest and they will be in as often as needed to make sure I had all I wanted.

After they left, I discovered that the only people who spoke English were the doctors, and very few nurses. As I was not allowed to get out of bed, and I mean for ANY reason at all, when the call of nature came I had to use what skill in mime I had to indicate "bedpan". Eventually the nurse, whose name was Orange, the same name as the Royal Family, taught me a simple Dutch phrase. "'een potje alsjeblieft".

I could now add to the very few Dutch words I had managed to learn, including the obligatory swear words, that of 'potty'. I was sure this would be of great help with any Dutch amorous adventure I might embark upon.

My final and most serious concern was when nurse Orange, in her crisp white uniform and cap, came in to take my blood pressure and temperature. She produced the largest thermometer I had ever seen. It was the size of the industrial kitchen models we used when melting sugar. She then put it in a plastic sleeve.

"Under my tongue?" I gestured with more than a little uncertainty.

At this point she produced a jar of vaseline into which she dipped the thermometer. It started to become hideously clear where it was going.

"Nee, nee," she replied with a bit of a giggle. With an interesting mime she indicated where it was to be put.

This manoeuvre wasn't as easy and most certainly not as comfortable as it may seem. Eventually, she had managed to take my temperature – for that day.

After various checks and x-rays they concluded that I did not have TB. I did, however, have a collapsed left lung. I had had a *spontaneous pneumothorax*, not caused by a rib fracture but no doubt a consequence of smoking. As a result there was a formation of small sacs of air, called blebs, in the lung tissue that ruptured, causing air to leak into the pleural space... and there you have it. I blamed those ghastly Caballero cigarettes. My note to self was to buy a better brand of fags in future.

The treatment was simply to wait and watch and see if the lung would heal itself, and then wait for it to inflate on its own. This could take a week or two. Meanwhile, Nurse Orange and I got on well, me practicing my Dutch potty requests while she practiced her English. She was always amused when it came time to check my temperature.

True to their word, Johan's family came in for regular visits and brought me clean clothes and fruit. They really were extraordinarily kind. Johan had returned to Amsterdam to sort things out with the hotel, to check my room and speak to the landlord. He promised he would soon get back to den Bosch and bring with him my list of items, my shaver, wash things, pyjamas, passport and some documents, with a few other bits and pieces.

As the trip to den Bosch was about ninety kilometres and took up to two hours, I wasn't expecting Johan to make the four-hour round trip the next day. But the following day he was back with all that I needed, and confirmed everything was sorted with the hotel and my landlord.

The following weekend, when dear nurse Orange was doing my 'vitals', I was manoeuvring the thermometer into place; it was a complicated procedure: lowering the pyjama bottoms, raising the hips, knees apart, maintaining balance, the device poised ready for entry. I was just completing the delicate insertion, when suddenly a number of heads appeared one by one around the door. Johan, then Tamir, and then the entire hotel team - even my Belgian friend.

I was now in a most precarious position as I needed to lower myself with great care in case I lost the entire thermometer in my nether passages never to be seen again. While all this was happening, each visitor approached my bed with the normal continental greeting of a kiss on either (facial) cheek except the Frenchman who gave me an extra one. I was then utterly taken aback when Tamir greeted me not with a kiss on each cheek but a kiss on the lips. This is not what I was expecting but I can only gather that it is a middle eastern custom. In my discomfort and confusion, I was past caring.

I managed to adjust myself with the thermometer safely withdrawn from the danger zone as far as I could tell. I discreetly re positioned my pyjama bottom. By now all had found places to sit around and on the bed and various chairs. The hotel had put together a box of fruit along with a nice note from Personnel, signed by Anna and the boss. Johan gave me my bag of bits and pieces and a couple of letters; one was from Mum and Dad, obviously following the kind phone call from Johan's father to assure them I was in good hands and they had nothing to worry about. The other was postmarked Eastbourne in a Grand Hotel envelope, which made me very curious, and I put them to one side to read later.

As with all hospital visits, it became a little strained after about thirty minutes, and everyone was trying to get more creative with the conversation. I was desperate to check on the whereabouts of my thermometer and, to this end, was applying my mind to find a way to give them a good easy excuse to leave. Of course, I did appreciate that they actually had taken a four-hour round trip at their own cost, on their day off. I thought back to England and felt guilty. How many times had I and others promised to visit a friend in hospital only a couple of miles away, but had always found an excuse as to why it didn't happen. The kindness of the team and the Dutch in general was something I would always remember.

I thought this avenue might work for them:

"I really can't thank you guys enough. To travel all this way? I mean - a FOUR HOUR round trip. What time will you get back to Amsterdam? What time is your train back? Nurse Orange will be in soon and getting upset with you, and me, and you don't want to see Nurse Orange upset, believe me. You might be OK, but I have no way of escape."

As if she had been listening at the door for her cue, in comes nurse Orange. She may well have just remembered the piece of medical equipment she had left behind. On seeing all the visitors, she said something in Dutch that I assumed was "I'll be back later", but this now gave everyone the opportunity to make good their escape. The visiting Dutch contingent started their exodus, saying that they had trains to catch, etc. Honour, courtesy and politeness now satisfied, I was again faced with a line of departing friends kissing me on the cheek. Johan was the last to go and explained that he was staying with his parents and would be in again tomorrow.

I was then left alone, with time to search and retrieve the errant thermometer prior to the nurse's return. When she eventually appeared she looked at me and presented another one, in its little plastic sleeve, liberally coated in Vaseline. What I really wanted to say was *'you know where you can stick that'*, which of course she did and in any event I feared my Dutch language was insufficient for the task. Obediently, therefore, I simply complied.

It wasn't long before my dinner arrived. Dutch hospital food is no better nor worse than hospital food the world over, with a Dutch 'accent' to it. I have never understood what happens to what is presumably fresh food at the point it arrives at the hospital. Whatever is done to it on the industrial scale, with the varieties of dietary restrictions to consider and the transportation process from kitchen to ward, is obviously the cause of the resultant tasteless, over cooked mush, naturally with some form of congealed gravy, a single flavour for all meats and fish, and, to crown the experience, served tepid. This has been held to be the universal truth in hospitals around the globe in which I have found myself: on no account should they provide a hot, interesting and flavoursome meal.

As I ate I opened my mail, I guessed the letter from home would comprise my mother saying how worried she was and shouldn't I come home, with a note from my father as to the need to keep a stiff upper lip, etc. I was more interested in the letter from The Grand. Jeremy or one of the other trainees had never been prolific communicators.

The letter was signed by M.A. Cairns. Why would he be writing to me? I really got excited when I read he was being promoted to General Manager of one of the De Vere Hotels, the company which had recently taken over The Grand Hotel. The hotel he was going to manage was the Castle Hotel in Norwich - and would I be interested in joining him as his assistant before the end of the year? I was stunned for a moment. I had worked for Mr Cairns during my trial at the Manor House Hotel in Leamington Spa, and then of course at The Grand. I liked and respected him, but had never thought that I might be in line to work for him again.

I needed to think this over. I knew him and he knew me. Getting that first assistant manager's job was so important in a hotel career. I knew nothing about the Castle and not much about the De Vere Group. It did sound like an awfully good opportunity. I needed to invest in a telephone call to Dad and ask his opinion, and see if he can find out anything about the hotel. I would sleep on it, if indeed I could sleep, as the more I thought about it the more interesting and appealing it became.

I re-read the letter from home. My mother was very keen on me returning home after my hospital internment, and the letter also held one bit of interesting news. My other brother Bob was engaged and planned to marry in September or October. He wanted me, as younger brother, as his best man. Bob and I had never been very close, but he was my brother and also in hotel management. I suspected this was as much about tradition as brotherly love, but was another reason to return home.

The reasons kept mounting as I pondered the issue. I was having a great time in Amsterdam, but wasn't learning much on the hotel management front. I was learning a lot on the *life experience* side, and, yes, this was also important in managing hotels and people. I ticked off that I had now got the Hilton on my resume, whether it be for six months or six years.

I had my visit from Johan, and we chatted and I told him about the offer I had received. He listened intently and then made a few points. First, I was twenty-one and to have an opportunity at that age was something to think about, as it certainly wouldn't happen in Holland. Second, his father had expressed concern at me remaining in Holland in winter with my lung problem, as Dutch winters can be very damp, cold and windy. Lastly, he broke the news that he was getting engaged and was planning to leave and go to the USA. We had become very close friends and he had taken me under his wing. He did not say as much, but I think he felt I might have difficulties in Amsterdam with no one to keep an eye on me.

I managed to call my father that same day. He was in agreement for the job shift in principle, and agreed to find out what he could about the Castle Hotel, Norwich and the De Vere Group. Being ever conscious of the cost of international calls, especially when I had reversed the charges, he kept it as short as he could and said he would write back in the next few days.

I then wrote to Mr Cairns, not wanting to keep him waiting, expressing my interest. Could he please give me some more information about the job, the hotel and about the company? I would then get back to him by return. The letter was in the hospital mail that night, courtesy of Nurse Orange.

The doctors, although pleased with my progress, were still not prepared to say when I would be allowed out. With all that was happening, I wasn't in a rush to leave, but even so it looked like I was facing another ten days. I heard back from both my father and Mr Cairns, both of whom offered a positive view on the hotel, and on Norwich. Mr Cairns added the point of salary, and, while not a fortune at £14 a week, it did include bed, board, an entertainment allowance, and a review after six months. Seemed pretty fair to me as a first assistant management position. The 'yes' side of the argument was stacking up. The more I thought about it, the more I believed it was the right move.

Johan arrived on Friday evening with his fiancee Janna, and we chatted about my time in Amsterdam and what we felt the future had in store for us all. I told him that I was going back to England, and what did he think was the best way of telling the hotel? Cunningly Johan suggested that I shouldn't resign, but should tell them that I was to go back home to England to recuperate, where I would have someone to look after me. This would keep my salary being paid and my options open, in case I wanted to return. An added bonus. I was to write the letter and he would take it in on Monday. What about my room and all the things I had there, I had my passport and papers but what about the outstanding rent? No worries, said Johan, he could sort it all out. All was now ready to plan my return to England.

I loved my time in Holland, especially the opportunity to have worked for Hilton Hotels. They were the first American chain to enter Europe, bringing the excitement of the new world. Hilton was way ahead of other hotel chains at that time; one might say a little brash or I rather put it as 'innovative' - a modern focus on marketing and promotion, activities that traditional hotels had deemed rather beneath them. A Hilton in-house magazine of the day promoted the idea of a hotel on the Moon, The Lunar Hilton, complete with an artist's impressions. Man did not actually land there for two more years, but it sparked our imaginations the way crazy unlikely plans always do. There was even an article written about it in 2013 - you can read it in Appendix C.

It was now September. The doctors agreed to release me, but not to an airplane's pressurised cabin. I'd have to go back on the boat that first brought me to Holland. My parents had sent me some money, funds to get back and, as I could not fly, it was a daytime crossing and I managed to stretch the funds I had to buy a first class ticket. Johan as always was true to his word, arranging the ticket and delivering my suitcase, and other belongings. There was little more than I had arrived with, due to a few obligatory souvenirs for those back home, so I needed a little extra pressure to shut the case.

On the day of departure, Johan's father very kindly drove me the one and a half hour trip to The Hook to board my ferry. We said our goodbyes and I thanked him and Johan for being so kind and hospitable during my time in Holland. I said, "It appears that I am the second Englishman whose life you saved." He looked most bewildered and, after a moment, simply said he was only too happy to help. He knew that Johan and I had been good friends.

I did write and thank Johan for all his kindness but I never felt it was enough. He married Janna and went to the USA. We didn't write after this and over the years I often wondered what had happened to my very good friend of that summer of 1967. I tried to trace him, first through a friend at the Dutch consulate when I lived in Melbourne, and when I moved to Thailand, through another retired Dutch friend who rather liked the challenge, I told him what I knew, and I was amazed when a week later he sent me an email with all of Johan's information. I wrote to him and soon had a reply from the now 78-year-old Johan in 2018. He was still happily married to Janna, with whom he had gone to America, and had worked for The Palmer House in Chicago. He had returned to Holland in 1970. He had one son and is now retired in Dordrecht, a lovely town about halfway between den Bosch and Rotterdam. Sadly, his father had died in 1970. We are still keeping in touch. The hospital I had spent time in had been demolished and replaced by an apartment block, so the residents can at least enjoy the beautiful view of Het Bossche Broek that I enjoyed from my hospital room.

Once on board the boat back to England, I immediately went to check out what first class had to offer. I found a very nice restaurant and cocktail bar, with not a piece of green vinyl in sight, and some very plush dining chairs and sofas. Having had no alcohol for what seemed like a *very* long time and only hospital food for the past few weeks, it was time to splash out and spoil myself, as was often my approach in life. I took my seat, even though we were still in port and were not due to depart for about an hour. A waiter appeared. "How may I help you sir?"

"Grilled fillet steak, French fries and a salad. Oh, and some mayonnaise as well. And a bottle of Beaujolais."

The steak was out of this world, the salad just a gesture to healthy eating. The wine was the crowning glory. How wonderful it was to eat good food again and enjoy a glass or two of red wine. As I was relishing the moment, a woman who had been eating nearby was rushed by the first class hostess in the direction of the ladies'. Good God, we haven't even cast off yet. Some people are so very sensitive to *mal de mer*, I smugly thought, especially as she was a woman. Ah, *schadenfreude*. My lack of sympathy was my downfall.

As the ship headed through the harbour entrance, I knew we were in for a rough crossing. It turned out to be the roughest crossing of the North Sea in ten years. Soon I realised that the steak and red wine were a grave mistake. My unaccustomed stomach now made me believe I was about to die. I raced to the loo; my steak and wine tasted nowhere near as good coming up. The flush was a lever next to my elbow, handily placed to align with where I knelt on the floor. My nausea did not stop, even long after the meal had been expelled from my system. I became adept at working the flush with my elbow. It was hell. Sea-sickness is the worst.

I have no idea how long I was in the loo, but I did not see another soul. The ship eventually docked in Harwich, and my brother Chris was picking me up. As I passed through Customs, I heard an announcement, "Would *Mr Won Long* of den Bosch, please go to the information desk where his brother is waiting for him."

I looked around for a Chinese man, who apparently was from where I had just been. No one to be seen. Doh! The penny dropped. Chris could not resist his little jokes. In tribute to my recent internment, I was now *Mr One Lung*. Oh very funny. My sense of humour had been lost down the toilet pan on the crossing. Chris was chuckling away, and I admit, I was delighted to see him. He took my case and we headed to the car and back to Warwickshire. I was back home in England at last, with a lot more experience under my belt, more than I might have wished for, but, as my mother might have said, not knowing the full extent of events, "Well dear, it's all part of life's rich tapestry."

The England I returned to was one where Harold Wilson was Prime Minister and the economy was in such bad shape that the pound was devalued. Breathalyzers were introduced. Britain was applying to join the EEC yet again and the *SS Torrey Canyon* supertanker ran aground off Cornwall leaking over 100,000 tons of crude oil into the sea, causing an ecological disaster. The average house cost £3,840, a Ford Cortina £749 and a gallon of petrol 5 shillings and 2 pence, all of which were out of my reach even on my new salary of £14 per week.

The Beatles released *Sgt. Pepper's Lonely Hearts Club Band* in 1967, which was to become one of the most acclaimed albums in contemporary music. I, however, did not like it, and so it was that that became the year I closed the chapter on my youth. With the hard years of training behind me, I was ready for a proper job in management, and to make my mark on the industry I had grown to love. My plan was to emulate a luxury lifestyle in the footsteps of hotel trailblazer Cesar Ritz.

It was nearly 50 years before I was to return to revisit The Grand Hotel, but this time as a guest. [56]

oOOOo

Appendix A

SCREAMING LORD SUTCH 1940 - 1999
(Chapter 7)

I truly believe he summed up what is most endearing about the English character - eccentricity! It is interesting to note that Screaming Lord Sutch started his party under the banner of the National Teenage Party but later decided it might be more apt, and possibly more appropriate, to rename it 'The Monster Raving Loony Party' The title rather speaks for itself and his manifesto was regarded as equally as absurd. Although he failed to win even a single parliamentary seat, as a result of which he never had an opportunity to implement his brilliant policy of: 'The constituency of 'South Hams' to be renamed 'South Hams Egg And Chips'', there were others included in his manifesto such as: Reducing the voting age to 18, 24 hours licensing, Abolition of dog licenses, Introduction of passports for pets, Pedestrianising Carnaby Street, Abolition of the 11 plus exam (he had my vote) and Legislation on commercial radio, all of which have now, believe it or not, passed through Parliament and accepted into law. He died in 1999 but the party lives on and are still on some ballot papers to this day, so when you see those hopeful politicians standing behind the *returning officer* on election night, the one in the eccentric outfit, enjoying the moment, will no doubt be the candidate for 'The Monster Raving Loony Party'.

Appendix B

THE GRAND HOTEL, EASTBOURNE.

*A*ccording to the contemporary fountain of knowledge, Wikipedia:

Eastbourne is a large town in East Sussex, within the historic County of Sussex, on the south coast of England between Brighton and Hastings. The modern town emerged in the early 19th century as a seaside resort, assisted by the arrival of the railway in 1849, and developed a spacious, regular layout.

Prior to its Victorian development, the area consisted of the estates of the Duke of Devonshire and others, which had evolved around the village of East Burne. Eastbourne's earliest claim as a seaside resort was a summer holiday visit by four of King George III's children in 1780. During the Napoleonic Wars, the Wish Tower and the Redoubt were built as defences. In the wake of the fall of France in 1940, the town's population fell sharply as this part of the south coast was considered a likely invasion zone. The town was badly bombed, achieving the dubious reputation of being 'the most raided town in the southeast'. Thousands of Canadian soldiers were stationed in and around Eastbourne from the summer of 1941 in the run-up to D-Day.

The sheltered position of the main town behind the cliff contributes to Eastbourne's title of sunniest place in Great Britain, and coined the promotional title of 'Sun Trap of the South' The town's reputation for health and sea breezes was a factor leading to the establishment of many private boarding schools in the 19th century. The town's climate, quiet charm and elegance have contributed to its popularity as a retirement destination and the number of resident pensioners exceeds the national average.

On 13 May 1874 the Eastbourne Gazette announced that a local resident William Earp was proposing to build a hotel with a 400-foot frontage at a cost of £50,000. The result was The Grand Hotel, constructed in 1875.

The Grand Hotel is well known for its long association with music. Claude Debussy corrected the proofs of 'La Mer' between 24 July and 30 August 1905 in Suite 200, which is now known as the Debussy Suite. The Grand Hotel has a rich history, as well as a stellar guest book of visitors since the hotel's opening, including Winston Churchill and Charlie Chaplin. Ernest Shackleton lived in Eastbourne and famously sketched one of his Arctic routes on The Grand's notepaper.

The Grand Hotel Orchestra used to broadcast live on the BBC from the Great Hall every Sunday night from 1924 to 1939 on the programme 'Grand Hotel'. During the Second World War, as Eastbourne was easy prey to air raids. The hotel eventually closed down and became a military headquarters.

The Hotel was handed back by the Government on 11th March 1946 (one month after my birth) when Richard 'Dick' Beattie became general manager, the man who was to be my boss when I first started my career seventeen years later on 15th August 1963

Appendix C

HILTON'S LUNAR HILTON (Chapter 17)

Reproduced from online '.Gizmodo' - What happened to the Hilton's 'Hotel on the Moon' by Matt Novak 7/12/13

B arron was elected as vice-president of Hilton Hotels in 1954, serving behind his father. Just four years later the Suburbanite Economist article appeared – the earliest reference to the idea I can find. I expect it will be difficult to find anything much earlier. That was the beginning of space fever in the United States, as the Russians had launched Sputnik in October of 1957, kicking off the Space Age - a period of tremendous fear and wide-eyed hope for what was to come.

Throughout later years, the idea appears again and again in popular culture. In the October 28, 1962 episode of The Jetsons, The Good Little Scouts, George brings Elroy's scout troop to the Moon and in a quick, fleeting shot we see the Moonhattan Tilton, a clear reference to the Manhattan Hilton hotel. And in Stanley Kubrick's classic 1968 film 2001: A Space Odyssey there is an office marked "Hilton Space Station 5" on the glass exterior, where people could presumably make reservations for the Hilton hotel on the film's orbiting space station.

Though it wasn't Conrad's idea he certainly didn't discourage the idea of a hotel on the Moon. The March 1963 issue of Cosmopolitan magazine ran a long and glowing profile on Conrad Hilton as the hard-nosed businessman who understood what people wanted and would stop at nothing to give it to them. Though not a quote from "Connie" himself, the article nonetheless ends with a space age promise from the writer: "it won't be very long before our astronauts land on the Moon and immediately behind them will be Connie Hilton with his plans for his Lunar Hilton Hotel."

Those plans began to take off in 1967. Barron, who was then president of Hilton, told the Wall Street Journal that he was planning to cut the ribbon at an opening ceremony for a Lunar Hilton hotel within his lifetime. He described the Lunar Hilton as a 100-room hotel that would be built below the surface. Guests would gather around a piano bar in an observation dome that allowed them to gaze back at earth.

Barron's desire to build a Hilton on the Moon - whether it was merely clever PR or something more sincere - struck a chord with people all over the world. The hotel group even printed promotional "reservations cards" for customers to reserve a hotel room on the Moon. "In the [Hilton] archive we've got hundreds, if not thousands, of letters of people writing in to him," says Dr. Young. "They'd seen the picture of the reservation form and they wanted to get their name on there.

"You read the letters, from all around the world - I always remember the one from Pakistan for some reason it stands out in my mind — but people really wanted to know that sometime in [their] lifetime we'll have hotels on the Moon."

Photographs

1. Grandparents John & Sarah Griffin, who had nursed with Edith Cavell, Kineton, 1915

2. My father Fred &elder sister Madge, 1914

n Griffin, uncle Will, my father, sister Madge, ah Griffin at home in Kineton, 1920's

4. My father and his Rudge Ulster 500cc Motorbike, c1933

t Grandparents John & Mary Walmsley (Rochdale Mill owners) & family; my grandmother, bottom in 1880's

6. Grandfather - James Langley, standing, right in top hat

7. Grandparents James & Annie Langley with Joyce, Mum Connie at Temple Grafton, 1912

9. The Griffins, father, mother, brothers Bob, Chris & me, in the garden in Swanage 1947

pped in and ready to go, Swanage, 1947

10. My first love - Elaine, my Nanny known as Yaiyai

1. Brothers Bob, Chris, sister Ginny & I

2. Eastbrooke School & Miss R C Bean - I'm seated front and centre, where I can be watched - other Bob, back 2nd from the left.

REPORT   DATE July...

...ck Griffin...   STBROOK
                REMARKS   TORY

Very interested. Good at answering up.

Fair

Very poor; hampered because he can't spell

Terribly weak. Should try   30th 1 95

Improved.

Untidy. Does not trouble over letter forms

    or spelling.

Interested in the stories.

Has done better work.

Improving

	REMARKS
...URE	
...ETIC	Very interested; likes discussing things
...S	"
...ETRY	" " "
...GRAPHY	" " " "
...TORY	" " " " if he could only read.
...IENCE	Would do well
...LOCUTION	Has done a little.
FRENCH	
LATIN	Loves his pencil & colours.
ART	Good, a promising — yes.
SINGING	Good. pro. Mr Bennett.
DRILL	Fairly good. B.H.
HANDWORK	

General Progress: Patrick is terribly slow and difficult.
Very ...tful and lazy. Does not seem to realise
that he is growing up. Signed... R. C. Bean   Principal

Conduct: ...must be more
...liable.

...awing.

...ny.

...OGRESS Patrick finds it difficult to concentra...
but he will improve. He is a very versatile chara...
& fond of fun

CONDUCT Very good.   Signed, Principal Rania C. Bean

13. One of many disappointing school reports

ndpa James Langley & I, at cousin Rosalind's wedding at Tachbrook.

15. My heroes of the French Resistance, 'Tantie' and daughter Jacquelin, from whose attic we 'rescued' arms left over from WWII

17. Me on Tim's BSA 350, scrambling in farmer Gilk's fields.

21. Putting on a brave face showing off my p listic skills

16. Uncle Douglas, Joyce, Tim & I - Pierrefonds, France - Looking innocent after our arms heist !

otor cycle antics with brother Chris & Ginny Lambretta.

19. In our teens, fellow conspirator & hero of my youth, cousin Tim

Crest School prospectus - The building...'is electrically lit and central heated'

23. School Rugby 1st 'XII' - 1955 - I'm the winger on the right

24. Hill Crest School photo 1957 - I'm right, standing 4th in next to best friend Simon Stone & well endowed Matron - on my right below, Nick Truswell who I met 40 years later in Sydney, he was GM o Sebel Townhouse.

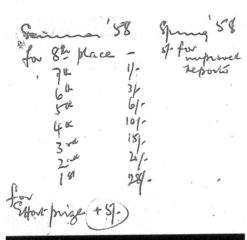

22. The stick hadn't worked so dad tried the carrot - didn't work !

27. A 'Pillbox' remains of Swanage beach re WWII in which we played.

Corfe to Swanage steam train (Corfe Castle in the background)

mer on the beach in Swanage 1947 - brother Bob, nanny Ayiyai, me, cousins Tim, Annabelle & y, Freda (Tim's nanny) & brother Chris

29. Chris, Bob & I in fashionable knitted beach attire, Swanage

30. My first attempt at riding (the second far less successful, see Part II)

34. As the Sailor I was to be

25. Sunday walk in Rempstone woods, me, mother, Chris & Bob

41. 'Tachbrook', Warwickshire, home to many Langley family gatherings

31. Me & the family with Swedish house guests. Thomas, seated front, far from impressed with an English summer, Ursel, German au pair, seated front

32. Chris & I with our pet squirrels we had rescued, their mother was shot by the local farmer

Camera Club outing, of which my father was president, my first press.

gnolia House - Our home in Swanage

36. Lord Wandsworth College, Long Sutton - My Public School

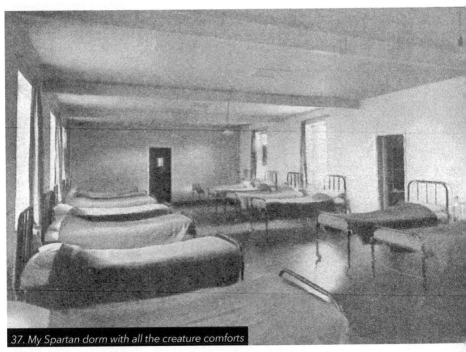

37. My Spartan dorm with all the creature comforts

outs on Parade - the notorious scoutmaster left is 'Happy' Nott, I'm front 2nd in from the right.

F Parade, Royal Engineers, on Founders
n 2nd from the rear

40. School friends, Lewis, Brett Morrell,
my fellow demolition expert & Bicknell

me from school with the latest in home entertainment, 14in black & white Baird TV & the Grundig
eel Tape Recorder -1959

44. Christmas at Tachbrook - Left-right, cousin Anthony 'Sos' Croft & friend Anne, aunty Bim, Annabe
Croft, me, uncle Ken, mum, Granny Langley, & favourite aunty Joyce

42. The Isles Hotel, Swanage, a holiday job to pay my debts but started a hotel career

e Old Red Lion, Stow on the Wold, where I spent a winter with the strange Reverend Burr

Manor House Hotel, Leamington Spa, where I started as a Trainee Manager August 1963

CONTRACTS OF EMPLOYMENT ACT 1963

STATEMENT OF TERMS OF EMPLOYMENT

NAME OF EMPLOYER: GRAND HOTEL EASTBOURNE LTD. AT ~~GRAND HOTEL EASTBOURN~~ MANOR HOUSE LEAMINGTO

NAME OF EMPLOYEE: MR./~~MRS~~/~~MISS~~ Patrick GRIFFIN

EMPLOYMENT COMMENCED: 25 August 1963

TERMS OF EMPLOYMENT AS AT 5 October 1964

REMUNERATION

WEEKLY REMUNERATION (EXCUDING GRATUITIES) FOR A WEEK OF 48 HOURS IS AT THE RATE OF £ 4 : 9 :

OVERTIME AND OTHER PAYMENTS SPECIFIED BY THE WAGES ORDER OR AGREEMENT AND NOT COVERED BY THE REMUNERATION REFERRED TO ABOVE WILL BE PAID AT A RATE NOT LESS THAN THAT PROVIDED UNDER THE WAGES ORDER OR AGREEMENT CURRENTLY IN FORCE.

INTERVALS OF PAYMENTS

WAGES WILL BE PAID WEEKLY

HOURS OF WORK

BASIC DUTY ROTAS WILL BE NOTIFIED WEEKLY IN ADVANCE BY THE HEAD OF DEPARTMENT. THESE DUTIES MAY BE SUBJECT TO VARIATION.

HOLIDAYS AND HOLIDAY PAY

PUBLIC AND ANNUAL HOLIDAY ENTITLEMENTS WILL NOT BE LESS THAN THOSE PROVIDE FOR IN THE CURRENT WAGES ORDER OR AGREEMENT.

SICKNESS OR INJURY

THERE IS NO ENTITLEMENT TO PAYMENT DURING PERIODS OF ABSENCE THROUGH SICKNESS OR INJURY. AN EX GRATIA PAYMENT MAY BE MADE IF A MEDICAL CERTIFI IS PRODUCED.

PENSION SCHEMES

THERE IS NO PENSION SCHEME OUTSIDE THE STATUTORY PENSION SCHEME.

LENGTH OF NOTICE TO TERMINATE EMPLOYMENT

	PERIOD OF CONTINUOUS SERVICE	NOTICE REQUIRED
FROM EMPLOYER:	LESS THAN TWO YEARS (104 WEEKS)	1 WEEK
	TWO YEARS BUT LESS THAN 5 YEARS (260 WEEKS)	2 WEEK
	OVER 5 YEARS	4 WEEK
FROM EMPLOYEE:	ANY PERIOD	1 WEEK

NOTICE BY THE EMPLOYEE MUST BE GIVEN IN WRITING TO EXPIRE ON A SUNDAY.

SIGNED ON BEHALF OF THE EMPLOYER

HEAD OF DEPARTMENT

I HEREBY ACCEPT THE TERMS AND CONDITIONS OF EMPLOYMENT AS STATED ABOVE.

The Grand Hotel, Eastbourne where I learn my 'chosen trade'

51. Les King, Chef de Cuisine, a lovely man, who wore more under his chef's hat than he let on.

53. The Restaurant at the Grand

GRAND HOTEL, EASTBOURNE

Managing Director : R. I. Beattie

Tele. Eastbourne 1600   Telegrams: Grand, Eastb

TARIFF

	ROOM including Early Tea, & Breakfast. Per Person.	INCLUSIVE TE Early Tea, Break Lunch, Afternoon & Dinner. Per person per da (for a minimum s of 3 days).
Front, with Bath & Balcony	65/6	97/6
Front, with Bath	55/6	87/6
Front, without Bath	48/6	80/–
Side, with Bath	50/6	82/6
Side, without Bath	43/–	75/–
Inside, with Bath	45/6	77/6
Inside, without Bath	38/–	70/–

MEAL PRICES

Breakfast	-	-	8/–
Continental Breakfast	-		4/6
Lunch	-	-	15/–
Afternoon Tea	-	-	3/6
Dinner	-	-	17/6

Clients are asked to inform the Reception (on arrival whether they wish to be charged incl Terms or at the room rate and to pay for their ▪ as taken.

These terms apply all the year round, ex that the following surcharges will be added duri

Christmas   35/–⎫
Easter and Whitsun   15/–⎬ per person pe
August and September   10/–⎭

GRATUITIES

12½% is added to all bills in respect of apartr board and restaurant meals and drinks. The ▾ of the sum is distributed to the staff as grat and no further tipping is expected.

DOGS

Dogs are charged at 7/6 per day and are allowed in Public Rooms.

56. 50 years later back at the Grand.

49. The hotels room tariff at the time

58. Charles& Oona Chaplin, the start of my hall of fame.

50. Wally Hawse, chauffeur to the eccentric Mr Myer's, with the Chaplin Children on 'Ge his horse

GRAND HOTEL
EASTBOURNE

A LA CARTE
(Cover Charge 2/6)

rs d'Oeuvre 6/6   Smoked Salmon 7/6   Caviar 21/- per portion
Strasbourg Foie Gras 15/-   Smoked Parma Ham and Melon 7/6
Fried Scampi 12/6   Scampi Newburg 12/6 (20 mins).
Liver Pâté 5/-   Melon 3/6 per portion   ½ Grapefruit 1/-
let and Entrecôte Steak Garni 15/-   Grilled Lamb Cutlets 7/6
Escalope of Veal Viennoise 15/-
lette Surprise 3/6 per person (20 mins).   Crêpes Suzettes 7/6

D I N N E R 17/6

Iced Water Melon
Liver Pâté with Hot Buttered Toast
Iced Orange Juice

Cream of Asparagus Soup
Consommé Petite Marmite
Iced Consommé Madrilène

Fillet of Turbot Waleska
Fillet of Sole Caprice

Vol-au-vent of Turkey and Mushrooms
Braised Ox Tongue Chasseur
Roast Chicken, Game Chips and Bacon
Leaf Spinach
Parmentier Potatoes

Cold Buffet

Pear Condé
Fresh Fruit Salad and Cream
Meringue Chantilly
Mixed Ices

Celery, Cheese and Biscuits

August   10% IS ADDED FOR GRATUITIES

le d'hôte, 7 course, Dinner Menu prepared by Les King in 1964 at 17/6d (75 pence)

MAITRE D'HOTEL

The Grand Hotel, Eastbourne Limited is a dynamic expanding organisation with an international reputation for cuisine and service.

It is due to promotion within the group that the above position has become available and we are looking for a person with extensive continental and West End experience who is capable of administrating and organising a staff of 50 and rates development as an important function. The ability to plan and supervise large scale banquets while maintaining the highest standard of service is also required.

Excellent remuneration and working conditions are offered for this senior post.

If you have the above qualifications please apply for an application form to:

M. A. Cairns,
Assistant General Manager,
The Grand Hotel,
Eastbourne.

54. An advertisement for the Maitre d'Hotel - to control a staff of 50, those were the days.

Doctor made his lavish lifestyle from death

WAS the doctor medically incompetent, did he carry out euthanasia — or mass murder? These unanswerable questions arise when considering the events autopsy done, but all it revealed was the presence of legally prescribed painkillers and tranquilisers. Bodkin Adams had already said he had prescribed these drugs during the couple's treatment. He had treated 71-year-old Mr Hullett, who had

Dr John Bodkins Adams: did he murder his patients?

55. Dr Bodkin Adams, the infamous 'alleged' murderer ! ..a well liked regular at the hotel

57. Tommy Steele, 1950's pop idol filming 'Half a Sixpence'

...nar Sharif who nearly put an end to my teen

59. Pete Murray, Radio Luxembourg DJ, who helped my teen love life take off.

...Bogarde, who was a hero of so many war ...t had a secret most never knew.

62. Violet Carson, very elegant and sophisticated not at all Coronation Street's Ena Sharples.

63. Grandma Langley, as Princess Ida, when she sang with The D'Oyly Carte Opera Company.

64. The Switchboard and how we communic in the '60's

66. The lovely Lorely, the boss's daughter, in Sydney 45 years later.

65. Catching up with my old boss Reg & Brenda Constable* 40 years later

THE

GRAND HOTEL

5 Star

EASTBOURNE

The Restaurant, beautifully decorated in soft shades of gold, grey, and warm white, is the perfect setting for fine food, and has an uninterrupted view of the sea.

GRAND WAY OF LIFE.

One of the most popular innovations at The Grand is the open—air, heated, salt—water swimming pool, beside the Sun Terrace and Lounge.

One of the 300 rooms

68. The Hilton, Amsterdam where I was to do my 'stage' (internship) in 1967's 'Summer of Love'

69. American Hotel, Leidseplein, Amsterdam - location of a few life's adventures

merican Cafe and Restaurant our local for a few more adventures

COFFEESHOP Mellow Yellow

ous 'Mellow Yellow Cafe' where I never inhaled

72. Two of the 'flower power' Hippies who did.

73. Amsterdam's famous canals ...for looking

INDEX

Lightning Source UK Ltd.
Milton Keynes UK
UKHW020633210121
377450UK00012B/964